Cornelius Cole

California three hundred and fifty years ago

Manuelo's narrative

Cornelius Cole

California three hundred and fifty years ago
Manuelo's narrative

ISBN/EAN: 9783743328983

Manufactured in Europe, USA, Canada, Australia, Japa

Cover: Foto ©ninafisch / pixelio.de

Manufactured and distributed by brebook publishing software (www.brebook.com)

Cornelius Cole

California three hundred and fifty years ago

CALIFORNIA

THREE HUNDRED AND FIFTY

YEARS AGO

MANUELO'S NARRATIVE

Translated from the Portuguese

BY A PIONEER

SAN FRANCISCO
SAMUEL CARSON & CO
PUBLISHERS AND BOOKSELLERS
NEW YORK: C. T. DILLINGHAM
1888

In Lieu of Preface.

THE preface to a book is usually nothing more nor less than an apology for its production, and is intended in some way to disarm criticism: an end, however, seldom attained, since the critics, as a rule, read no further than the preface, taking it for granted that a work which needs an apology is not worth the perusal. If no preface is furnished, then these censors will have no alternative but to read the book through before pronouncing judgment upon it.

ESCRITOR.

CALIFORNIA 350 YEARS AGO.

I.

THE BEGINNING.

NOT very many years ago, but prior to 1847, an event, most important to the world, occurred in the city of Evora, in the little kingdom of Portugal. It was nothing less than the discovery there of an old, musty manuscript relating to Alta-California,* a country until then, and for some time afterwards, only known in Europe as an obscure Spanish possession on the far-distant Pacific Coast of North America.

The manuscript was written in a sort of mixture of the Spanish and Portuguese languages, liberally interspersed with Indian expressions, and owing, undoubtedly, to that cause, as much as to its extreme age, it attracted considerable attention, when first brought to light, although it was not regarded with very great interest till some time afterwards.

---

* It was called Alta-California—*alta* meaning higher or upper—because it was supposed to lay well up towards the North Pole, and not for the reason that it was originally more elevated, in any sense of the word, than Lower, or *Baja* California, as the peninsula was called; or possibly it may have taken that lofty appellation from the fact of its being approached by a voyage on the high seas, while Lower California could be reached by merely crossing the gulf.

While the precise date of the discovery cannot now be ascertained, it is known with certainty to have occurred before the breaking out of the great gold excitement in the United States, in 1848 and 1849, for had it been subsequent to that important event, the notoriety of California, on that account, would have riveted attention to it at once, and fixed the date with certainty.

The scroll being observed, as stated, to relate to a country scarcely known in Portugal, what wonder that it should have been regarded at the time as of little value. As often remarked by Thucydides, "it is desirable to be accurate in all things," but it sometimes happens, as in this instance, that the exact facts cannot be obtained.

It was only afterwards, when the name of California became blazoned forth throughout the world as the depository of nature's choicest mineral treasures, that the attention of the finder of the manuscript was turned towards it again. Then, and not till then, a knowledge of the discovery spread abroad through the ancient city of Evora, and became the subject of much discussion among the priesthood.

It is well known that the early history of that particular part of the New World to which the scroll related had always been shrouded in the deepest mystery, and every attempt theretofore made to throw any considerable light upon it had failed.

The visit of Sir Francis Drake to that region in the year of grace 1579, was supposed by some to have been the first by any European; but all the accounts of that celebrated visit are quite unsatisfactory, so far, at least, as relates to the inhabitants of the country. That distinguished navigator, it is presumed, was deterred, by apprehensions of danger, from exploring the interior of the land to any considerable extent, and his observations, so far as known, were all made from the quarter-deck.

There is nothing authentic to show even into what waters

his ships penetrated; in short, everything that has come down to us concerning his discoveries is uncertain even to the verge of perplexity. Some writers have attempted to prove that he actually entered and anchored his vessels in the harbor of San Francisco instead of Sir Francis Drake's Bay, as it is now called. But that, I think, will appear in the sequel to be erroneous; and it is equally an error to suppose, as some writers have, that Viscaino, or Cavendish, or Rogers, or any other one of the bold and venturesome voyagers of that and the following century, either penetrated into, or knew anything at all about, the great harbor of the North Pacific.

A few Franciscan friars, it is true, came lumbering along some two hundred years later, and, after that, gave to the church, but not to the world, some little insight into the original condition of the country and its people; but these monks were, to all appearances, as chary of imparting information concerning their observations as if they had been in mortal dread lest their new dominions should be encroached upon by somebody; as, indeed, they actually were in the next generation or two by the advent among them of Rocky Mountain trappers, and, later still, by traders in hides and tallow along the coast.

But the old manuscript already mentioned has unexpectedly, and we must think most fortunately, opened up to the world a chapter in the remote history of that part of America, which antedates them all by many years, and which is far more instructive than anything heretofore disclosed concerning that region, a region which, it may be remarked, had been to all the rest of the world for unnumbered generations a *terra incognita*.

Evora, within whose sacred precincts the scroll was discovered, is the capital of the well-known province of Alemtejo, and was once a more populous city than it is at the present time, though it continues to be the seat of numerous convents and other religious establishments.

A university founded there about the year of our Lord 1550 was suppressed by the authority of the Government of Portugal in 1767, at the time of the expulsion from that kingdom of the order of Jesuits, by whom that same institution had been successfully conducted for more than two hundred years.

Among the many monuments of antiquity pointed out to the traveler in Evora is a ruined temple of Diana, older than the Christian era, and also an aqueduct of Roman construction which still supplies the city with water; but the object of greatest interest, in the opinion of the people, though by no means so ancient as some of the others, is the splendid old cathedral in which the manuscript alluded to was discovered. Designed, as this building was, for the accommodation of a numerous priesthood, there were in it, above and below ground, not a few but many apartments, in one of which, long neglected, this literary treasure lay hidden away. It was found in a secret closet, closely wrapped in an envelope of untanned skins and covered with the accumulated dust of many ages. No one at the time it was brought to light or afterwards could tell exactly whence the manuscript came or give any very intelligent account of its origin, and its discovery, which was entirely accidental, excited less curiosity at first than might have been expected, but subsequently and not long after, the Dominican Brotherhood, in charge of the place, for reasons already hinted at, set themselves about the business of investigating it with commendable zeal.

The wrapping about the bundle indicated unmistakably its origin to have been some frontier town in America, and a single expression observed on one of its pages pointed towards Acapulco as the place whence it might have been brought, and where it may have been written. But, strange to say, no date was discovered in the entire roll, a fact which, perhaps, will be satisfactorily accounted for hereafter.

A thorough search of all the records of the establishment

threw but little light upon the subject, and was in the main unsatisfactory, but not entirely so, since it disclosed the circumstance that an old member of the Dominican order, Justino by name, a native of Evora, had returned from Mexico about three hundred years before, broken in health, and that he soon afterwards died. It was conjectured that the manuscript might have been brought into the monastery by him, and its age, as evidenced by its dilapidated condition, went some ways towards confirming that conclusion. A careful examination of all the archives and old papers of the church was made by the priests, to find, if possible, some of the handwriting of Friar Justino with which to compare the writing of the manuscript; but the search proved in vain. The records likewise failed to show what particular apartment in the monastery had been occupied by him on his return, and even his burial-place was forgotten. Neither was it known in what part of Mexico he had wandered; but this is not so much to be wondered at, since the members of the Dominican brotherhood were migratory in their habits, and seldom remained more than a single year in the same locality. In fact they were, in the true sense of the word, missionaries by occupation. Armed with no better weapons than scrip and staff, they were always traveling from place to place. Father Justino's one aim in life had doubtless been to instruct the rude natives of the New World in the sublime doctrines of the Christian religion, and his home at any time was likely to have been wherever he could accomplish most for the welfare of that class of his fellow-beings. It was, evidently, after a life thus spent that he had returned to the scenes of his childhood, there to render up, in peace, his weary soul to its divine Master.

It is no slight evidence of the self-sacrificing devotion of Justino, that the manuscript contained almost no account of his own career, which is therefore left largely to conjecture; but it gave much information concerning what was then, or not long afterwards, known as California, and its early inhabitants, derived mainly from the evidence of a Spanish sailor who had spent many years in that mysterious country.

The writing may have been, and probably was, intended as the basis of a missionary movement in the direction of Alta-California, and for that reason the character of its people, their habits of life, their capacity for civilization, and, above all, their fitness for conversion to Christianity, were largely dwelt upon. If, indeed, the manuscript had been known with certainty to have been prepared by pious hands for the specific purpose of inciting the Dominicans to undertake such an enterprise, it could hardly have been more complete in detail; and we may well believe that, if Father Justino was really its author, of which there is less doubt the more the subject is considered, and if his life had been spared but a few years longer, it is altogether likely that the renowned Franciscan friar, Junipero Serra, would have been anticipated in his labors of love, in that uncultivated field, by at least a couple of centuries.

There is this drawback, however, about the whole matter, which ought in fairness to be laid before the candid reader. The ink of the writing in the scroll had become so far obliterated by age as to render its deciphering extremely difficult; and what was still more discouraging to the young priests, the vermin had attacked one end of the bundle, actually destroying a portion of the text, and probably that very portion on which the date should have appeared. But these misfortunes only added to the interest taken in the subject by the persons in whose hands the manuscript had fallen, and, naturally enough, their pious enthusiasm was kindled by such untoward circumstances to work out to an intelligent conclusion the contents of the whole document. Had it been simple, easy reading, as most of the literature of the church is known to be, it is altogether probable that this remarkable production might have been, like much of such literature, passed over lightly and been forgotten; but somehow it is so ordained by Providence, that in matters of history as well as of science, and even of religion, difficulties thrown in the way of their development only add to their value in the estimation of mankind. The more ancient and obscure the record of events, and the more uncertainty surrounding them, the higher the appreciation of them, as a general rule. "If gold could be easily procured," as remarked by one of the monks, "it would be of little value;" and on the same principle, as reverently declared by another, "He who bears the heaviest cross shall wear the brightest crown." The worth of any commodity depends largely upon the amount of labor expended in its production ; and so the very great work necessarily bestowed in digging out, as it were, from a mutilated mass, the hidden meaning of this musty old manuscript, has invested it with most unusual interest.

It is probably owing to this circumstance, more than to any other, that it possesses at this time any considerable importance, for it is, after all, when dispassionately considered, only the story of an obscure sailor man, and as likely, for aught we can see, to be as untrustworthy as other stories of a similar origin.

Should the reader be inclined to this view of the case, he might as well now discontinue the task of perusing it, and permit the narrative to pass, either as the doubtful yarn of a seaman, or else, if he prefers it, as the idle tale of a Dominican friar—one or the other of which it certainly is, but which makes little difference, since either is liable to be discredited. But the next chapter may possibly disclose something of greater interest, and the perusal of that much more is therefore recommended before dropping the subject entirely.

II.

THE NEXT CHAPTER.

THE story runs that very many years ago a large man-of-war—large for those times doubtless, though of only about five hundred tons' burden—was cruising along the northwestern coast of the newly-found continent of America, but upon what particular errand she was bound is not stated, nor is that of any consequence so far as at present appears, though it is presumed she was on a voyage of discovery, seeking for the Northwest Passage. But what is important to know is that she bore the Spanish colors at her mast-head, a flag in those days emblematic of by far the most powerful maritime nation in the world. She was a full-rigged frigate and was thoroughly equipped and provisioned for a long voyage, and therefore presumably the more venturesome. It being well understood that she was now in waters that had never before been disturbed by the vessels of civilized men, she was handled from day to day by her officers with all the caution that prudence required under the circumstances. She had been abroad on her lonesome cruise for many weeks and had penetrated far into the "Northern Indian Ocean," as that part of the Pacific was then called, feeling her way, as it were, along the coast and among islands, when, as it happened, on a clear afternoon a narrow opening into the land was observed by her commander, and her prow was at once turned thitherward. After several ineffectual attempts to reach the channel, rendered abortive by adverse tides and currents, she succeeded at last in making an entrance into a wide and beautiful harbor, noticed in the report as being completely landlocked. This harbor was bordered on every side by uneven, if not rugged, woodlands, and in some directions mountains were plainly visible. According to the description given in the manuscript, the harbor was much larger from north to south than from east to west, although it was represented to be some leagues in width.

These casual observations touching the geographical formation of the harbor and country about, give us a very satisfactory clue to its identity, and though its waters remained unnamed for generations afterwards, unquestionably the good ship was then riding securely in what is now known, the world over, as the Bay of San Francisco. In a little while soundings were taken, sails furled, and anchor dropped.

The extreme newness of the country, like many other parts of America when first visited by Europeans, was fairly bewildering. The all-pervading silence was spoken of as oppressive, but the locality was none the less interesting, on that account, to men who were eagerly searching in an unexplored field for the wonders of nature and of Providence. This was really a far more inviting region than they had expected to find, promising, as it did, to the leaders of the expedition great renown in case of a safe return to their native country. They could confidently expect decorations from their king for bringing to light a land of such varied promise. And as to the men, each and every one of them, from common sailor to cabin-boy, could hopefully look forward to a supply of shining silver from the plethoric Spanish treasury as a reward for his participation in the discovery.

The good ship had been inside the harbor only a day or two when, in want of fresh water, as ships usually are, a boat's crew, well armed and equipped, was sent ashore to reconnoiter the land in search of the needed beverage. The country bordering on the Bay, though extremely wild in appearance, was obviously inhabited by human beings of some sort, since fires were observed to blaze on certain of the hills by night, and smoke to ascend therefrom by day.

There must have been, at that remote period, vastly more timber in that region than was found in later times, for the shores were represented as thickly covered with trees of large growth, almost down to the water's edge; and even the islands in the Bay were said to be studded with oaks and evergreens. The country was described as marvelously picturesque and beautiful when viewed from the deck of the ship, or from aloft, and it is to be inferred that even then it possessed in profusion those fascinations for which it has since become famous.

But the evident shyness of the natives, not one of whom could anywhere be seen, created a suspicion that they might be hostile, as, indeed, the Indians in many parts of the New World had proved to be, and on that account as favorable a location as possible was selected for the landing. It was on a low, sandy spit extending into the Bay, and so situated as to be covered by the guns of the ship as she lay in the offing.

The shore was reached by the boat's crew without interruption, and, so far as could be determined from appearances, not one of the inhabitants was within leagues of the place.

The Spaniards, full of good spirits, and growing bolder by degrees, proceeded inland, lured on, not more by what they were in pursuit of, than by the attractiveness of the surroundings. Delighted with being once more on *terra firma*, and in such a pleasing locality, they had pushed far into the heart of the forest, when the foremost of the men espied skulking in the undergrowth, not a hundred varas away, what at first appeared to him, and which he supposed really was, some new species of wild animal, but which, on closer inspection, proved to be a human being clad in the skins of wild beasts.

This sudden development created no little commotion among the Spaniards, and all, with one accord, rushed forward to obtain a better view for himself. The Indian, not disposed, as it seemed, to quit his ground without some reluctance, one of the sailors, with a recklessness wholly unaccountable, considering their situation at that moment, cast a weapon of some sort at him, severely wounding him in the leg. A cry of pain was immediately raised by the native, and in less time than it takes to relate the fact, a hundred or more stalwart warriors, all armed in their way and ready for battle, sprang from cover and advanced upon the Spaniards, who, perceiving themselves outnumbered, at least ten to one, beat a hasty retreat. The enemy followed, with a fearful clamor, but for the best of reasons soon learned to maintain a respectful distance. After several halts on the way, merely to show that they were not wholly demoralized, but losing no time unnecessarily, the boat's crew, nearly exhausted by the race, at last reached the landing and all safely embarked save one, a young man, who was left prone upon the ground, not far from the water's edge, where he had been stricken down by the enemy's weapons. The boat's crew hovered near the shore for some time to ascertain the fate of their comrade, and then put off to the ship. The young man making no movement that was observed, was believed to have been killed outright, and his shipmates abandoned him to his fate. This young fellow, who was, in fact, only wounded, and who, in due time, recovered his senses, is the one from whom was obtained the facts which go to make up the narrative contained in the manuscript of Father Justino, as we assume it to be, and of which we are now giving a somewhat liberal translation.

In the series of little conflicts occurring on the retreat of the boat's crew, a number of other natives, besides the one already mentioned, were wounded, more or less seriously, which caused great commotion among them, and a most frightful war dance was presently inaugurated over the prostrate body of the sailor.

The captain of the man-of-war, in doubt as to the nature and numbers of the natives, weighed anchor and hastily pulled out into the stream, awaiting only for the crew to come on board before departing for some place of greater safety.

The wounded man, abandoned as he was, expected no better treatment from his enraged captors than to be dispatched at once, and, crossing himself, with a spirit of resignation, as a good Christian should, he calmly awaited his fate. In afterwards describing his sensations at that particular time, he was exceedingly animated, and indulged in more levity than Friar Justino thought was warranted under such serious circumstances, and accordingly the good priest, as is stated in the manuscript, administered to him a fitting rebuke. But the sailor's excuse, and a sufficient one it would seem to be, was his marvelous good-fortune in escaping death, which to him just then appeared inevitable, and it may well be conceded that his feelings at the time of relating the joyful events were not altogether his own.

To his surprise and unutterable gratification the enemy, when the dance was ended, began more coolly to contemplate his person, as he lay stretched upon the ground, and on their approaching him more closely he was enabled to perceive in their faces expressions of great curiosity, and this inspired new hope within him. It was the first time the Indians had ever beheld a human being of a race different from their own—a circumstance to which the sailor certainly owed his life; and to this same fortunate circumstance the world is now indebted for this extremely interesting narrative. The anger of the savages rapidly yielded to their astonishment, and the wounded white man was not after that seriously molested.

Not long subsequent to the occurrences just described, he was visited, where he lay on the shore, by a number of the women of the country, whose countenances, more than those of the men, beamed with compassion towards him, and he found far less difficulty in gaining their good-will than could have been expected, considering, as we must, that they were only barbarians, and he an utter stranger among them. But for the kindly offices of these gentle creatures, he always insisted he must have perished miserably where he lay, for such was the character of his wounds that he was not at all in a condition to care for himself. In this time of sorest need assistance was thus rendered him by the more sympathizing sex. His experience under these most trying circumstances it was that incited in his breast that respect and partiality for women which ever afterwards graced his character, as will appear in the subsequent pages of this history. He certainly had abundant reason to be grateful to them, and it is to his everlasting credit that he never afterwards neglected an opportunity to show his gratitude. A flint-headed arrow had penetrated one of his legs, going quite through the fleshy part, flint, shaft, feathers, and all; but the most serious wound was inflicted on the back of his head, with a stone hatchet, fixed in a wooden handle—a native weapon quite common, as he afterwards observed. It was this blow that rendered him, for the time, insensible, and came so very near costing him his life.

III.

MANUELO.

WE almost forgot to mention the name of the individual through whose kindness we are enabled to continue this most eventful narrative. It was Manuelo, and nothing more. If, perchance, at any time another name belonged to him, the fact was nowhere disclosed in the manuscript, and his possession of one is therefore thrown in doubt. A single name for a person of obscure origin was no uncommon thing in those days, and even the ownership of one good name was more than some people could boast. If peradventure Manuelo possessed, by right of inheritance, a family appellation, it being nowhere disclosed in the writing, it is now wholly lost to history, and the responsibility for that public calamity rests upon the author of the manuscript. It is possible, however, that his patronymic may have been eaten away by the rodents, and if so, the responsibility would be removed entirely from the shoulders of Justino. It must be considered a misfortune, nevertheless, that the first white man whose feet ever pressed the sacred soil of California, is compelled to go down to posterity under the simple appellation of Manuelo; but it is none the less a duty to perpetuate what is certainly known concerning him, and we proceed accordingly to relate, or, rather, to permit him to relate, the further occurrences of that time,—how the native women, prompted by their natural goodness of heart, hastened to bring him water and food; and how they tenderly bound up his wounds, applying to them the wilted leaves of medicinal plants, held in place by thongs of buckskin; and how they treated him with more than sisterly kindness, during all the years he remained among them.

IV.
SOMETHING ELSE.

THE precise location of the village to which Manuelo was removed, after the lapse of some days, can never be known with certainty, since the fact is disclosed that at least a dozen large villages, and many smaller ones, were scattered around the great Bay at intervals. One town, however, much larger than the others, was situated "over against the entrance to the harbor," and this was, so to speak, the capital of the whole country. Here resided the head chief, or king, who maintained a sort of court, surrounding himself with all the paraphernalia consistent with the degree of civilization enjoyed by his people. This capital was on the opposite side of the broad harbor, and quite away from where the white men had landed. Becoming acquainted with all these facts, as he grew better of his wounds, and, true to his sailorly instincts to seek the largest centers of population, Manuelo early resolved, when sufficiently recovered, to pay a visit to that city, which purpose he afterwards carried out, but under difficulties, as will appear.

His recovery was more rapid than could have been anticipated, in view of the serious character of his injuries, and much more speedy than it would have been but for the unremitted attentions of the Indian women. Indeed, their manner towards him was so considerate and thoughtful of all his wants, that he could with difficulty persuade himself that his wounds had been inflicted by people of the same race with them, and it is but just to say that his heart overflowed with gratitude in contemplation of their kindness. Such magnanimous conduct on the part of those unlettered barbarians towards an unfortunate and perishing Christian should convince us all, as it did Manuelo, and Justino as well, that the better qualities of human nature are confined to no particular race, and belong exclusively to no condition in life. It teaches, also, as plainly as anything can, that we should always brace up against adversity, and under no circumstances give way to despair, since none are gifted with foresight to know what the end of apparent calamity may be; nor is anyone able to control, in all things, his own destiny.

Pious Justino took occasion here to remind his informant of the great religious truth that the winds were always tempered to the shorn lamb, and that there was certainly a providence in his escape, which lesson Manuelo, sailor-like, but not irreverently, accepted, with the proviso that the lamb should be shorn only at the proper season of the year, in which case he maintained there could be no doubt about the truth of the saying.

V.

NATIVE HABITS AND RELIGION.

SATISFACTORY though the progress of Manuelo's recovery was, nevertheless weeks elapsed before he was able to stir forth from the wigwam in which he had been laid. The arrow in going through the fleshy portion of his limb had grazed the bone, and for a time he greatly feared it might result in permanent lameness. The wound on the head was of a nature to dislodge the scalp for a space, and the process of healing was necessarily slow; but being frequently admonished by his attendants to remain quiet, he was as often assured that the end would be well. He was able the more readily to conquer his impatience since his confinement, with its agreeable companionship, afforded him an opportunity to make progress in mastering the language of the people, and at the same time to learn something about their habits and general disposition—an opportunity of which he availed himself to the very best advantage.

Their language he found to be simple, but expressive, and by no means harsh in sound. It was not difficult for him to acquire a sufficiency of it to make known his wants, while his native tongue was freely used in expressions of thankfulness, which his attendants—as he insisted—understood full well. Their habits were in many respects entirely primitive, but in others they were marked by a degree of civility quite unaccountable in a people who had never enjoyed the blessings of Christianity.

Extreme delicacy of manners and modesty of demeanor, it was observed, characterized the conduct of the women, young and old; and even the men, on all occasions, were sufficiently polite, evincing thereby a liberal endowment of native goodness. He could plainly see that the most warlike amongst them had come to regard him with sympathy and favor, and all apprehension of ill treatment in the future gradually wore away. With the children of the village, possibly because he was a sailor man and a stranger amongst them, he became a great favorite. This fact must be taken as demonstrating the excellent natural disposition of Manuelo himself, for we learn that the partiality of the children for him was abundantly manifest, long before his proficiency in the language enabled him to entertain them with stories of his own adventures.

Owing to the uncertainity, or perhaps it would. be more proper to say the certainty, of his stay among them, it was clearly his duty, as well as his interest, to observe with care whatever might be peculiar, or otherwise, in the customs and mode of life of this people; and he was not long in learning that the young men and women were addicted to many innocent pleasures, and that mirthfulness was a leading characteristic of the race. Their lives were taken up with a round of domestic duties, interspersed with a variety of games, each in its season. It is worth relating that these sports were seldom interrupted, even by the occurrence of a death in the tribe, for these people looked not upon death as a calamity, unless it might be the result of accident or violence. They were firm believers in the future existence, and through their seers, prophets, and priests, assumed to hold communication with the spirits of the departed. This fact Justino regarded as of the highest importance, and he made it the basis of a lengthy disquisition in the manuscript, upon their susceptibility to the influence of gospel truths, which, though it might have been interesting enough to the Dominican brotherhood centuries ago, can hardly be worth recording here, and is therefore omitted. He described with great particularity their incantations and ceremonies over the dead, whose bodies, by invariable custom, were consumed on a funeral pyre. He told how their preparations for this last rite were made. On every such occasion, in a beautiful wooded valley, hemmed in on either hand by a dense forest of evergreen trees, the body, on the day following the death, would be borne on the shoulders of four stalwart men. The hour chosen for the funeral ceremony was always near the setting of the sun, when the litter would be preceded by the eldest prophet of the village, arrayed in a long robe of the skins of black animals, and bearing aloft a lighted torch.

Following the bier would come the family friends of the deceased, in single file, and each with a bundle of fagots, to be added to the pile, after the body was placed thereon. Next in order after the immediate friends of the deceased followed a band of female singers, all arrayed in picturesque costume. The dirge-like music of these, interrupted only by the incantations of the priest, was kept up, with brief intervals, till late at night, and until the body was consumed. The most impressive part of the ceremony occurred just at the time of setting fire to the pile, when the solemn voice of the priest, mingled with the loud lamentations of the mourners, could be heard afar, and was re-echoed back from the neighboring hills. Only a select number of the men, and barely enough to perform well these last sad obligations to the dead, ever attended on these occasions, and the children never. As a general thing, all the people of the village, of every age and sex, would follow the procession to the outskirts of the town, when, with demonstrations of friendly regard, they would bid adieu to the departed and with measured tread return to their homes.

The sorrow of these simple people over their dead was undoubtedly softened by their faith in the future existence, and by their confidence in the power of their prophets to communicate with the spirits of the deceased, which was unbounded. Justino argued from this fact, and very properly, that they were most fit subjects for missionary labors, and the good man longed to be the one to impart to them the sublime mysteries of the true religion. In this ambition he was doubtless greatly encouraged by the genial Manuelo, who, though a sailor, was nevertheless a good Christian, and never forgot entirely his obligations, either to the church or to these miserable barbarians.

[From the Napa *Register*, December 20, 1886.]

Desiring to obtain some fine loam for the Insane Asylum grounds a short time ago, the gardener resorted to the site of an old Indian rancheria at a short distance in the rear of the Asylum. It was found upon reaching the depth of three or four feet that the locality was an Indian graveyard, and several skeletons of the aborigines were found. These were covered with only a few feet of earth, and from the position in which they were found, and from their surroundings, much interesting information was obtained in regard to the manner in which the Indians of Napa Valley buried their dead.

As a general thing, the bodies were doubled up, the chin resting on the knees and the hands clasped about them. Then the bodies were bound with bark, pieces of which were found on the skeletons in a fair state of preservation. Bright-hued stones, beads, and other trinkets were also found. The bodies were buried, not in a sitting position, but upon their sides. Continuing the excavations there were found at the depth of six feet indications that the Indians practiced cremation, as the ashes of human bones were discovered, and also large numbers of beads united by the action of fire.

Little thought is given by the busy, driving whites of to-day, to the countless numbers who once roamed over every part of this valley. They lived their day and passed off the stage of life, leaving behind them but few traces of their existence, swept away by "the flood of years."

VI.

THEIR SPORTS.

A FAVORITE sport of the children, and indeed of the youth of both sexes, was hiding and seeking, the facilities for which, in so wild a country, were practically unlimited. In following this diversion, frequently they would wander off to great distances alone, and thus incur risk of destruction by wild beasts. Nevertheless they pursued this sport without restraint and with a zeal and daring quite surprising. Instances were related to Manuelo where children had been lost or destroyed in their efforts to escape detection; but the diversion was none the less applauded, and, as Manuelo believed, because it encouraged adventure, and at the same time increased their expertness in forest tracking and trailing.

The women had an amusement, practiced by them exclusively, which consisted in the throwing and catching of forked sticks, prepared for the purpose; but exactly how it was conducted is not so described as to render the account intelligible, although it was a game, he said, in which they freely indulged and became exceedingly expert.

The men of the tribe, old and young, had a variety of sports, such as foot-racing, wrestling, and ball-playing. Instead of a ball, a round stone, or, more commonly, a piece of wood, worn down to the proper shape, somewhat oblong, with the ends smoothed to avoid the infliction of wounds, was used. Not unfrequently the men were so swift of foot as to elude wild beasts when pursued by them, or to overtake in the chase the fleet animals of the country. They were expert hunters, and were little in fear of the most ferocious tenants of the forest. Two or three of them could at any time conquer a huge bear or a full-grown panther, of which large numbers were in the forests about. Some of their exploits in this line exhibited a daring and hardihood unexampled in story. Their weapons were few in variety, and simple in construction, consisting of the bow and arrow, flint-pointed, the javelin, with point of bone, the stone hatchet, and the war-club, in the use of all of which they became exceedingly expert. Like the Spanish bullfighter they were accustomed to study with care the vulnerable points in their four-footed adversaries, and seldom failed in a contest to gain a victory.

Manuelo, in the exuberance of his admiration for their skill, was wont to say that no matadore of the old country, in the arena, ever displayed greater coolness in danger than these people were in the habit of showing in their contests with wild beasts. In other respects, no less than in those mentioned, these denizens of the forest exhibited a peculiar nobility of character, which they probably acquired from the nature of their surroundings. Their self-sacrificing magnanimity was always equal to their bravery. They never failed to render assistance to a companion in distress, however great the peril or severe the sacrifice; and this it was that called forth from Justino the philosophic reflection that cowardice and cruelty go hand in hand, while bravery and generosity are inseparable companions.

It was a leading tenet of their religion, if they may be said to have had a religion, never to shrink from responsibility, and they understood their obligations to each other as well as any people under the sun. The most enlightened nations of that century, it was thought, might have learned much from these half-naked savages, touching the duty of man to his fellow, and it was regretted by the good friar that others, more in need of it, could not have enjoyed the benefit of their example.

While he remained among them Manuelo could not but frequently reflect that if his Christian companions, meaning those of the ship's crew, had possessed only half the chivalry of these barbarians, they would never have left him to an unknown fate. This never-failing unselfishness of his captors was exultingly adduced by Manuelo as evidence that they really enjoyed a civilization of the very highest order compatible with entire ignorance of the Christian religion. But Manuelo's glowing account of the magnanimity of the men was even more than surpassed by the exuberance of his opinions touching the virtue and excellence of the women. Indeed, he had far greater reason to regard the gentler sex with favor, inasmuch as to them he was indebted for the preservation of his life. But, independent of that obligation, and even if it had never existed, he must have pronounced them among the very best specimens of womankind, and a higher compliment no man could pay the gentler sex.

VII.

CHAPTER SEVEN.

THESE children of nature having few wants they were easily satisfied. In truth, they knew nothing whatever about the outside world, and were troubled with no cares beyond those incident to their simple mode of life.

Until the advent, in this great unknown harbor, of the *Don Carlos La Grande*, for such was the name of the man-of-war in which Manuelo had come, they were oblivious of any other race than their own, and happy for them had they been permitted to remain forever in that state of blissful ignorance. Free from a desire for change or improvement they were content with their present condition, and with what they possessed, as indeed, had been their ancestors for, possibly, thousands of years before them.

There were evidences among them in abundance, observable mainly in the formation of their villages, and particularly in the wonderful size and growth of their mounds, of a remote antiquity, and who shall say that, as a people, they were not contemporaneous with the oldest of which history gives any account? But there is in this, perhaps, too much of speculation to be incorporated in a record of actual events.

So rarely has it happened that the historian has been able to transmit to posterity accurate information, even concerning transactions of his own time and country, to say nothing about those of other times and other lands, gathered, as they must needs be, from many sources, and often untrustworthy, that the public is to be congratulated upon the specific and evidently reliable character of the intelligence furnished by Manuelo concerning a people and country hitherto unknown, and after a lapse of hundreds of years. It has been remarked that fiction predominates in history, and likewise that much truth is to be found in works of fiction; whether that be so or not, it is certain that the remark cannot apply with any fitness to the present narrative, since the only point in it upon which there is any considerable doubt is as to the time of the visit of the *Don Carlos* to the Bay of San Francisco, and even that can be fixed with a tolerable degree of certainty, since it is known that the king after whom the good ship was named the great Charles the Fifth of Spain, became famous in the early part of the sixteenth century, subsequent to which event the vessel must have received its christening. The period of her cruise is therefore set down, with much confidence, after, but not long after, the year of our Lord 1525.

There is no account anywhere found in all the Spanish archives of her return, and the presumption is raised that she was lost, with all on board, on her way home, somewhere in the Pacific Ocean—an occurrence by no means uncommon in those times. If such was unfortunately the case, Manuelo, after all, though alone stricken down, was the only lucky man of the crew.

It is not even known to this day where the *Don Carlos Le Grande* was fitted out, nor by whom, nor yet who was her master;* but that she was an armed vessel, and on a voyage of exploration, is clear enough, both from the account of Manuelo himself, and from the testimony of the Dominican friar, as transmitted through this old Evora manuscript.

Had the *Don Carlos* been a piratical cruiser, Manuelo might not have disclosed that fact to Confessor Justino; but his excellence of character, as everywhere developed, is of itself a sufficient refutation of any such uncharitable assumption. His uniform kindness of heart repels the idea at once that he could ever have been engaged in the wicked pursuit of a buccaneer, and the bare suggestion of such a thing calls for an apology to his memory, which we freely render.

Whatever his companions, who so basely deserted him on the beach, may have been, it is certain enough that Manuelo himself could never have been a pirate at heart, and we hasten to exonerate him from any such wicked suspicion.

---

* Since the completion of the translation, it has been suggested that the ship was commanded by either Cortez, Ulloa, or Cabrillo, each of whom was in that part of the Pacific between 1535 and 1541; but a mere translator is at liberty to indulge in no opinions of his own, and therefore I express none.

VIII:
THE SUBJECT RESUMED.

THE place where Manuelo and his shipmates landed was to the north of the entrance of the great harbor, probably several leagues away, and on the westerly side. A sailor never fails to note and seldom forgets the points of compass, and to this circumstance must be attributed our own good fortune in being able to designate with reasonable certainty the quarter of the Bay where the debarkation took place. Without doubt it was not far from the site of some one of those charming villages which adorn the great interior waters of California; but whether near where the lovely village of San Rafael now nestles among the wood-clad hills of Marin; or where Petaluma reposes, intoxicated with the sweet fragrance of a perpetual summer; or where the village of Napa luxuriates amidst her soul-inspiring vines, may never be known, for there is nothing in the manuscript to guide the translator to the exact locality, and the matter must ever remain enveloped in some uncertainty.

But after all it is less essential to ascertain the precise spot first approached than it is to know that a landing was actually effected by Christian white men upon the shores of San Francisco Bay, more than three hundred and fifty years ago. Our own opinion is that it occurred not far from where the flourishing town of Petaluma now stands, and that the early inhabitants of Sonoma Valley first enjoyed the advantage of a sojourn among them of Manuelo; though it must be confessed that if Napa had been more accessible to the sea, her residents might well dispute the honor, for it is related that during his stay in that vicinity, frequent excursions were made with hunting parties to the interior, and through a most delightful region, the description of which, as given, would apply as well to the one as to the other.

The valley visited is represented as one in which all nature sported in primitive loveliness. It was covered entirely over with a carpet of green, and was embellished in the spring of the year with a profusion of flowers of every color, giving it, when viewed from a distance, as Manuelo aptly expressed it, the appearance of a piece of the costliest tapestry. To add to its magnificence, the plain was studded, at convenient intervals, with groups of wide-spreading evergreen oaks, the whole differing not essentially from an extended park in the countries of Europe.

The mountains on either hand though high were not precipitous, and were covered with a growth of graceful pine and fir trees, which, whenever approached, were found to be vocal with the songs of birds. The valley itself was enlivened by the presence of whole herds of deer and antelope, remarkable for their tameness, and countless numbers of skurrying rabbits were darting hither and thither in the exuberance of their playfulness. The place seemed to the romantic Manuelo a veritable paradise, ever exhibiting its attractiveness in entrancing profusion. But if captivating to him, it was even more so to the simple children of nature, in whose company he was in the habit of resorting to its peaceful shades, not less for pleasure than in the pursuit of game.

IX.

THE ABANDONMENT.

THE *Don Carlos Le Grande* remained in the Bay some days after the loss of Manuelo, but was constantly cruising about in pursuance, it may have been, of her first purpose of obtaining a supply of fresh water, of which, as we know, she was in need. But whether she obtained it, or exactly what course she afterwards pursued, Manuelo could never ascertain from the natives. He was made aware at the time of her delay, and hoped it might be continued until he should be sufficiently recovered of his wounds to enable him to reach her deck once more, but in this, alas! he was doomed to disappointment. Not recuperating sufficiently while she remained in those waters to hold communication with her, he saw the ship no more. Her little experience, resulting, as we know, in the loss of one man and probably in the wounding of others, admonished her captain to give the place where Manuelo was left a wide berth, as the sailors phrase it.

The survival of their companion, whom they had left for dead, must have been entirely foreign to the thoughts of his shipmates, but Manuelo himself was not equally disposed to forgetfulness. He continued anxiously to look for her white sails long after his restoration to health, and when in all probability the ship was hundreds of leagues away on the ocean.

With her departure, had he known it, would have vanished all hope of ever again seeing his native country, and it was well for his happiness that he remained in ignorance of the event, at least until he might learn to appreciate, as he finally did, the kindness of the people in whose hands he had fallen. But contentment, like confidence, is a plant of slow growth, and the soil in which it was now struggling for existence was, to say the least, not wholly congenial. Homesickness is induced by no definable circumstances, nor does it pertain to any particular race. It is a malady to which all mankind alike are subject. A savage in the palace of a king would suffer from it as poignantly as an exile in the bleak forests of Siberia, and Manuelo, though, for the best of reasons, as much pleased at times where he was as thousands have since been in the same locality, could never entirely obliterate from his memory the scenes of his childhood. It was not therefore on account of dissatisfaction with the country, nor yet for ingratitude towards his benefactors, as Justino is careful to inform us, that he was led to hope that the time would arrive when he could make his escape from a land even then as beautiful as Eden, and which was destined in the far-distant future to become extremely attractive to all the rest of mankind.

X.
PROVIDENTIAL.

WHAT with good nursing and care, as already hinted, Manuelo, in a couple of months, was sufficiently healed of his wounds to move forth in the world; and in the meantime he was not neglectful in acquiring information concerning this singular people. His estimation of their character underwent a complete change. In fact, he found them, when properly approached, so far from being blood-thirsty savages, as at first regarded, to be extremely gentle, and possessed of hearts overflowing with the milk of human kindness. It became apparent to him that their attack upon the boat's crew was the result of misapprehension, and merely the outburst of just indignation for the injury wantonly inflicted on one of their number. It is an improbable supposition, but the theory nevertheless was indulged in by the Portuguese priests, that the sailor who threw the first weapon may have remained under the delusion that the skulking Indian was really a wild animal of some sort, a belief rendered barely possible by the fact of his having been clad in skins. Be that as it may, the conduct of the sailor appeared in its results to be disastrous to the last degree, nearly costing, as it did, Manuelo his life. But however it may have appeared at the time, it can hardly be denied now that good eventually resulted from the affair.

It is written, as Justino remarked, that "man shall do no evil that good may follow," but it is always safe to leave the result of one's actions to an overruling Providence. In this instance an apparant disaster certainly opened up to mankind the remote history of an extremely interesting country, which history otherwise must have remained in obscurity forever.

XI.

THE PEOPLE DESCRIBED.

THOUGH not particularly tall, the natives were well formed, athletic, and agile. For an Indian race their complexion was unusually light and their features regular. They were, upon the whole, a comely people. Their hair, as black as the raven's wing, grew to great length, and was closely coiled on the top of the head by the women, and by the men braided in a queue, much after the manner of the Chinese. The gay plumage of birds, curiously wrought, constituted the principal head ornamentation of both sexes; but it was the custom of the women and girls to indulge in wild flowers also, in their season, for the purposes of adornment. The appearance of the people on festive occasions, when gathered together in large numbers, and particularly when engaged in a lively dance, was extremely picturesque.

Always proud of their embellishments, these children of the forest were, probably, the only people in all the world who did not regard some others as more fortunate than themselves. Being entirely satisfied with their condition, and limited possessions, the passion of envy was a stranger to their bosoms. Even the young women were moved with sincere delight by the more brilliant appearance of their companions, and were unremitting in their exertions to add to the attractions of each other. Tne dark-eyed maidens of the Spanish race of that day not unfrequently essayed exhibitions of equal generosity; but their real sentiments were too often betrayed by the illy-concealed manifestations of malignity. Nothing of the kind, however, was ever observed by Manuelo in the expressions of these more tender-hearted and better-bred women of early California.

XII.

MATRIMONIAL AFFAIRS.

IN pursuance of an old established custom of these Indians, all matrimonial alliances among them were contracted in accordance with the united judgment of the leading people of the village, and nothing, in that regard, was left to blind passion, or the foolish indiscretion of youth. It was observed by Manuelo that alliances thus publicly formed were maintained with the utmost fidelity, and any violation of them was visited with the severest penalties.

Their children, though few in numbers, were remarkably robust, sickness being almost unknown among them. Paternal no less than filial affection was a distinguishing feature of their peculiar civilization, and manifestations of love, of both kinds, were most common among them. A want of care for their young by the mothers was never observed, and the domination of the fathers, though sufficiently absolute, was always marked with tenderness.

The chief of the tribe, alone of them all, indulged in a plurality of wives; and to him were allotted two, and no more. The selection of these was not accorded to that high functionary any more than in other cases of matrimony in the village; but the wives of the chief were chosen for him at a council of the people, in which the high priest acted a most conspicuous part. On these interesting occasions of the selection of wives for the young men, which occurred at the season of the year when the flowers were in bloom, the prophet would assume, as a general rule, to be advised and directed in the choice by the spirits of the departed friends of the parties; but whether he was really and truly so influenced or not, Manuelo was unable to say, and Justino ever remained in doubt upon the point; nevertheless, we have the assurance of the keen-eyed stranger, that the selections thus made were uniformly marked with wisdom, and, moreover, that marriages so contracted were sometimes highly spiritual in their results, as instanced in his own particular case, as will appear in the sequel.

After betrothals effected in this manner, months, and even years, would often elapse, precisely the same as in Christian countries, before a final consummation of the unions, during all of which time the parties engaged would remain irrevocably bound to each other, in this respect differing somewhat from the practice prevailing in many of the more enlightened nations of the world, where engagements of marriage are only voluntary.

XIII.
THEIR HABITATIONS.

THE houses of the chief—for as he was furnished with two wives so two houses must needs be provided for him—or lodges, perhaps, more properly to be called—and the lodge of the prophet, were centrally located in reference to the others of the village and were placed upon the highest part of a huge mound, which seemed, to the observing Manuelo, artificial in its formation; but how or when constructed, or by whom, or for what purpose, he could come to no satisfactory conclusion, and so the matter is left to the determination of archeological societies.

The dwellings of these functionaries were surrounded by hundreds of other domiciles, but all erected with care and arranged with a fair degree of regularity and taste. Each of these lodges was tenanted by a single family, and each possessed many of the characteristics, if not the conveniences, of a European home.

The site of the village was originally selected in reference to a stream of pure water, and no pains were wanting on the part of the people to keep good its supply. To avoid the danger of a possible diminution of the stream by drought, pits were sunk and dams erected at convenient intervals along the channel of the rivulet. Nothing was permitted to impede the water's pure flow, and access to the same was never obstructed. Their only means of handling the water was in baskets closely woven and lined with pitch. In these it was borne with safety and kept indefinitely. These vessels, made of reeds and grass, were of all sizes, of many shapes, and extremely useful. Even cooking was accomplished he said by casting a succession of heated stones in them, when partly filled with water, by which means the fluid was kept boiling as long as desired and until the contents of the basket, whether vegetables or flesh, were fitted for food.

As with most nations, the domestic duties were performed by the women, but unlike the practice with many other people, both savage and civilized, the men were in the habit of applauding their wives' exertions, and alleviating their labors by words and acts of kindness. Their politeness was not of that hollow sort made up of pretensions; it partook largely of genuine, self-sacrificing benevolence, leading Justino to the conclusion that by proper exertions they could be converted into most excellent Christians, a work he had at heart, but which, unfortunately, he was never permitted to accomplish.

XIV.

THEIR NAMES.

THIS particular tribe about which the story has thus far been running was called the Yonos, which is the Indian name in that country for deer. It was, doubtless, bestowed upon them, or assumed, by reason of their swiftness of foot; and there was equal significance in the names of the individual members of the tribe, whether male or female. As to the children, they were allowed to go without any certain appellation, except that each was known by a name sounding not unlike that of its father or mother, according to the sex, until, in advancing years, some particular characteristic was developed, when a fitting appellation was given, by which the individual ever afterwards would be known.

The name of the maiden selected at a grand council of the village for the wife of Manuelo was Noña, applied to her because of some resemblance to the quail, she being of an exceedingly shy and untamable disposition. But it ought to be mentioned in this connection, inasmuch as Manuelo himself was emphatic upon the point, that he never considered it worth while to try to capture the girl, since, as he affirmed, even before her selection, he had perfected his plans, and, so far as he was able, made arrangements to abandon the village of the Yonos for a more congenial residence.

From the descriptions of the city over the Bay he concluded it would be more agreeable to his tastes to reside there. This he protested to the Father Confessor was the only reason for his coolness, or, more correctly to speak, for his want of ardor towards his betrothed, and he asseverated repeatedly, and with earnestness, that his conduct towards Noña was not to be attributed to the fact of her being the choice of others only for his wife. Had the privilege been left to him to make a selection from all the damsels of the village, he acknowledged it would have fallen on another, for there were in his eyes more comely persons, and those who, at the same time, were less disposed to avoid his company. One in particular who had been most attentive during his confinement, but whose name is not given, so won upon his regard that the recollection of her ever afterwards remained fresh in his memory, as he confessed. This person scrupled not, on all fitting occasions, to exhibit towards him her good temper; and the difference in the demeanor of the two extorted from Manuelo the reflection that kindness grudgingly bestowed is seldom grateful, while a spirit of generosity increases the reward many fold. Bounties conferred with an unwilling hand are shorn of half their value, while the smallest favor proceeding from a full heart assumes the amplest proportions.

From the manner of Manuelo in detailing this part of his experience, the confidence of Friar Justino in his magnanimity was somewhat impaired, and it can easily be imagined that this interposition of the Yono people in a matter and manner adverse to his tastes, tended not a little to increase his desire to leave them. While his gallantry might have stood in the way of his admitting the facts, it is fair to conclude that this action of the tribe had much influence in hastening his departure. But justice compels the acknowledgment that he would in all probability have left the Yonos had he never even heard of the maiden. But more upon this subject in the next chapter.

XV.

A DOUBTFUL TRICK.

THE assignment of a wife by the village council being equivalent, under the strange customs of that country, to actual marriage, and being looked upon as a most sacred obligation, it was not surprising to find, on the part of the leading people of the tribe, the strongest opposition to his departure. As soon as his purpose became known, and it was in vain for him to attempt to conceal it, obstacles were thrown in his way, and the persistency of the people in thwarting his purpose led to much embarrassment.

The large town on which his heart was set lay leagues away, and the only means of reaching it, so far as could be perceived, was by water. As time rolled by he became convinced that the longer the delay the greater would be the difficulty in his escape. The matter was the subject of discussion everywhere, and he could plainly see that complications were increasing. He had often heard, in his youthful days, that delays were dangerous, but he never till now realized the full meaning of the saying. To tear himself abruptly away he felt would be to sorely offend the Yonos, and to attempt flight surreptitiously by seizing one of the canoes, of which a number were always moored by the shore, might prove fatal to his plans, for, in that event, he would surely be pursued, and, if overtaken, which was but too likely, would be punished.

Reconnoitering the great Bay, as opportunity offered, in either direction far up and down its borders, and thus satisfying himself beyond pervadenture that to pass around it by land to the north or south was quite impossible, he was compelled, as it were, by the force of circumstances, to resort to a species of strategy, justifiable, it may be, but which the pious Justino was convinced would have been highly reprehensible had it been practiced upon a more enlightened and Christian community. Instead of appealing directly to their reason, as possibly he might have done with success, he cunningly wrought upon their heathenish credulity in a manner we are about to relate.

Well knowing the belief of this people in all manner of supernatural interpositions, and their faith as well in admonitions from heavenly quarters, the crafty Manuelo falsely pretended to hold communications with the spirits of his deceased friends and to be directed by them. In order to make this imposition the more complete he accustomed himself to imitate, as nearly as he was able, the incantations of the high priest himself, going through a variety of ceremonies which seemed to be understood by the natives themselves; but to these he added certain maneuvers entirely his own, and by such conduct imposed upon the credulity of those simple-minded villagers.

Fortunately for him, when stricken down upon the beach, he had retained upon his person, besides a cutlas of Moorish pattern more than a vara in length, a pair of large Spanish pistols, and likewise a few rounds of ammunition. Of the latter he had been exceedingly careful, knowing full well that when it was gone there would be no possibility of renewing his stock. From the first he had concealed from the natives the use of these arms, apprehensive lest, should they become instructed in handling them, he would be deprived of their use altogether, or at least be compelled by their childish curiosity to exhaust his last grain of powder, in which case the pistols would have lost all their value to him. Impelled by such motives he had already taught the natives, both young and old, to look upon the weapons as something sacred, little dreaming at the time how important and peculiar an end was to be subserved by the lesson. Prudent man that he was, he never forgot how indispensable these firelocks might be to his safety in some conflict, it might be with man, it might be with fourfooted beast. Had Manuelo been as vainglorious as many another sailor would have shown himself to be under similar circumstances, he would have taken delight in surprising the Indians by experimenting with his pistols in their presence long before there was any occasion for his doing so. But, thanks to his good sense, his few rounds of powder were preserved, and proved useful in a direction little anticipated by him, as we shall presently see.

In addition to the impressive ceremonies usually adopted by the natives for the citation of spirits, Manuelo made full preparation for firing off one of his pistols at a certain stage of the proceedings, and for kindling a fire at the same time with the burning powder. And though he warned the people beforehand, as well as he was able, of what he intended to do, and, after the manner of jugglers, required them to join at a particular time in the performance of his trick, yet it seems they could have formed no adequate conception of his purpose, for when the explosion took place the spectators, more than astonished, fell prostrate upon the ground, hiding their faces in their hands. To say that they were, one and all, completely dumfounded, would be to express what occurred in the most moderate language.

Differing from the Spiritualists of later times, these held their meetings in the open air, and under the spreading branches of some ancient oak. Their mystical performances, though in the night-time, were open and above-board. The priest, who, in this particular instance, be it remembered, was the irreverent Manuelo himself, occupied a mound constructed partly of stones near the sacred oak. By his side stood a rude altar, upon which, during the ceremony, a fire was usually lighted; but by the direction of Manuelo this fire had now been carefully extinguished. We have said there were no preparations made for hiding anything from the assembled multitude, and, indeed, on this occasion there was not the slightest necessity for concealment, since a far greater wonder to them than visible spirits could have been was the terrible power of gunpowder. A heavy clap of thunder from the clear blue sky of that summer evening would not have astonished them more. In fact, the poor, ignorant barbarians believed, from that moment that their stranger friend could command, at will, the artillery of heaven. Combustible material, laid by Manuelo in advance upon the altar, was set on fire by the explosion, and the amazement of the people at the report of the pistol was a thousand times increased when they saw a fire blaze forth, apparently created instantaneously from nothing.

The force of genius is irresistible, and Manuelo was no longer a prisoner. He had conquered his liberty. From that hour he was able to command and direct in whatsoever he would. The Indians seemed to forget that he had once been a helpless, wounded sailor; they now regarded him as little less than divine. The women almost worshiped him, and Noña herself ceased, in a measure, her foolish coquetry. From that time all the prerogatives of the high priest and chief combined were accorded him. Without difficulty he caused his admiring friends to believe that he was divinely inspired to leave them, and all opposition to his departure subsided. It was with reluctance, nevertheless, that they consented to the loss of so renowned a person as he was regarded, and not until a faithful promise had been extorted from him that at some time he would return to them, a promise which truth compels us to acknowledge he never intended to fulfill. He did return, however, though long afterwards, with great gladness, and under circumstances so strange as to leave on the mind of the good Justino the impression that it was intended in some sense by Providence as a punishment for his perfidy.

XVI.

HIS DEPARTURE.

IN pursuance of his plans, Manuelo at an early day bade his Yono friends, not forgetting his betrothed, a gentle *adios*, for a trip across the broad Bay. Clad in the best robes the natives could furnish, and crowned with a *tiara*, woven of the brightest of feathers, by the fairest of hands, he was placed in the middle of a large canoe and paddled by stalwart men in the direction of the greater village. Armed with his trusty saber, which hung by his side, and with loaded pistols, Manuelo felt like a veritable prince of the realm. But the result showed that he presumed more than was warranted upon his newly-achieved dignity, for his approach being observed from the other side, he was menacingly repelled and not permitted to come within rods of the land. Neither the head chief himself nor his followers had ever so much as heard of the Spaniard, and from his curious appearance they feared he might be some hostile prince, from a long way off, come upon some mission they could not divine, and which they feared might bode them evil. His Yono companions were not entirely unknown in that country, for their tribe was really but a branch of the same great nation, and acknowledged allegiance to this king. To be compelled to remain in the boat while his men were permitted to land, was no less humiliating than unexpected to Manuelo, and at first this treatment disposed him, in true Spanish style, and with weapon in hand, to enforce a landing. This purpose he would doubtless have carried into execution, regardless of the cost to himself, but for the timely remonstrance of a member of his crew, better known on the shore than the rest, having been at this place before. This cool-headed person at last succeeded in persuading his master to possess his soul in patience for a time, and until himself and another could proceed to the king's headquarters and thus pave the way for an interview. Better counsels prevailing with Manuelo, he contented himself on the wave while his two companions sought out the dignified chief in the city not distant, and laid before him an account of the marvelous achievements of the stranger; the result of which was that in a short time the king, attended by a large retinue of his subjects, himself in the van, came down to the water's edge to welcome the stranger ashore. Their approach was surveyed by Manuelo at first with misgivings, but he was soon made at ease, where he sat, by such demonstrations of good-will on the part of the king as the grandeur of his character would allow. The visitor was conducted at once to the great wigwam of the chief, on the top of a high mound, in the center of the town. His familiarity with the Indian dialect, already acquired, put Manuelo upon terms at court without the usual delay, as he alleged. It is possible the story told by the men who preceded him, touching the wonderful powers of Manuelo to create thunder and lightning, to kindle a fire at will, and to invoke the spirits, may have contributed not a little to his welcome by the king, for it is hardly presumable that a mere stranger, unaided by reputation, would be received, in so short a time, on terms of familiarity at any court, savage or civilized. The treatment

Manuelo experienced was all that could have been desired. Not only was he awarded an apartment by himself in the chief's great lodge, but he was furnished with attendants to observe his every want. In the manuscript occurred the equivalent of the expression so often repeated since, that he was the observed of all observers. The first white man that had ever set foot in that considerable capital, he was, of course, the special wonder of the inhabitants. It was the principal ambition of the men to observe his actions, and of the women to note his style of dress. The curiosity of the children foreshadowed at first so much of annoyance to Manuelo that he found it advisable to assume much more reserve towards them than naturally belonged to his character He was, however, now no longer a seaman, but in truth, in this country, a prince and a prophet. With pistols, and powder, and prudence, he expected to maintain this character, but without these, or deprived of either of them, he was in danger of losing his standing. It was a subject of no little solicitude with him, therefore, as with all countries in those days, to preserve both his dignity and his weapons, not that he needed either for his protection, for, in the event of a collision, this brave race, in spite of his arms, would have overpowered him in a moment; but they were required for show,—his side arms on state occasions, it might be, and his pistols for a service not known to other kings and courts, but nevertheless well understood by Manuelo.

XVII.

HIS MAJESTY.

THE Indian name of the king, for some unaccountable reason, is not given by Father Justino, but the meaning of it, according to the authority, was bear-slayer—an appellation bestowed upon him on account of his skill in hunting that ferocious beast. In stature he was among the largest of men, and otherwise distinguished by the peculiarity of his adornments, and likewise by a deep scar on his face, the result of a wound inflicted by some wild animal. He was a person of much reserve of manner and quiet dignity when at home, but, like his warriors, was greatly addicted to manly sports,—to hunting and fishing, to wrestling and racing,—and with his men he frequently indulged in such pastimes.

In athletic exercises the king was seldom surpassed, but if it chanced that any, in such contests, were able to excel him, courtesy and good breeding forbade their doing so; in this respect imitating people of the highest known civilizations.

It was the custom of this nation to choose their king at a convocation of warriors from all the villages, summoned together for that purpose by heralds, sent out weeks in advance, and long enough beforehand to allow of the preparation for a great feast in commemoration of the event. The king was selected for his strength, both of body and mind, due regard being paid likewise to his manly virtues and moral worth. His continuance in office would last while all these qualities endured and no longer. In the event of his becoming infirm by reason of age or other cause, or in case of the impairment of his intellect or virtues, he was constrained by his people to retire from his high position. When driven from power, even if for lack of moral integrity, if not too flagrant, the deposed chief would be permitted to take refuge in the priesthood, and generally to assume high rank in that order.

The present king, who had been upon the throne many years, was observed to incline to habits of ease. This was remarked by Manuelo and others more distinctly than by himself. As usual with mankind, he was slow to perceive and still slower to acknowledge his waning strength, but, not entirely oblivious of it, he sought to conceal his infirmity under the cloak of reserve. His conduct, for this reason, on all public occasions, was marked with a show of dignity, which Manuelo, being a member of his household, could plainly perceive was more apparent than real.

XVIII.

THE HIGH PRIEST.

The chief priest at the time, a venerable man, as full of excellence as of years, had formerly been king, but had been deposed, it was said, by reason of some bodily infirmity and not on account of his age. Be that as it may, he bore the change patiently and appeared not in the least humiliated by his deposition, for of him it is related that he retained in his new sphere all the gravity that naturally belonged to both positions. Had he really been endowed with all the wisdom indicated by his manners, a dethronement for decadence of intellect would have been out of the question. Such was the propriety of his conduct that dereliction of duty was never suspected, and at no time in his long life had he betrayed a lack of manly virtue. Pokee, for such was his name, had been a good king, and he was now no less worthy a priest. There were other seers and prophets in the city, all venerable men, but none at all comparable to him. It was observed that the priests in that country were accustomed to provide their own living, after the manner enjoined upon all men, "by the sweat of the brow," so that the people were priest-ridden in no sense of the term. There was no tithing nor taxation in all that country in those halcyon days. The king and the high priest alone were publicly supported, and that was done by voluntary contributions, which were more than sufficient for the purpose. Gifts of delicacies, in their season, the best that the country afforded, were liberally bestowed upon these functionaries, and, as remarked at the time, the generosity of the people was greatly augmented by the appearance of Manuelo among them.

The habits and customs on this side of the Bay differed not essentially from those on the other, excepting, perhaps, that here everything was on a much grander scale. The laws of the whole country, it is true, were the same, and similar superstitions prevailed everywhere, but the religious rites, while, as in other places, performed in the open air, were here more impressive.

XIX.
EMBARRASSMENTS.

MANUELO soon saw, and much too soon for his peace of mind, as many a fledgling priest in other lands before him had seen, that much was to be learned before he could be confident of success in his new calling. He had shown himself a good prophet for one occasion and when his liberty was at stake, but it was another thing to keep up the delusion, in the presence of this brighter and more critical people, and before so grave and reverend a dignitary as the great Pokee. The more this subject was weighed in his mind, the more oppressive it grew. He even thought, at times, his freedom had been purchased at too high a price, when paid for in the doubtful barter of falsehood and deceit. To be plain, it was not his conscience that troubled him so much as the dilemma of being compelled to keep alive indefinitely a delusion, or suffer ignominious exposure, and much worse it might be at the hands of an indignant people, some of whom, for aught he knew, might be acquainted with the use of fire-arms. These considerations determined his mind to seek a postponement of the further exercise of his priestly functions as long as possible, in the hope that some lucky turn in his fortune might relieve him altogether from embarrassment, or, at all events, until he could ascertain whether or not, in repeating his trick, he would be treading on solid ground. To his relief at this time, happily, came the remembrance of a Spanish proverb learned in his childhood, which says, "When you are in doubt do it not," and his purpose was strengthened.

But the advent of Manuelo having been heralded by his renown as a conjurer, and all the people believing in the power of the priesthood to call up the shades of the dead on proper occasions, he was confidently expected, and particularly by the old chief, to give some demonstration of his powers. In this, as in other countries, the wish of the sovereign being equivalent to a command, the heaviest draft ever made upon Manuelo's artfulness was to avoid being compelled to put his powers into practice before he was ready. But, as ever before, so in this emergency his genius forsook him not. He was the guest of the king, and his safety depended upon his obtaining such influence at court as would enable him to control, instead of being controlled by, his majesty; and this is not the first instance recorded in which a courtier has realized that necessity.

While Manuelo had come to this place in the guise of a prophet, he had likewise assumed the airs of a prince, and the better to carry out his purpose, he now pretended to belong to a powerful empire far to the southward, which was true enough; but it was not true, as he further stated, that his father was king of that country, and that himself was heir to the throne. Knowing full well, however, there was no one to contradict his assertions, he took on his new character with the greatest confidence and maintained it with far better success than could have been expected of one who had never before seen king, nor court, nor courtier been.

XX.

PRETENSIONS.

THOUGH as friendly to Manuelo as anyone else, the translator is not so blinded by partiality as to claim for him more than is justly due. Unquestionably, Manuelo was distinguished for the originality of his resources, while in other respects he may have been in no manner superior to many

---

NOTE.—To avoid a waste of time (unless, indeed, the indulgent reader should be a person of leisure), it might be as well to skip over the next chapter, it being the one of no particular interest.

another Spaniard of that generation. But no one is great in all things, nor even in many, and it is most difficult, sometimes, to tell who of a number is superior. It might be possible to distinguish the grandest tree if the forest were all of pines, but it is made up of many species. The largest oak may be overtopped by the slender fir, while in strength the oak may far excel. The oak and the pine may both be inferior in fiber to the maple, and all again be eclipsed in usefulness by some other species. As the trees of the forest are valued according to their several qualities, so with men; some excel in one, and some in another direction, but none in all. Qualities are measured, and weighed, and gauged, and the standard of one may be wholly inapplicable to another. Cloth is not measured by the gallon, nor wine by the yard, nor is superiority determined by any particular criterion.

Our new-fledged prince, for prince Manuelo must now be considered, found little difficulty in retaining his arms, a thing he greatly desired. They were, for greater security of possession, always borne upon his person when awake, and kept by his side when sleeping. His cutlas, which was most prized, as of more lasting utility than the pistols, attracted but little attention from the natives for the reason that they were wholly unacquainted with the uses of metals, with the single exception of gold, which was valued for ornament only. He was at some pains to keep his keen blade concealed in its scabbard to avoid their prying curiosity, and perhaps also to escape an occasion for proving the real purpose for which it was intended. As to his pistols, they were looked upon by the natives as curious ornaments, and were worn in a manner best calculated to sustain that delusion. The difference, in reality, between what is for actual use, and what for mere show, even in the most enlightened of countries, is not so marked as to render absurd this notion of these barbarians.

NOTE.—There is evidently something lacking in this chapter, but

XXI.

NATIVE WEAPONS.

OF the various arms of these Indians it is difficult to say which was most needful. Their javelins were pointed with bone and were handled with skill, and often with fatal effect. A small spear, like a dart, was thrown with a sling attached to the end of a stick, and revolved in its course. This instrument was sent with remarkable precision, and was useful in war, but chiefly in hunting. Every man in the tribe and every lad of sufficient age was armed with one or the other of these missiles; but the javelin was more commonly the arm of the adult. Bows and arrows were likewise in general use among them, the latter always tipped with flint, or obsidian, and as sharp as a knife.

The expertness of certain artificers in working out these arrow-heads was the more astonishing since it was all done by hand, and with remarkable facility. A skillful artisan could easily turn off half a score in a day, perfect in shape and ready for use. Of the same materials, and in a similar way, their knives were produced, almost equal in keenness to knives of steel, and hardly less useful for the cutting of skins and food. Their hatchets of stone were likewise quite sharp. Set in handles of wood, these were formidable weapons, both in war and in the chase, as Manuelo could testify from his own personal experience. Like the javelin and arrow they were capable of being thrown a great distance, and with an accuracy of aim never equaled by Europeans unless, perchance, in the most ancient and barbarous times. This last remark is an interpolation by the translator, for neither Manuelo would believe, nor Justino admit, that the people of Europe, much less the

---

whether to charge the omission to Manuelo, or Justino, or to the priests at Evora, the translator is in doubt. The character of the subject discussed, however, points suspicion strongly towards the priests.

good people of Portugal, had ever been other than most enlightened Christians. It is undeniable, nevertheless, that in the far-distant past, and before histories were thought of, every part of the world, in its time, was in a savage condition; for have we not found, even in Spain, implements of stone similar in construction to those here described by Father Justino?

XXII.
THE KINGDOM.

THE country occupied by this considerable nation, who, by the way, called themselves the Santos, had no definite and fixed boundary, except so far as formed by the ocean on the one side, but it included, altogether, a large number of villages scattered throughout many valleys. It comprehended a wide range of territory, but how wide Manuelo's conception is at fault, or else Justino has unwittingly failed to transmit the facts to us. All the people, however, who acknowledged the supremacy of Bear-Slayer were, figuratively speaking, under the same flag. They possessed no banner, in fact, but their national emblem, which served the same purpose, was a white bird's wing which every warrior was accustomed to wear as a part of his head-gear.

The name by which these people were known, when rendered in Spanish and then again in English, was "The Pines." Whether this appellation was assumed by them because of their resemblance in numbers to the pines of the forest, or whether because they were tall and strong like the pine, is not known, for the manuscript is silent upon this point. But as it is a subject of speculation, we may repeat the suggestion that their extreme fondness for the nut of the pine may have had something to do in conferring upon them this peculiar cognomen.

A marked feature of the country as then described was its well-rounded mountains and smooth sloping hills, covered with timber of every sort. Another characteristic, hardly less conspicuous, to which attention was especially called, was its many beautiful valleys all studded with evergreen trees, and coated, perennially, with a carpet of grass, interspersed in the springtime with bright-colored and sweet-smelling flowers. Barring from his description most of the trees, which, however, may have become exterminated in these three hundred and odd years by forest fires, and we have in Manuelo's account a picture which will be recognized as nearly correct, even at the present day.

Another circumstance mentioned by him, and one which must go far toward identifying that part of California as the scene of his trials and triumphs, was its liability to earthquakes. These, he informs us, occurred almost every year of his stay in that country, and as often caused great trepidation among the women and children. One shock in particular he mentions, because more severe than the rest, drove the waters of the Bay quite into the town, but did no further damage than causing great fright to the people, and washing away all the boats that lay moored on the beach, many of which, however, were afterwards recovered. This earthquake was followed closely by a dense cloud of smoke, which enveloped the land, but whence it proceeded, or how it was produced, no one at the time could tell. As soon as a moment was allowed for reflection, after the shock, the sacred groves were sought by the populace, and from there the loudest incantations were sent up by the priests, the result of which was a quiet earth once more, and in due time a clear sky, greatly to the gratification of the people, who were by no means slow in manifesting their appreciation of this most opportune service of the prophets.

XXIII.

THE CAPITAL.

IF Manuelo was not mistaken, which does not seem likely, the chief settlement of the Santos was located on the opposite side of the Bay from where the great commercial city of San Francisco was afterwards built, but just at what point is not known, nor can that now be of much consequence, since the ruins of the same, after this long lapse of time, have in all probability become totally obliterated. If known to have been where the considerable city of Oakland now stands, it would not add much to the interest, since the name of the first city is now entirely lost, and any account of it would apply as well to one locality as to another. What's in a name? has often been asked. The reply is, that whatever is famous in the world's history is exclusively so from the preservation of names. Had the name of Alexander the Great been suppressed, all his mighty achievements, if known at all, would have inured as much to the glory of any one of his million men as to himself.

Without doubt, in the long series of ages unrepresented by written history, hundreds, and perhaps thousands, of heroes have existed, no less famous in their day and generation than Alexander, or Cæsar, but whose ashes now repose in unknown sepulchers. The importance of perpetuating a name, whether for good or evil, cannot be better shown than by the mention of Bucephalus, most famous of horses, whose glory, like that of his proud master, has been, most fortunately for him, transmitted to us.

It is an interesting fact, and one deemed worthy of mention by Justino, that this horse and his rider are the only two prominent characters, in all that vast multitude, whose history is preserved to this day.

But the reflection arises, unbidden, that had the name of the

Santos capital been rescued from oblivion by Manuelo, even that might not have aided in fixing its locality.

Babylon, the most magnificent of cities, was located somewhere on the River Euphrates; but beyond that its site is unknown. And so of the city of the Santos; we only know that it was on the Bay of San Francisco. If Babylon possesses an advantage over this, it is only in name; for, thanks to the good Justino, a description of the one is as well preserved as of the other. The city of the Assyrians, it is known, was rectangular in construction, and occupied both sides of the river, while the city of the Santos was circular in form, and was on but one side of the Bay.

In the center of the latter city, as we have already seen, were situated the dwellings of the king and of the principal prophet. Surrounding these, and at regular intervals, in numerous rows, were the tenements of the people. In rows did we say? and that was correct, for the city was built from the interior outwards, and the last of the rows was never completed. In the first of the circles, near the center, dwelt the priests, and the seers, and the principal men of the nation. Each one of the lodges in the outer circles was a family dwelling, and these were numbered by hundreds and thousands. Their houses, not large, were ingeniously constructed of wood, and of wattle, and reeds, and were plastered within and without. While not remarkably imposing, they were well calculated to afford protection against the winds and rains, and the heat of the summer sun. Their carpets were matting, and their beds of the same material, spread upon dried grass. Their household utensils were such as have been described as in use by the Yonos, to which, perhaps, may be added knives of flint and needles of bone.

Their dwellings were always kept clean, and in person they were seldom untidy. Their clothing, of which they had but a limited supply, was made of the skins of wild beasts. The elk alone of all animals was domesticated, and elk in large herds were maintained in the neighboring valleys. Occasionally these were used as beasts of burden, to bring home booty and game; and, presumably for this reason, their flesh was seldom eaten by the natives. The horns of this animal, though abundant, were highly prized. They were used for the making of spearheads and fish-hooks, and for other like purposes. The flesh of the deer was the principal meat of the people, and was prepared for use by drying in the sun. A goodly supply was always on hand in every household.

But of all the fourfooted animals found in this country, the hare was the most abundant, and perhaps the most useful. In parts of the land these nimble little creatures literally swarmed, and their skins were in constant demand for the making of garments. Owing to this fact, due care was observed in keeping good their supply. Being protected from wanton destruction, they were killed only as their skins or their flesh might be needed. The same regard, and for a similar reason, was paid to the antelope, the pelts of which were even more highly prized. It may be said of these wise Santos that they were never improvident or wasteful of whatever was useful for clothing or food; and in this it will be admitted they exhibited a higher degree of civilization than is enjoyed by many of the most enlightened Christian nations.

NOTE.—The following extract from the Solano *Republican* of very recent date is so strikingly confirmatory of our history that we cannot forbear to make a note of it:—

"The primeval Caucasian commenced his existence in the garden of Eden, and may not a beneficent Deity have placed the primeval inhabitant of California in an Eden no less suited to his happiness and the supplying of his physical wants? The wide-branched oaks showered down their annual fruitage of life-giving acorns to feed the dusky matron and the tired huntsman and warrior, as the manna fell upon the Israelites in the wilderness. The wild grasses growing in grandeur upon the silvery plains bowed over in thrifty bearing of nutritious seeds. The rippling

XXIV.
THEIR OCCUPATIONS.

BY observing these just relations towards the brute creation, it was noticed that a sort of harmony sprung up between the natives and the animal kingdom, at least so far as the inoffensive portion of it was concerned; but towards those more ferocious beasts of the mountain, as the bear, the lion, and the wolf, an unrelenting warfare was waged. Even the birds of the air seemed to look upon these rude masters of the soil as their friends. Quail, grouse, and other birds of that species frequented the hills in vast numbers, and water-fowl of every description, from swan to swift-winged widgeon, swarmed on the lakes, rivers, and bays, apparently unmolested by man. Never frightened by the report of fire-arms, these birds were likewise half tame. In taking so many of them as were needed for food and for feathers, the people proceeded with such quiet and skill as to create but little alarm. Whatever the fact may be, Manuelo asserted it as his firm belief that many of the water-fowl looked upon the noble Santos as their natural protectors against the fox and the cunning coyote. Large numbers of these ravenous creatures were destroyed by the natives, and greatly to the relief of the feathered tribes; but the object of their destruction was to obtain their pelts, rather than the protection of the birds, and so it happens, remarked Justino, that man often receives credit for his actions regardless of his motives. The beaver, the otter, and other amphibious creatures, were sought for their furs, which were worn by the princi-

---

streams were filled to overflowing with toothsome trout, and the elk, the deer, the antelope, and the hare fell at the demand of the swift-flying arrow, and as the winter rains came on, so came the heavens aglow with myriad numbers of wild fowl from the far distant North to supply their portion to the aboriginal necessities. It was an Indian's paradise in the long, long ago."

pal chiefs and prophets. In the taking of fish, considering their appliances, the Santos, both male and female, displayed unexampled skill, and fish constituted largely their diet, being freely indulged in every day of the week, and not on Fridays alone. All kinds of fish were captured by them, except the great whale, which sometimes came rolling and tumbling into the Bay, but was never disturbed by the natives, being always regarded with feelings of awe.

Though fishing and hunting supplied their principal wants, they were not without berries, wild fruits, and nuts, in considerable variety. These were gathered in their season and when dried were stored for future use.

As wise and as happy as these people were, they knew nothing whatever about the cultivation of the ground. This will excite less wonder when it is reflected that all their wants were satisfied without a resort to any of the more slavish methods of obtaining a living. Their means of subsistence were ample in the lines marked out for themselves, and it may well be doubted if their enjoyment would have been augmented by adding any other. Bread they had not; bread they knew not; bread they wanted not. The curse pronounced against Adam and his descendants, "In the sweat of thy face shalt thou eat bread," had no application whatever to them, and Father Justino was confronted with the apparent exemption of a whole people from a malediction which he had been taught to believe was universal in its application. The anxiety of the friar to find an explanation for this remarkable fact led to a diligent searching of the Scriptures, and there he discovered, to his great joy, that the occupation of Abel had been the keeping of flocks and herds, the same exactly as these people; and the good friar reached the conclusion that this son of Adam might have left progeny of his own, the descendants of whom these people may have been. This opinion was strengthened by the further observation, likewise recorded in sacred history, that "unto Adam also and his wife did the Lord God make coats of skins and clothed them," a custom faithfully followed by these, their supposed descendants. As with our first parents, so here also the garments in use were better calculated to hide their nakedness than to protect their persons from the cold and heat of the seasons. Coats, indeed, like Adam and his wife, the Santos possessed, made of skins like theirs, and long, but other garments had they none. This robe-like vestment constituted the dress of the men, women, and children, indiscriminately, and none were provided with better, not even the king.

XXV.

SETTING THE FASHIONS.

MANUELO soon discovered the great necessity that existed for a change in the form of clothing of this people, and he wisely concluded it would detract nothing from his dignity as prince or prophet to suggest some improvement in the same. To this conclusion he was partially driven by his own necessities. The scanty supply worn by himself ashore from the ship, had already become the worse for usage, and he was constrained to replace it with new. The only materials for his purpose at hand were the skins of beasts, and with these he must needs fashion his garments. His experience on shipboard, and ample enough it had been, in patching and mending his clothes, now stood him in excellent part. His first great need was new pants, to replace the old ones, now fairly reduced to tatters. The pelts of the deer and the wolf were in plenty, and of fur-bearing animals not a few. There was barely enough of his old garment left to serve him the turn of a pattern, and he selected the soft yellow skin of the deer as the best with which to replace them. It need not be stated that while he was thus engaged in playing the part of a tailor, he was constrained to adopt the scanty costume of the natives. His trusty saber served the purpose of tailor's shears, and for a needle he ground in the form of an awl, a bolt from one of his pistols. Leathern thongs were used in the place of thread, and so all his wants were supplied. The finished garment was tasty enough for the time and the place, and Manuelo was proud of his achievement. Every step in the work, as he wished it might be, was closely observed by the women, a goodly number of whom were all the while present.

With a fair stock of patience, and encouraged by his former success, he presently fashioned also an excellent waistcoat out of the skins of the fox; and he then made a coat in the form of a blouse, with sleeves of full length, from the pelts of black bears, the hair being left on the outside. His head-dress was wrought from the skin of the beaver, but not after the modern style of hat from that same fur, and a good covering for his feet he was able to make from the thick, tough hide of the grizzly bear. Fully arrayed in these garments, Manuelo was more than ever the admiration of the people, and certain it is he had good right to exult, for the triumph of his genius was never before so complete. His fame on account of these successes soon spread throughout the city, and there was no longer any limit to his influence. It was readily seen by all that the style of his new habiliments was better calculated to impart comfort than the old, and he found less difficulty in setting the fashions than he had anticipated.

In imitation of his example, the whole population, so to speak, set themselves about the business of making pantaloons, vests, coats, caps, and shoes, and before many weeks had elapsed, almost every man, woman, youth, maiden, and child in the city was attired in one or another of these useful articles. Seldom, if ever, had fashion spread more rapidly, even in the most enlightened country. But a complete dress was rarely indulged in by any one person, unless we except the king and his courtiers, including Manuelo, of course. As a rule, only one or two articles of apparel were worn by the same individual, and on public occasions, it is related, the assemblages presented a highly picturesque, if not a comical, appearance. The pantaloons and the blouse became the favorite garments of both sexes, and the wearing of neither by either sex created no disturbance in that country.

Manuelo was wont to say that next to his achievement as a priest and a conjurer among the Yonos, his success in establishing new styles at the capital was the grandest triumph of his life, and he congratulated himself most of all that in this latter case he had contributed very largely to the happiness of a whole class of his fellow-beings. In this, again, is displayed his never-failing goodness of heart, for though afterwards he acquired distinction as a warrior, he counted not his successes in that direction as superior to his attainments in a peaceful way; and so it should be, thought Justino, the man that promotes the welfare and adds to the happiness of his race, is really entitled to more consideration than the one who, for his own glory, annoys and destroys mankind. True civilization is indicated by the prevalence of the former sentiment, and barbarity by the latter. It was wondered by the priest if the world would ever arise to an appreciation of its civic heroes, such as Manuelo surely was.

XXVI.

THEIR SUNDAYS.

BECAUSE the Santos were ignorant of the laws of Moses, they paid little respect to the Sabbath day. Even in times of peace, and notwithstanding the pious instructions of Manuelo, they could never be brought to a comprehension of the distinction between Sunday and another day of the week. They were less to be condemned on this account, however, from the fact that Manuelo himself, by reason of wounds, or for some other cause, lost his reckoning, and was uncertain during all of his stay among them whether Sunday was Saturday, or Monday, Sunday. But this was not a matter of so much importance at the time, since there was no place of worship in that country for him to attend, and no Christian priest to whom to confess his sin of forgetfulness. But he made the best reckoning he was able to under the circumstances, and always observed one day out of the seven for pious meditations, except indeed when abroad on some warlike expedition, or other important business, exceptions recognized as proper by all Christian nations.

But the Santos were not without their own Sundays, if such they might be called, which occurred twice a month, or just at the full and again at the new of the moon. These were days of rest from secular pursuits, unless it might be the pursuit of a bear or the like, and were observed with almost as much show of piety as characterizes the Sabbath day in gospel lands. These were called the Prophets' days and were devoted to religious observances.

The places of worship recognized by this people, as in the case of the Yonos, were in the open air and under the spreading branches of trees. The pulpit or rostrum was a mound overgrown with grass, and surmounted by an altar of stones, upon which a fire was kept burning during the whole of the Sabbath day. Their hours of meeting were at the rising and setting of the sun, and their ceremonies consisted of chanting and the invocation of spirits. The priests, as Manuelo would have it, pretended to be on familiar terms with the souls of the dead, and at certain times would appear to converse as freely with them as with their own flesh and blood. Their gravity of manner and apparent sincerity were no less than that of the Dominicans themselves, and Manuelo was so impressed thereby that he might have accepted their creed as his own but for his success in the same direction, which he knew but too well was attributable to his pistols alone. By this fortunate circumstance alone, Justino thought, Manuelo's conversion to heathenism, and the loss of his soul, were prevented.

Such faith had these heathen in their own particular mode of worship that no expedition was undertaken unless by direction of the priests. Their esteem for their friends in the other world was unbounded, and the good friar believed, from the account that was given, that they were addicted to the pagan practice of ancestral worship, and his pious desire to be the bearer among them of the only true religion was depicted on many pages of the voluminous manuscript.

In the main the Santos were a peace-loving people, and strifes were uncommon among them; but if war was proposed, the oracles were consulted, and the same resort was had in the case of deposing a king. From this it will be observed that the priests were all powerful, and that the king himself held his place subject to their will. But, unlike the practice in other countries, where a similar rule prevailed at the time of that writing, the king of the Santos could only be deposed for some moral, intellectual, or physical infirmity, whereas in other and more enlightened lands the reigning prince was sometimes set aside by the pontiff for an offense against the church, and without a formal invocation of supernatural aid.

XXVII.

SUN WORSHIP.

SITUATED, as these people ever had been, beyond the reach of interruption from the outside world, they enjoyed that independence in social life, as well as in religious belief, which immunity from intrusion would naturally confer. There was no adversary to their opinions, and no enemy to their institutions. They were alike free from fear and free from importunity. The only disturbers of their peace were the prowling bear and the insidious panther. In this primitive condition they might have continued, we know not how long, but for the greed of the Spanish race, which eventually led to encroachments upon them. In religion, as in other habits of life, they were peculiar. From some unknown incentive, the Santos were in the habit of paying reverence to the sun, which we are informed they regarded as the source of all light and life. In pursuance of this unchristian notion, the people assembled in the early morning of each Prophets' day, in their places of worship, and, with faces all eastward turned, anxiously awaited the coming forth of that great luminary. On his first appearance over the distant hills, the sun was greeted with demonstrations of joy. After giving expression to their feelings, with no less earnestness than if his coming had been in answer to their prayers, they bowed down before the full-orbed king of day, and covering their faces with their hands, remained in silence for some time. In the evening, again assembled in like manner, they awaited the slow sinking of the setting sun into the western ocean, when, on a signal from the priest, all broke forth into lamentations, which, continuing until the curtain of night shut down upon the scene, one and all would retire to their homes and to peaceful slumbers.

The world they regarded as something within, and not upon which they dwelt; in this belief differing not from the erudite Urban VIII., the Atic Bee, so called, who about this time was inflicting punishment upon the heretical Galileo for proclaiming a different theory.*

---

*It may be remembered that Galileo lived many years subsequent to these adventures of Manuelo, and it is impossible, therefore, that Justino could have introduced this illustration in his manuscript. The only way to account for its appearance is to suppose that it may have been injected into the narrative by some one of the meddlesome priests at Evora, an explanation somewhat fortified by the fact of the well-known jealousy existing between the Dominican brotherhood and the order of Jesuits. The perse-

But with infinitely less knowledge of heavenly affairs than was possessed by that learned pope, these Indians looked upon, or rather up to, the sky above them as to the dome of a mighty tabernacle, arching over their inheritance, which was regarded by them as the very center of creation. The stars were believed to be within the dome, and set like gems to adorn the ceiling of the great structure. The silent moon was an interesting object to them, so far only as it marked the recurrence of their sabbaths. In other matters of astronomy they were uninformed, but the phases of the moon seemed to be understood by them perfectly, it being the duty of the priests to keep these things in mind, and errors in calculations seldom or never occurred.

XXVIII.

FESTIVITIES.

THE regular festivals of the Santos were but two in the year, one in the spring and the other in the autumn; the one in the season of blossoms and the other at the time of ripe fruits. These productions of nature were intended to give character to the occasions, and were the distinguishing features of these festivities, the one being called the Feast of Flowers and the other of Fruits

These gatherings were subject to the call of the high priest and were held with great regularity. They were believed to be religious assemblages, as well as occasions for all manner of games, each feast lasting three days and no longer. Large delegations of people from other villages and tribes poured in

---

cutions of Galileo were instigated by the disciples of Loyola, and a Dominican never permitted an opportunity to slip of giving his rivals a rub. This much is stated in order to vindicate the translator from the possible charge of an error in dates. As the work came to him in Portuguese, so he is bound to render it in English, leaving discrepancies to take care of themselves.

at such times, coming by land and by water, each delegation bringing a liberal supply of food to contribute to the general festivity. In reference to the ages of the persons attending, there was this wide difference between the two feasts: the Feast of Flowers was more for the delectation of the young; and the Feast of Fruits for the older people of the nation—so that in reality it may be said there was only one feast in the year for the same individual.

At the Feast of Flowers, and at no other time of the year, marriages in the nation were celebrated. On these happy occasions all the young men and maidens appeared in their gaudiest attire, wearing the best of their clothing of skins, and each embellished with a profusion of the gayest ornaments, fashioned of feathers and flowers and shells, and some of the finest of gold. As in other lands, more favored by civilization, engagements of marriage were made in advance, but here, as with the Yonos, such engagements were invariably effected by the friends of the parties, with the advice and consent of the prophet or priest, and nothing was left to the foolish caprice of mere boys and girls. Though made in this way, betrothals were kept in good faith, and at the Festival of Flowers consummated with many demonstrations of joy. The wisdom of the practice was fully vindicated by the happy results of the unions. In nothing did the good Santos exhibit better judgment than in making these matches, as shown in the physical perfection of their offspring. Of sickly and deformed there were none among them, and as a race they excelled in vigor of body. If weakness of mind there was any, or lack of true virtue or moral integrity, it was not observed by Manuelo, and certainly never reported by him. Marriage, with them, was never solemnized except between persons of mature age and perfect development, and only then when the parties were congenial in temper and harmonious in purpose, of which the parents and priests were regarded as the best judges. But notwithstanding their extreme austerity in some respects, the Santos, from oldest to youngest, were addicted to sport, and no people on earth were more merry than they.

At the Feast of Flowers every kind of amusement that could be invented was indulged in by both sexes. But the principal sports of the youth were the dance and the chase, and hiding and seeking, and surprises of various kinds. The young and vigorous men of the nation, the warriors and hunters, including some priests and the princes, spent much of their time on these festive days in leaping, and running foot-races, in shooting the arrow and dart, and in throwing the javelin and hatchet. Shooting birds on the wing with the arrow was a favorite sport, and in this alone were they cruel, unless also we except their trials of strength in desperate wrestling matches. Stripped quite to the loins for these exhibitions, most violent contests ensued; but the victor and vanquished were both crowned alike, and never the former alone. The applause of the crowd, so far as was seen, was bestowed upon each. To do all one could, though failure ensued, was with them a virtue as great as success, and a failure from whatever cause was ascribed to blind chance or ill luck, so the vanquished was never disheartened. In throwing the hatchet and javelin they were hardly less certain of dropping their game than had it been done with the rifle, and neither in war nor in hunting would they seek a close contest, since, from a great distance, their weapons were cast with deadly precision. In a strife with the grizzly bear, or the panther, or lion, which they never entirely declined, they thought themselves safest when out of its reach.

In a race at the time of their feasts, it was never their habit to take a straight course, but to double some object and back; and racing in boats as well as on foot was among the displays at their games.

For amusement, the women and girls resorted to many devices, both pleasant and sportive, but never immodest or rude.* From the advent of Manuelo among them, a leading diversion became the making of garments from skins, after the fashions already described, and this custom, as stated, spread rapidly throughout the whole country. The expertness of the women in this, if the story is worthy of credit, was hardly inferior to that of the faithful housewives of Castile. But something in such a remark must be set down to the bias of Manuelo, who took to himself all the credit of imparting to them the instructions by which they were guided, an honor to which he was clearly entitled, but whether as great in degree as was claimed, is a point upon which there is doubt.

The children that attended the feasts engaged in all manner of games such as children are wont to enjoy when aided by elderly women. Less absorbed in matters of fashion than maidens and mothers, the grand dames of the tribe devoted themselves, in the main, to the care and amusement of the young.

On every day of the feast, if the sky was not overcast, the sun, in the morning, at rising, was greeted with long and continued acclaims, in which all the people, old and young, joined. And on the close of each festive occasion, at the end of the third and last day, the sun was dismissed from the heavens with a song so wild and so weird that once heard it was never forgotten.

At the autumn festival, intended, as the name would indicate, to celebrate the ripening of fruits, berries, and nuts, the

---

*Here, again, Manuelo's recollection is at fault. He was asked how the native mothers exercised restraint over their daughters, and could not answer the question. He was sure, however, that they did it in some way; for in the matter of dancing, he said the Indian girls were exceedingly circumspect, and even more so than the fine young ladies of old Spain.

usual diversions of the country were indulged in by the great body of the people assembled, but it was also the occasion for serious business consultations between the king and his chiefs, priests, seers, and prophets.

At these times matters of the highest importance to the whole nation were passed upon. It was the custom then to discuss the relations of the Santos to neighboring nations, and to determine questions of peace or war; but war was never fully and finally decided upon without first seeking supernatural instructions; a practice entirely similar, in all respects, to that of the ancient Greeks, who, as history informs us, would never commence hostilities without first consulting the Delphian oracles. This is no mean proof that the real civilization of the one people was equal to that of the other; though, by the common consent of mankind, that of the Greeks is counted of the very highest order, while the equally unanimous judgment of inimical nations places the civilization of the Indians of the New World much lower down in the scale. But it is probably best to accept Justino's conclusion, that the one was advanced in one direction, and the other in another, and that the Santo was as much enlightened in his way as was the Greek in his, and neither too much so since both were alike miserable pagans, and both equally outside of the pale of the church.

To the credit of the fates that presided over California three hundred and fifty years ago, it ought to be remarked that their decisions, unlike those of the Delphian oracles, were generally in favor of peace, and not in the direction of inciting mortals to the wholesale destruction of each other.

If at a council of this nation the question was raised concerning the king, and his fitness to reign, the chief priest presided and ruled upon matters with fairness. The obligations of the sovereign to his people were freely discussed, and his duties prescribed. Aside from the maintenance of a fitting amount of dignity, as in other kingdoms, the reigning prince of the Santos was required to act the part of an arbiter between disagreeing subjects, and to enforce his awards in all cases.

When, the oracles being adverse to peace, war unfortunately arose, the king was expected to assume at once the command of his forces; not to direct, from some safe retreat, his military movements, as is uniformly the custom with generals in other countries and in these later times, but to take an active part and lead the fight in person, however dangerous or distasteful it might be. If a similar rule were applied to all kings, fewer wars would occur in the world. Between the post of his majesty and the post of danger there is usually a very wide distinction. But not so with the king of the Santos; if there was peril in war, his duty was there, and no path of escape from danger was open to him. In peace alone was his safety, and peace with a throne was better, in his estimation, than war and a home with the dead.

XXIX.

ABOUT WAR

WAR, says Justino, though always destructive, is not in every instance an unmitigated evil. Although to be avoided when practicable, it is not always to be declined. The relations of nations to each other are such that a passage at arms, now and then, may be for the benefit of both parties, and by no means prejudicial to the rest of the world. Periodical conflicts among the elements are indispensable to the purification of the atmosphere. Storms, however severe, result in replenishing the earth. Nature is full of contentions at times, and her forces are equalized thereby. Man is but part of a great system, whose diversified ends are worked out, under the direction of the Almighty, in many mysterious ways. Even the brute creation is incited by love and hatred, by fear and jealousy, to mortal combat. Bickerings, argued the good friar, have occurred even among the angels, and why should mortal man hope to escape them? The only being who ever taught absolute peace on earth was the divine Master, and even he, unmindful for the moment of his own teachings, overthrew, with violence, the tables of the money-changers, driving them forth from the temple with scourges.

On looking around, Justino could see that even the gospel of truth had been propagated by wars, and those, too, of the bloodiest sort, and he took occasion to justify all that had been done by the brave Ferdinand, referring, doubtless, to the great Hernando Cortez, in whose warlike wake the church had traveled and triumphed. The good friar knew full well that by war Christianity had been enabled to penetrate the benighted regions of Mexico, and by that means alone its inhabitants had been brought to a comprehension of the only true religion. By this agency immortal souls without number had been snatched like so many brands from the burning. Without wars they must have perished by thousands, yea, millions; and why should not wars, therefore, he exultingly asked, be sometimes justified? Continuing, he remarked that "peace on earth and good-will towards all men" may possibly become the universal law, when the world is brought, as he hoped it might eventually be, under the domination of the wholly Catholic Church.

These reflections in justification of war, or similar ones by other members of the Dominican brotherhood, may have had some influence upon the Christian princes of that time, but they could have had none whatever upon the mind of Bear-Slayer, for there is no evidence that they were ever brought to his attention by the only person entertaining them that could have done so. But had Manuelo presented them in their most attractive form, it is doubtful if a favorable impression would have been produced, since it is recorded that in the councils of his nation Bear-Slayer invariably voted for peace, regardless of the extent or enormity of the provocation. Other rulers of his time, and in all ages, might have followed his example more frequently had they been under a similar necessity of exposing their persons to the dangers likely to follow an opposite course.

XXX.

THE MODENS.

NOTWITHSTANDING all that could be said or done in opposition, wars would sometimes occur, forced on, as it were, against the will and wish of the principal chief. The nation with which the Santos were most apt to fall into collision was the one lying to the north, called the Modens, or Oaks, a name presumably bestowed upon them because of their strength, or, mayhap, on account of their fondness for acorns. The Modens were well known to be an exceedingly warlike people, and between them and the Santos many bloody fights, in past ages, had occurred, and often with doubtful results. These two nations were hereditary enemies. Like the Greeks and Trojans, or like the Carthaginians and Romans, they were implacable foes, and hostilities were liable to break out between them at any moment and upon the slightest provocation.

A wide space of territory lay spread out between the Santos and the Modens, unoccupied, except now and then by hunting parties, or in case of war by the armies of the respective nations. Though untenanted, this region was far from being, in any proper sense, neutral territory, for it was claimed by both peoples, and had been the scene of many a desperate conflict. A much more fitting appellation would have been "the dark and bloody ground," for such it really was.

The undisputed country of the Modens stretched far to the northward, and was watered throughout by a great river with numerous tributaries. The river, the one afterwards named the Sacramento, was then known as the river of the Modens. In like manner their capital city, which rivaled in extent the one on the Bay, was called the city of the Modens. Its exact situation, from the facts that are transmitted, if properly sought out, would be found to have been where a branch from the mountains comes down on the plains and unites with the principal arm of the river. In long after years a town was there built on the site of the first, by the conquering whites, and was called by them the city of Uba; but that, like the first great city there built, has gone into lasting decay.

From the best information that now can be had concerning the land in dispute, it is that which spreads out between the two rivers, in after times known as the American and the Cosumnes, and the most famous battle that ever took place between the two belligerents was fought near the site of the capital of that great commonwealth which now comprehends the land of both nations. At that time the Santos, like the French afterwards at Austerlitz, were victorious and drove the enemy into the river, where great numbers perished by drowning. For ages following, the place was famous on account of this battle, and it is a notable circumstance that the works from which the Modens were then driven were long afterwards occupied as a place of defense against the descendants of its constructors, by a military chieftain of an entirely different race, and became widely known as Sutter's Fort. The data, in the manuscript from which this conclusion is drawn are not altogether distinct and legible, and the inference itself may not be in strict accordance with what is stated in the scroll, but it is none the less reliable on that account, since all history, and especially history of wars, is largely inferential, and seldom more authentic than this.

XXXI.
SOME REFLECTIONS.

BUT in order that we may follow with fidelity the thread of this narrative, it will be necessary to return to the chief's home, where some little time since we left Manuelo arrayed in his new garments of skins, the admiration not more of the common people than of the head chief himself. His influence in his capacity of prophet and prince was all that he really needed; but it was immensely augmented by his success as a tailor and a leader of fashions. But it is well understood that influence implies obligations, and Manuelo could not expect to retain his power and standing at court without the performance of such duties as his reputation imposed upon him.

It is one of the consolations of poverty, says Justino, and at the same time no slight compensation for humility in life, that little is required of persons under such circumstances. Instances are many, and as sad as numerous, where sudden transitions from want to affluence, and from humiliation to authority, have resulted in great embarrassment, and even in misery. We are taught that happiness at best is but fleeting and illusory. Some philosophers have maintained, on the authority of personal experience it may be, that true enjoyment consists in the pursuit of blessings, and not in their fruition,— in hope and nothing more. The consolations of religion are all of that character. It is the hope of Heaven alone, says the good friar, that makes us happy in this world; and without that hope he thought all mankind must be miserable. That happiness is more in the anticipation than in the enjoyment is abundantly shown by the increased anxiety always entailed upon those who are supposed to have actually attained it. The most successful in the pursuit of wealth and honors are often the least contented of mortals; and the Dominicans in their pious wisdom argued as follows: "To want is to be miserable;

who wants most is most miserable; who has most wants most; therefore, who has most is most miserable."

Authority is sometimes useful no doubt to him who possesses it, but in the hands of the upright it is more frequently wielded for the benefit of others. To some it is an absolute burden, and so it proved to be in the case of Manuelo; for though inclined to ease and comfort, he was not permitted to enjoy those blessings. That *otium cum dignitate* which often falls to the lot of hereditary princes, was never accorded to him. The fates were adverse to such a consummation; but this must be attributed largely to the natural beneficence of his character. So far from wielding his power, extensive as it now was, for purposes of oppression, he was absolutely oppressed by it. Nor did there appear to be any relief in his case. The future, so far as he could perceive, was beset with darkness and despondency. Princes before him have found themselves in a similar dilemma, and a conspicuous example was the mighty Charles V., whose faithful subject Manuelo had been before setting up the standard of royalty on his own account. But that renowned monarch was able to elude his troubles by taking shelter under cover of monastic life. When political storms were howling loudest, he abandoned his throne and retired to a friendly convent. But there was no resort of that sort for Manuelo. In all that country, afterwards so distinguished for its religious establishments, there was not then a single one to which he could have fled, and those with whom his fortunes were cast expected of him far more than was ever demanded, by his subjects, of Charles, who was only king or emperor at most, while Manuelo was at once prince, prophet, and tailor, and so conspicuous in each of these lines that the people were ill-disposed to concede any limit to his power—he could not, without great danger to himself, disabuse their crude minds of this notion. To have done so might have proved fatal to him, and it certainly would have been disastrous to his hopes of escaping from that country; for be it remembered, if the fact has not already been stated, that he ever entertained the idea that at some future period he would be able to reach a Spanish settlement by traveling to the southward.

Sailors, as all are aware, are proverbially restless, and so was Manuelo by nature. Even the character of prince, which he now enjoyed, or rather, we should say, which he suffered, for there was little enjoyment in it for him at this time, did not enable him to entirely conquer that disposition. Indeed, it was by maintaining that assumed character that he hoped eventually to make good his escape from Bear-Slayer's dominions. For these reasons his embarrassment was greater than that of King Charles, since the danger to the latter was only in retaining authority, from which danger he was able to escape by divesting himself of the same; while the danger to Manuelo was in retaining his power and as well in laying it down, and as much in the one as the other.

Manuelo's uncomfortable situation was cited by the good friar as a timely warning against persons assuming to be what they are not, and for the avoidance of undertakings which cannot be performed. He thought the dilemma might well be regarded as evidence of heavenly wrath towards Manuelo for pretending to priestly functions, for which he was illy prepared by study and pious reflections. Nevertheless the sympathetic heart of Justino was moved towards him, because, as has been argued, one's commiseration for others is measured, not by the amount of their sufferings, but by their supposed sensibility. Even beggars are sometimes moved to tears by the misfortunes of the great, while their own are borne with the utmost indifference. We are most apt to pity in others those evils from which we think ourselves not exempt, since we hope at some time to enjoy the like commiseration. It is not in human nature to sympathize with persons happier than ourselves, but only with those who are thought to be more miserable.

These seasonable reflections of the good friar, or, possibly, of the monks of Evora, must have been intended more for the consolation of mankind in general than Manuelo, who could see no alternative but to make the most of his situation. The line of deception which he had been practicing for some time, and which in fairness, it should be confessed, had been partly forced upon him by circumstances, must needs be followed out at all hazards.

The world in which we live is full of delusions, and so much satisfaction do people in general derive from their contemplation, that it is often counted a crime to dispel them. By far the larger share of the laws of all enlightened countries are enacted for the protection of delusions, and why should Manuelo be condemned for practicing what is so common. Princes and priests alike pretend to the possession of divine authority, and the claims of Manuelo were surely no more to be doubted than theirs. The difference between him and other princes and priests was, that while he was greatly distressed by such pretensions, they usually rest but too easily under them. His claims to distinction ought to be counted even better than theirs, for his were not founded upon supernatural authority at all, but were the legitimate creation of his own genius.

But Manuelo's assumptions were not all delusions; his pretensions were by no means all hollow. A veritable tailor he had proved himself to be, and had succeeded so well in that character that he very properly concluded it might be in place for him to impart instructions to these rude people in other branches of industry. For such duties he regarded himself as eminently fitted by his superior knowledge and Christian education. But coming, as he did, with only his arms, and without industrial implements, he found himself wofully wanting, in the means of carrying out his intentions, and it was impossible in that country to supply the deficiency. In the matter of cooking, he sought to impart information, but did not succeed as he hoped, for the want of the requisite implements. A still greater obstacle that stood in his way as a cook was a lack of the needed experience. A mere sailor-man had he been on shipboard, and never at all a sea-cook, though from aught that appears, as Justino most gravely suggested, in view of his undertaking, the descendant of such a person he might possibly have been. But his efforts in this direction were largely a failure, and were, therefore, from the necessities of the situation abandoned.

XXXII.
FISHING.

WHILE failing in some, Manuelo enjoyed the completest success in other pursuits. With a sort of harpoon made in form of a spear, for that purpose, he boldly attacked a huge whale in the harbor. In the earliest part of his life he had been on a voyage or two in search of those monsters of the deep, and understood full well just how to approach with safety and to conquer that formidable creature. To the boundless astonishment of the natives he now put his knowledge and skill in successful practice.

With the aid of a host of the men in their boats, he towed the huge carcass ashore, and with his sharp sword hacked it to pieces, in presence of the multitude. The blubber was used for both fuel and light, lamps being constructed out of sea-shells. From the fibrous bark of a tree wicks were prepared, and thus he taught the Santos to illuminate their dwellings. From the limber bone of the whale many curious articles were made, but none of particular use.

In fishing Manuelo was expert, excelling, in that particular sport, all others. He invented new methods of taking the salmon, which abounded in the rivers and bays of that country, and he instructed the people in the art of drying and preserving that fish.

The man-eating shark, of which all the natives were in horrible dread, he could handle with ease, and of these he destroyed not a few, his feats in that line commanding unbounded applause.

On the islands of the Bay, there were, at that time, swarms of seals, and sea-lions, or lobos, wolves of the sea, as termed by the Spaniards, between whom and the natives a mutual fear existed; but Manuelo taught the men how to capture these brutes, and of their skins to make couches and carpets, thus adding to the comfort and pleasure of the people.

XXXIII.
A SHIPWRECK.

IN all that pertained to the water, Manuelo's skill, as remarked, was complete; but, lacking the tools, he was baffled in building a boat. This difficult task, however, was in a manner overcome by placing two canoes side by side, and binding them together, by lashing timbers athwart-ships, fore and aft, with rawhide. In this manner he constructed a craft quite new to the natives and very convenient withal. Sails were made for this boat out of skins, and with these unfurled, the Bay was navigated, hither and thither, by the force of the wind, to the great delight of the people, and without the use of the paddle. So marked was his success in this line, that he might have added to his other distinctions, it was thought, the title of Great Admiral. But this, adds the author, was only a little piece of pleasantry of Manuelo's, and belongs not to the body of the history.

But what does belong to it, as of much more serious import, is the fact that he discovered, even at that early day, the danger to small craft of being carried out to sea, on ebb-tide.

Through the narrow entrance to this harbor, widely known, in after ages, as the Golden Gate, then as now rushed the currents of the ocean to and fro at the rise and fall of the tide, with great impetuosity. This phenomenon, so shrewdly observed by Manuelo, might not have been mentioned but for the circumstance of his having been incautiously borne, together with eight stalwart Santos who were with him in the boat, out to sea on one of those fast-ebbing tides.

By education, if not by nature, he was fond of the sea; but this particular voyage was nevertheless undertaken most unwillingly, though his reluctance to entering upon it proved of no avail. The sails of his shallop, on that occasion, were of little use, and night coming on with a fearful storm, he was carried far away from the land. Without chart or compass, he must have been lost on the watery expanse, but for the unremitted exertions of his brave companions, who vigorously pulled all the while for the shore.*

As it was, and in spite of their efforts, they drifted many leagues down the coast, and only succeeded in landing at great peril of their lives. The vessel itself was wrecked and soon went to pieces on the rugged, rocky shore.

Owing to good management, it must have been, rather than to the favors of fortune, the lives of the men were all saved, and a landing effected. More dead than alive, from rolling in the surf, the men crawled ashore, and eventually finding their way to a neighboring settlement were kindly cared for.

On the following day the shipwrecked crew took up their line of march, single file, but empty-handed, through forests

---

*It is a strange coincidence, and worthy of note, that the very day this chapter was completed and ready for the printer, eight small boys drifted far out to sea on the receding tide, in a punt, a craft not unlike that of Manuelo's, and were rescued from their exceedingly perilous situation by one Antonio, presumably a countryman of our hero. For particulars see San Francisco papers of September 27, 1887.

and over mountains to their homes, but too glad to make their escape in that way.

Hitherto good luck had attended Manuelo in all his voyages, this being the first disaster of the kind that had ever befallen him. It was a sort of turning-point in his career, and was followed by other calamities, which he attributed to this as the beginning. It was true then as now that misfortunes come not singly but like birds of evil omen, in flocks, and he was consequently doomed by irresistible fate to undergo trials which might have discouraged a person of less fortitude.

This little experience of Manuelo in the breakers not only thoroughly wetted his garments but it likewise dampened his ardor somewhat for maritime pursuits, for though he afterwards constructed a new boat precisely after the form of the one lost, he was much less venturesome in it than he had been in the first, and only indulged in sailing it up and down the smooth waters of the Bay, always keeping near the shore and closely observing the tides. One calamity of this kind, he thought, ought to suffice for a life-time, and he wisely determined that his experience just narrated should have that distinction.

XXXIV.

A SEA FIGHT.

IN one of those ventures with his new craft in the interior of the country, it being at the time of a flood, when the plains were all covered with water far and wide like a lake, as since they have frequently been, he mistook the true course of the river, and was himself, with his men, somewhat bewildered. Not knowing just whither he went, and encroaching upon the enemy's territory, he was, as might have been expected, hotly pursued by many hostile canoes. When overtaken, as he soon was, a most desperate encounter ensued, which resulted in wounds to himself and his men. Though a running conflict, from beginning to end, it was fought with remarkable valor. The Modens, for it was they who were then giving chase, outnumbered the Santos many times, which greatly inspired the pursuit. Warmly waged was the battle, and it appeared nearly lost when the new-fangled bark fortunately striking a current in the river, and at the same time a friendly breeze filling her sails, she made good her escape.

Manuelo fought bravely, as, inspired by his courage, did likewise his men, and not one was seriously injured, while some of the Modens were killed outright, and their bodies next day floated out on the tide. This is thought to have been the only engagement of the kind that ever took place on those interior waters, and for cool daring and skill, from beginning to end, may never be equaled again.

The reputation of Manuelo as a nautical man, which had been seriously impaired by his shipwreck, was fully restored by the tact displayed in this encounter, and again he would have been happy but for the wounds he received, which after all were not wounds, in the strictest sense of the word, but only contusions. His thick bear-skin blouse proved a good coat of mail, and shielded him from the enemy's darts; but it could not protect him from a sound beating, from which he suffered many days.

His trip out at sea had taught him a lesson of caution against such adventures in future, and so, in like manner, his fight on the river and narrow escape had the effect to make him more prudent and to turn his attention towards peaceful pursuits on the shore.

XXXV.

SANTOS INDUSTRIES.

THE domestic duties of those early dwellers on the Bay of San Francisco were divided between the sexes as with people in some stages of advancement the world over. Upon the men, as among the Yonos, devolved the duty of hunting and fishing, and also, in part, of drying and preserving the fish, and the flesh of their game, for subsequent use. It was in like manner their duty to construct their weapons of war, their traps, their hunting implements, and fishing tackle. Not unfrequently, also, the obligation devolved on the men of providing their own clothing and shelter. Their houses were built by the males as a rule, though in getting together materials for their construction, the women were expected to take an active part. But the dwelling once completed and furnished, it became the duty of the wife to keep it in order, a duty she never neglected. The preparation of food and the cooking thereof, when that was required, ever after Manuelo's unfortunate failure, devolved on the gentler sex.

A calling in which the women and girls were particularly expert was the making of baskets. These were constructed of various sizes and shapes, and tastefully ornamented. They were fabricated of different materials carefully selected. Some of the wild grasses used in their construction were as fragrant as roses, and such were highly prized by the maidens for their sweetness.

Gifts of berries and flowers were presented in these baskets, a practice quite common among them, and one which Justino thought extremely befitting in that land of perennial spring.

Wild cherries and plums, in profusion, were found on the mountains, and grapes and nuts in abundance on the slopes of the hills. Berries of various sorts were obtained in the valleys and gulches and were picked by the women and children. Far and near were they sought, but whenever they were gathered in dangerous parts, an escort of young men, well armed with arrows and spears, attended the party to protect the industrious women and children against the attacks of wild beast, or perchance wilder men from some other nation.

XXXVI.
SOME LEGENDS.

OF the bounteous products of nature, large store was laid up by these people for use in the lengthening winter season, at which time, while enjoying the same, thrilling stories of adventures were narrated. Tales of hair-breadth escapes occurring on these expeditions formed largely the staple of entertainment for children, if not of adults, during these long, peaceful evenings. By custom long established, their stories were told in rythmical numbers, and were thus handed down, like the works of old Homer, by word of mouth, from one generation to another, and some from the remotest of times. It will be deplored by the reader, as it is by the translator, that Manuelo, when relating these occurrences, not being in a fanciful mood, failed to preserve the rythm of the tales. Since, then, we must needs disregard their harmony, we will greatly abridge the few that are cited, and relate them in the plainest of prose. In the first it was told how an infant was left by its mother to rest in the shade of a tree while she wandered some distance away; but too long neglected, the babe awoke from its sleep, and, by its cries, attracted the attention of a she-panther, and before the distressed mother could come to its rescue, the babe was borne away by the brute to its lair. The young of the panther, like the babe, were crying with hunger when the old one returned, and the motherly heart of the dam, it is said, with pity was moved, and she nursed the young child with her own progeny. The babe and the whelps, in the same hollow tree, were protected; but the Indian mother grieved over the loss of her infant, and remained in despair till a fairy informed her, while sleeping, as plainly as anything could, that her child was still living and well. The fond, weeping mother, inspired by this comforting dream, wandered forth from her home, and sought for her little one by night and by day, regardless of danger, all the while roaming through woods dark and dismal, when at last, from afar, she espied, or, perchance, it was that she heard the child cry, and approaching discovered it nestling by the side of its captor. They told how she longed to go near it, but could not with safety for fear of arousing the panther, and she therefore waited and watched where she was a night and a day, expecting in case she disturbed the fierce brute it would quickly devour her poor child, and how she continued in frightful suspense till the panther went forth seeking food, when the mother, with caution advancing, seized the child and made good her return to the village.

It was also related, or rather was sung, how a beautiful maiden was seized by a great grizzly bear, and was carried away to the woods, and when this became known, how her lover pursued in hot haste, and boldly attacked the huge beast. A frightful encounter ensued, unequaled in strength, it is true, but likewise unequaled in skill and in courage. Greater strength was possessed by the bear, but more skill to the young man belonged, and so, in the end, he recovered his sweetheart, but not before he was himself severely wounded. The cries of the maiden helped much in the fight, and it may be presumed the young man was encouraged thereby, while the bear by the same was rendered more shy. This lover, contending so bravely for his sweetheart, became very great in his subsequent life, and the same was Bear-Slayer the king.

It was likewise related how persons were lost and wandered away many leagues among mountains and valleys, unknown, subsisting on berries for days and for moons; how some of such perished of hunger and cold, as their ghosts on returning would tell, while others, more lucky, would find their way home after dangers and privations so great as to baffle description.

Still others, in seeking wild grapes and in hunting for nuts and for fruit, would venture too far to the east, or the north, and be seized and enslaved by the men of some cruel, inimical nation.

Such is the brief outline of a few of the stories the Santos were accustomed to relate in their long winter nights in order to while away time, which otherwise might have hung heavily upon their hands.

XXXVII.
WINNING A SWEETHEART.

WITH less purpose to gather berries than to protect those who gathered them, Manuelo sometimes accompanied parties going forth for that purpose. On such occasions he had the forethought to arm himself properly, and was therefore never without the means of defense. Owing to this precaution, he was fortunate enough on one of these expeditions to have a successful encounter with an animal of the feline species; but whether panther, or tiger, or only a huge wild cat, Justino has left us in doubt. Whichever it was, the creature had climbed a large inclining tree, and crouching on one of its branches, was pelted with stones by the natives, and pierced by some of their darts.

Manuelo, who seldom knew fear, approached too near to the tree, when the monster, quickly descending, came with great fury upon him. At first he thought to use in defense one of his pistols, but time was too short to restore his lost priming, so he drew his sharp sword, and with one fell stroke cleft the head of the brute quite in twain. Writhing in agony for a few moments on the ground where it lay, it expired.

From this sudden encounter, he came off without so much as a scratch, but it was by a scratch, as he remarked, that he escaped. When the creature was first observed to approach, Manuelo, like the more prudent of the boys, was inclined, for his safety, to run; but a moment's reflection dispelled that purpose. There were two considerations then pressing upon his mind, either of which was sufficient to deter him from such a course. To escape by running he might not be able, and to have done so, at that particular time, would have been, as it plainly appeared to him, both cowardly and disgraceful, since it must have exposed to the fury of the beast certain maidens who were gathering berries close by, and among them one who seemed to him the fairest and brightest in all the land—a young girl whose Indian name was Alola. Of this fair damsel Manuelo was then the particular friend and self-constituted guardian. Indeed, it is thought he would not have gone after berries at all if Alola had not led the way, and it would have been base for a Spaniard like him to have abandoned such a beautiful girl to be torn by a monster of any description.

On his killing the cat, or whatever it was, loud praises went up from the crowd, but the loudest acclaims were less valued by him than the blushes of the charming Alola. When she saw the encounter, she cried with affright and almost fainted with fear; but at the result she screamed with delight, and for joy shed many a tear.

It can hardly be necessary to add in any plainer language than has already expressed it, that Manuelo had conceived a strong attachment for this girl, and the saddest thing that could have happened, and worse a thousand times than any calamity to himself, would have been the mutilation of her prepossessing features by the claws of some wild animal.

NOTE:—Here a very considerable space in the original, nearly a whole chapter, in fact, has been omitted entirely by those meddlesome gentry at Evora, for no other or better reason than that, in their judgment, it was too light reading for history, and might prove interesting to young and giddy people only.

XXXVIII.
A BEAR FIGHT.

FEROCIOUS beasts of different species, and particularly grizzly bears, were then quite common in that country, as indeed they continued to be long years afterwards, and even down to the time when California was finally overrun by other races of men. These huge animals, many of which far exceeded in weight the ox or the horse, were a source of great annoyance to the Santos nation. They abounded in certain parts of the country, but were migratory in the season of fruits and nuts, foraging far and wide, and not unfrequently making serious inroads upon the native settlements. Their natural home, no doubt, was in the mountains, but they were by no means content the year through with what could be obtained for food in any one locality. Sometimes in gangs numbering from half a score to half a hundred, they would descend into the valleys, coming quite down to the borders of the rivers and bays with great boldness, causing infinite trepidation among the women and children, and even among the men.

Next to the vigorous Modens, the most dangerous enemy of the swift-footed Santos was the grizzly bear, and it is hard to say which of the two was at times the more dreaded. Of these enemies the bear was certainly the more insidious, often making his appearance at dead of night, and on most unexpected occasions. The half-domesticated animals of the natives were frequently carried away by them, and now and then a child, venturing too far from its home, shared the same fate, to the immeasurable distress of its parents.

On occasions like these the alarm spread abroad, and the men of the tribe, the fleetest and best, all armed to the teeth, in great haste sallied forth to avenge the offense, which was all that could be done, for the child was seldom recovered alive. At the head of a crowd in pursuit of the bears, as in duty bound, the chief always appeared, and whenever the alarm occurred in a large village, the head chief himself was found in the lead. But whether chieftain or king, he was never deserted in the fight, for his men would never abandon him, however dangerous or desperate the conflict.

As a usual thing the bear or other animal pursued in such manner was captured and slain, for these Indians as hunters were extremely persistent. At the end of the chase a great shout arose, and joy pervaded the whole camp, every heart apparently being filled with gladness, save that of the bereaved mother whose child had been borne away by the brute.

It is a notable fact, as Manuelo informs us, that if the child was not devoured by the beast the hunters would feast on the flesh of the bear; but if the bear devoured the child, they would leave the huge carcass, hacked and torn, for the wolves to devour, or cast it headlong into the Bay for the sharks and sea-lions to feed upon. It would seem from this statement that these considerate men of the forest scrupled to partake of the flesh of a beast that had fed on their kind, and thus it would appear that, though heathen, they were sometimes inclined to good taste. In this, it was the opinion of Father Justino, they manifested a higher state of enlightenment than is shown by many a more fastidious people, and that they were, in fact, as far removed from cannibalism as it was possible for a people to be.

In this same connection it was related by the author that on a dark and stormy night, in the fall of the year, while the people were all locked in the profoundest slumber, a monstrous she-bear, with two cubs at her heels, impelled no doubt by hunger, invaded the city, and actually demolished the lodge of a native family near where Manuelo was sleeping. The tumult caused by this unexpected incursion surpassed everything of the kind, unless it might be the commotion arising from the violent shock of an earthquake, a thing but too common in that country. The women and children were frightened nearly out of their wits. To say that the men, and the bravest of them, were unmoved by fear, would be claiming too much for their courage, unless we except the only white man in the place. Before the native hunters could gather their strength, the old bear had made good her escape, but not so with her young, or at least one of them, for being seized by the ears by the doughty Manuelo, a violent struggle ensued, but he did not loosen his hold, though he would gladly have done so on account of the scratching the cub persistently gave him.

This unlooked-for achievement of Manuelo added much to his fame in the city, and more, as Justino assures us, than was gained by another of a similar nature that followed soon after, and to which he was emboldened by his former success. In fact, it is shrewdly suspected, though not so recorded, that he was deluded, by the capture of one little cub, into the belief that he was an experienced bear-fighter, for he hesitated not to join the very next hunting expedition organized under Bear-Slayer.

An opportunity to display his prowess a second time was not long in coming. That same autumn, as fortune would have it, a whole troop of bears of large size, some thirty or more in number, came down on the plain, one dull, cloudy day, to forage. When their approach was discovered the people became much excited, and the men with one accord, seizing their weapons, prepared to resist the invasion. The force that went out against this bristling foe was at least four hundred strong, well armed for assault, or defense, each having his javelin or hatchet of stone, and some with their bows and arrows were armed. But Manuelo with his cutlas alone was equipped, for his pistols, it will be remembered, were regarded by the natives as ornaments only, an opinion he could not afford to dispel, as his powder was scarce; so he left those weapons behind. With himself, he is supposed to have argued that if he could capture one bear, without arms, and with his naked hands alone, he would surely be safe with his keen saber, in any contest with another.

The strength of the attacking party was in a measure concealed by the clouds and mists of the morning, and the bears, relying upon their numbers, were not easily frightened. Before fairly scenting the danger, they were completely surrounded by the swift-running Santos, who, fetching a large circle, advanced towards the center in good order. The brutes, comprehending the situation, and seeing the circle contracting about them, pricked up their ears, looked wildly around, and foamed with anger. But the men still advancing, the fight was begun, and some of the monsters were wounded. The bears huddled together for better resistance, while the men kept off at a respectable distance, well aware of the ferocity of the grizzly bear, like other wild beasts when held at bay. At length a large masculine bruin, more bold than the rest, with his white teeth exposed and fire in his eye, made a break for that part of the line where the only white man happened to be. The supple natives fell back, but did not retreat, while the brave Manuelo stood firm, and with weapon in hand awaited the attack of the beast, which, quickly as thought, arose upon end, and with his huge paw fetched our hero a stroke on the ribs, which sent him rolling away twenty varas or more, upon the smooth, grassy plain. Manuelo, of course, was badly disabled, but the bear was prevented from following up his victory by the quick advance of the Santos, who plied him so vigorously with spears and stone hatchets as to cause him to withdraw.

The blow that was dealt with his sword, at the time Manuelo was attacked, brought the blood in torrents from the head of the daring old grizzly. This would have afforded some consolation to the one who caused it had he just then been in a condition to enjoy anything, but, alas! he was not. The assault upon Manuelo was the signal for attack along the whole line, and the fight from that moment became general. It was waged for some time, with changing results, when, at last, as they say in speaking of wars, victory perched upon the banners of the swift Santos. The rout of the bears was complete. Leaving six of their number, including their leader, the one that began the affray, dead and stark on the plain, they began a hasty retreat. The pursuit was as quickly begun with terrible yells, and the bears were kept running till far in the hills.

On the part of the natives not a man was slain, and Manuelo alone was seriously wounded. The conduct of the chief, on this occasion, was observed to be most gallant, and worthy of all praise. He was near at hand when the Spaniard fell, and was the first to come to his rescue. But for him Manuelo maintained he must have been killed on the spot, for the bear, as he thought, had observed that his coat was made of the skins of his kind, and his rage was increased by that fact. As it was, Manuelo was severely contused, if indeed his ribs were not broken, and many a long day passed slowly away before he was fully recovered.

It is an ill wind, says the old proverb, that blows nobody good. This was paraphrased by Justino, so far as to say it is an ill blow that brings not good to somebody, and so Manuelo thought in this case, for it was his good fortune, during his illness, to have the attendance and care of the kind-hearted Alola. This fair young creature, in the most touching manner, bestowed her sympathy upon the wounded sailor, and was unremitting in her exertions to soothe his sufferings. Strange to say, her ministrations were more than gratified, for was not his recovery even too rapid, since the pleasure she enjoyed in attending upon him must needs come to an end when he was once more restored to health?

XXXIX.
TRIALS.

CAPITALS of all countries are especially attractive to people of an ambitious and overreaching turn of mind, and persons distinguished for those qualities are found there, in greater numbers than elsewhere. To these characteristics are usually superadded an abundance of sycophancy, and more than a sufficiency of assumed dignity.

Commonly known as courtiers, these people swarm about the gates of royalty, contributing, by their presence, to that motley mass of mankind more frequently designated as "the world at large."

The capital of the Santos was no exception to this rule. It was visited from time to time by persons coming on missions of pleasure or curiosity, and some upon errands of business. Among these visitors now and then appeared representatives of the Yonos, the faces of whom were familiar to Manuelo, as was doubtless his to them, but his new character of prince, upon the preservation of which depended his standing at court, forbade his recognition of these old acquaintances except in the most formal manner.

It stood him in hand to look well to the dignity of his position, and he neglected none of the means requisite to maintain it; nevertheless, it was impossible for him to wholly ignore the many courtesies received at their hands in the time of his sorest need. His real feelings towards these visitors, therefore, were but poorly portrayed in his manner towards them.

More cordiality would doubtless have been shown them, but for a lingering, and perhaps too well-grounded apprehension, that a return to his former intimacy might lead to a demand of marriage on behalf of the timid Noña, which would now have been more embarrassing than ever on account of his relations with Alola. If he had ever entertained any feelings towards the Yono maiden beyond those of pure friendship, they were now entirely supplanted by his warmer and more tender attachment for the chief's daughter, for such the fair and confiding Alola really was. Upon her his heart had become firmly fixed, and she in turn as freely bestowed all the wealth of her affections upon him.

A double purpose, therefore, it would seem, had Manuelo in playing the part of a prince. First, he had hoped thereby to avoid those complications growing out of his first matrimonial engagement; and in the next place, by the same means, to promote his suit with his new and more charming sweetheart. For the latter purpose he needed, above all things, the favor of her immediate friends, and how better could he expect to obtain it than by playing the part of a prince?

While he believed that he was loved by Alola for himself alone, he was confident that the attentions of a person of standing would be far more acceptable to her relatives than of one without rank. For reasons which will presently appear the two lovers endeavored, as far as practicable, to conceal their mutual regard from the men and women of the place, but they were at no such pains to hide it from each other. As is usual in cases of the kind, too fond of each other's society, they consorted more than was prudent, considering the feeling that existed in that community regarding such matters.

It is true that all this time they were members of the same household, and her attendance, therefore, upon him during his infirmity was but natural; nevertheless, envy was engendered in certain quarters, on their account, causing them, in the end, no little inconvenience.

Manuelo himself was endowed by nature with a fair share of sensibility, and it was with some reluctance that he permitted matters to drift along as they did, even to the point of public dissatisfaction, but there seemed to be no alternative for it. The difficulty was that the Santos had but a meager appreciation of the feelings of these two young people. Saving and excepting Alola alone they were far from possessing a sentimental turn of mind; on the contrary, they were, in reference to affairs of the heart, as in other matters, eminently practical. In very truth it was this characteristic of the race that had almost bound Manuelo, without the slightest regard to his own wishes, to the shy Noña; and the same was now likely to interfere seriously with his honorable attachment for the fair young daughter of the chief.

An old Spanish proverb likens love to a perturbed river, which never runs smoothly, and Manuelo greatly feared lest the stream of affection that flowed so gently between himself and Alola, should be obstructed by the meddlesome matter-of-fact friends of the latter.

The ex-king and high priest, the venerable Pokee, had a son named Gosee, a most comely and valiant young man, to whom this fair maid had already been promised in marriage, and an engagement when made, as this was, by the highest authority in the land, was almost as good, or, as Manuelo remarked in reference to this case, almost as bad as a marriage.

This established custom of the country as now applied being directly in opposition to the wishes and purposes of Manuelo and Alola caused them many unhappy reflections.

Manuelo was aware, but kept it to himself, that from time immemorial it had been the practice in Spain and in other Christian and civilized countries, to effect matrimonial alliances for members of royal families without regard to the tastes of the parties to be joined, and often in direct opposition to the inclination of those who, as he thought, might well be regarded as most deeply interested in the event. Under wise State policy in many countries, so slight a consideration as personal affection had ever been made to yield to the welfare of the whole nation. The good of the people at large has even required in conspicuous instances the consummation of matrimonial relations under the most repulsive circumstances. A practice which could lead to such results Manuelo concluded might possibly have been sanctioned by time, but he was sure it could have been hallowed in no other way. But he was not in a condition of mind just then to take an impartial view of such matters, even though he had been a veritable prince of the blood, for the custom was, as he expressed it, directly athwart his purposes. Not being in reality of true royal descent, he was by no means, as Justino contended, a competent critic of the practices of the genuine and pure-blooded hereditary princes of the earth.

Confined to royalty alone as was this custom in other kingdoms,—this custom of arranging connubial relations without reference to the wishes of the parties,—it had no such limited application in the New World. Here it was common to all classes alike, and it is believed affords some proof that even in those early times, as subsequently, the good people of this country possessed by nature certain of the more prominent characteristics of sovereignty.

If, then, neither the people, nor the king, nor a prince of the realm, nor yet the high priest, could select his own wife, much less could Manuelo, who, while a prince, was yet a mere stranger in that country, be expected to enjoy that high privilege.

This reflection might have brought some consolation to the mind of the man, and, possibly, also to the object of his adoration, had his love been, or if love ever was, under the control of reason. But, unfortunately for their peace of mind, it is not. The more love is confronted with argument, no matter how logical or convincing, the more perverse it becomes. The tide may be resisted for a time, but it will rise higher and higher, like an obstructed stream, and eventually break over all opposition.

It was Justino's opinion that had Manuelo's success in this

love affair depended upon it, he would unhesitatingly have renounced even his title to royalty.

After what has been said it need hardly be added that many obstacles were thrown in the way of the lovers, but Manuelo, in nowise discouraged, set himself to the task of overcoming them in a true, manly way. He had the cordial co-operation of some of the best matrons in his endeavors to obtain the consent of the chief and the high priest to a recision, so far as his case was concerned, of this arbitrary custom. Though in the hands of the best of advocates, these efforts were unavailing. The old ecclesiastic set his face like a flint against it, as did also his son, the youthful Gosee, and of course their objections were potential. The unimpassioned high priest took such a view of the matter as might have been expected from one of his advanced age and forgetfulness. The maiden, he thought, by Manuelo's dress might have been captivated, or else because of his being a mere stranger she was unduly influenced by him. It was against these considerations that the artillery of his eloquence was directed. Little attention, however, was paid by the lovers to the vaticination of this crusty old functionary. The suggestion of such childish motives, in an affair of so much gravity, tended rather to excite ridicule than to produce conviction. All others plainly saw at the bottom of their attachment a vastly more powerful incentive than the one proclaimed by the senile Pokee.

Finding it impossible, by argument, or honest persuasion, to overcome the opposition to their desires, both Manuelo and the young woman were on the brink of despair, and were ready for almost any emergency that promised well to their hopes. Manuelo, himself, was so incensed by the fruitless result of his importunities that he could have taken vengeance on his rival, and seriously contemplated that course; but fortunately for all parties, he was dissuaded therefrom by the cooler judgment of his fair inamorata, who, with womanly tact, devised a way out of the dilemma by proposing an elopement, not, however, to be carried out immediately, but only as the pressure of circumstances might require.

XL.

A CHANGE.

WINTER passing rapidly away, the lovers feared lest the next *Fiesta* of Flowers, which would come in the spring, might be concluded upon by the priest and the chief as the time for solemnizing the proposed alliance between the son of the one and the daughter of the other, and the contemplation of this danger was a constant alloy to their happiness. It is true that Gosee and Alola were both yet quite young, and the time for their marriage, according to the considerate custom of this country, would not have arrived, in due course, for a couple of years; but it was apprehended that the growing attachment of the intended bride for the mysterious stranger would induce precipitation in this particular case. Her infatuation for Manuelo was becoming too conspicuous for concealment. The fire of her love would burst forth, at times, with such ardor as to baffle all attempts at suppression. In this matter she exhibited less prudence than belonged to her nature; in truth, she was more of a girl than a woman, while Manuelo, in the case, was more of a man than could reasonably have been expected. The affair grew into public prominence, to the no slight annoyance of Alola. It seems the Santos single dames were no less addicted to meddling in matters of this sort than is a similar class in any other nation. Their gossip very naturally annoyed Manuelo, as well as Alola, since it tended to frustrate his plans. For this reason alone he regretted the notoriety of the affair, for would he not have esteemed the partiality of the princess for himself a very great compliment but for the danger it involved?

It is not stated in so many words in the manuscript, but the inference is plain that had Manuelo never appeared at the capital the union publicly planned for this fair maiden and the high-born Gosee, would have been considered, even by herself, as all others regarded it, highly advantageous. But the genius and wisdom displayed by Manuelo as a leader of fashion, and in other directions, rendered his suit irresistible, and ere the girl was aware of the peril her heart was gone. There is a power about love that has never been fully accounted for, even by the wisest of philosophers, and that power, whatever it is, seized upon the innocent Alola with irresistible force.

It is often asserted, and truly, that love is blind, and it was quite impossible for the chief's young daughter to discover any defects, if such there were, either in the person or character of the winsome Manuelo. To her, at least, he was perfection, and every attempt to turn aside the strong current of her partiality for him by pointing out his faults, whether imaginary or real, only made it the stronger. But for this mysterious, this unaccountable, this irresistible influence, which at times seizes upon and possesses man and woman alike, Manuelo might well have been censured for what Justino regarded as a gross violation of the laws of hospitality in accepting and reciprocating the love of the chief's daughter against the protest of her parents, while a guest in their house.

But in a case of this kind much must be set down to uncontrollable fate, and the two lovers are entitled to a charitable judgment upon their conduct, notwithstanding the opinion to the contrary of Father Justino, who, it must be remembered, was only a Dominican friar, and, therefore, by no means a competent judge in matters of secular love.

The devotion of Pericles to the noble Aspasia, a similar case, was not more sincere than was that of Manuelo for the royal object of his affections. The more he saw of her charms the more irresistibly was he drawn towards her; and she, in like manner, overcome by the contemplation of his many virtues, reached, at last, that point where life itself was counted as naught in comparison to his love, and where she would willingly have sacrificed all other friendships for his.

XLI.
AVOIDING DANGER.

WHETHER well or ill grounded, the apprehensions of Manuelo and his sweetheart touching the speedy marriage of the latter with the priest's son made no difference, since those apprehensions were sufficient to render them both thoroughly unhappy when left to themselves and uncheered by each other's society. This danger haunted them constantly, and would not be dismissed until Manuelo, prompted by his usual, or rather unusual, foresight, bethought himself of the necessity of allaying suspicions regarding his purpose, which was, as he confessed, to possess himself, at all hazards, of the pride of his heart. In this firm determination he was met fully half way by the courageous young creature who was to share with him the risk of the venture, and likewise the spoils, so to speak, if it succeeded.

Though careless at first, as young ladies too often are in affairs of the heart, Alola had, by this time, become fully aroused to the exigencies of the situation, and Manuelo came to rely largely upon her discretion in the management of this delicate business. It is said to be always the safest in affairs of this kind to submit to the guidance of the gentler sex, since they, in such matters, are controlled as much by instinct as reason, while man, relying on his intellectual faculties alone, is undoubtedly often quite stupid.

Manuelo and Alola, accordingly, putting their heads together, concluded upon a line of policy the success or failure of which will be discovered further on in this history. It was agreed between them that Manuelo should leave the king's dwelling and take up his lodgings in another part of the city, and that he and Alola thereafter should be seen as little as possible together. It was thought best there should be in their outward demeanor some evidence of a growing alienation between them, or, at all events, that it should be made to appear to the public that they were not wholly dependent upon each other for the air they were breathing, as was sarcastically hinted in the current gossip of the day.

With Manuelo there was another motive for pursuing this course, which he did not disclose, at the time, to his faithful companion, but it doubtless aided in giving direction to his conduct. When a youngster at school, in old Spain, his master had taught him this lesson, that "too much familiarity induces contempt," and these words had been written so often by him that their meaning was never forgotten. Mindful of their wisdom, he dreaded the more to remain in the home of his truelove, lest she should conceive in some way a dislike for his person. It had also been inculcated by the same schoolmaster that "to one's body-servant no man is great," the meaning of which, as explained at the time, was that all defects, whether of the person, mind, or morals, of a notable character, must needs become known to one in such close relations with him, and Manuelo feared not a little lest Alola at length might discover that he was not, in reality, either prophet or prince, but only a tolerable tailor. He had no apprehension that the discovery would be made that he was a mere sailor, for his achievements in that line during his stay with the Santos, among which were his shipwreck and his sea-fight, had not been of a character to inspire confidence in his ability as a seafaring man.

By removing from the king's own dwelling, therefore, he would not only relieve the mind of the maid, but at the same time free himself from much apprehended embarrassment. The natural inclination of the gentle Alola was, of course, to have her lover always near, and the poor creature consented with the greatest reluctance to his going away. But discretion, she realized in her cooler moments, was the better part to be chosen, and especially since it was pregnant with promises of future happiness, while a little want of discretion might dash all their hopes. To use his own apt figure of speech, suggested by his early experience, they were by this move taking in supplies and mending their sails for a long voyage, and a slight miscalculation was liable to wreck their prospects.

This being the situation, the two submitted cheerfully, though she reluctantly, as was said, to what Manuelo was constrained to believe to be the will of Providence, but which the innocent Alola regarded as altogether too cruel for that. She had been instructed by her lover to look up to the Almighty, as the embodiment of goodness alone, and she could not see how it was possible for a being whose every impulse was fraught with benevolence, to impose upon her the cruel necessity of a separation from her lover. Hence she questioned the conclusion of her Christian companion, that Providence had anything whatever to do with the movement; and the utmost endeavors of the good Manuelo to impress upon her crude intellect the idea that divine Wisdom was at all responsible in the case, were unavailing.

A person of Manuelo's popularity could easily find other quarters, and straightway he removed to a house of his own, partly built by himself, in another portion of the city. The ruse was complete, suspicion was allayed, and slander ceased wagging her tongue, and when afterwards the two met, it was in a manner becoming their high positions.

The spring wore away, and the flower festival came in due time, but no marriage between Gosee and the rosy-cheeked damsel was suggested for that occasion, the two being considered as yet quite too young for that event. This being determined upon, Manuelo was greatly relieved, but not more so than was his gentle sweetheart.

XLII.

ANOTHER TACK.

THE gentle reader has already been informed that the course of true love seldom runs smoothly; when least expected the stream is liable, as is the case of rivers in that country, to sink out of sight, beneath the surface, only to appear again further down the channel of time; and such proved to be the experience of Manuelo and his intended.

At the Feast of Flowers, mentioned in the last chapter, an incident occurred which came near putting a permanent period to their engagement, for it nearly cost Manuelo his life. A wrestling match in the camp was progressing, and all the young men of the nation were trying their strength, while the maidens were watching the game. Manuelo's success in the contest of love wrought in him the foolish idea that in other contests he might be equally strong. Impelled by this notion and not less by the smiles of Alola, who was sitting among the spectators with her brilliant dark eyes on her lover, he thoughtlessly challenged the son of the priest, his unhappy rival, to a trial of strength on the green. Manuelo well knew that in the matter of swiftness he was not a match for the stalwart Gosee; but he thought that in strength, of which he could boast, he might be his equal at least; for on the ship's deck, in his earlier days, he enjoyed a high reputation for strength. But Manuelo reckoned too much on the past, and in this was his judgment a failure, as was likewise his strength, for the son of the priest at the very first bout threw him heels over head, and he fell on the ground with terrible force. So severe was the fall that he lay on the plain for some time, nor could he arise, and so great was his pain that he could not refrain from moaning aloud; and his cries pierced the heart of Alola, who rushed to his aid and bathed his head with her tears. No bones being broken, he soon recovered from his fearful mishap, the wiser for it.

Explaining his unexpected discomfiture to his sympathetic mistress, he attributed his fall to an unlucky slip of the foot on the smooth, grassy plain, which he assured her would never occur again, as it never did. But he was wont to say to others that a fall from the yard-arm to the deck of a ship would have been no more dreadful than this fall from the arm of Gosee.

The lesson thus received was of value to Manuelo, and probably saved him from other disasters. He learned to rely not on his physical strength, but to trust solely to his genius, which had never failed him. He said to himself, "Let the shoemaker stick to his last, to the last, and to his awl, after all," and he applied these words to his own case in a manner that need not be stated.

XLIII.
WAR BREWING.

FROM an intimation or two already dropped, touching the relations that existed between the Santos and the Modens, one ought not to be surprised to learn that war broke out that summer between these two powerful nations, and the account of it as given by Manuelo himself may not be uninteresting to the general reader of history. If to no other people, it will, in all probability, be entertaining to those who now occupy the territory which was the theater of the conflict, and future generations likewise, upon the same ground, may possibly peruse his dramatic account of it with profit, if not with pleasure. It is for these reasons that the translator gives it with a great deal of particularity, and to him, therefore, on that account, may be due some little share of the credit which belongs, it is readily conceded, in much larger part to Father Justino, of rescuing from oblivion a considerable chapter of history which can nowhere else be found, and which, but for the kindness of that great and good man, must have been irretrievably lost. But the impatience of the reader admonishes us to proceed with the narrative without further delay.

In point of military preparations and strength of numbers the belligerents on either side were nearly equal, in this respect bearing a striking resemblance to the Romans and Carthaginians; but here the parallel ends, for though there were leaders not unlike Scipio and Hannibal among these early Pacific Coasters, the nations themselves differed from those more ancient ones in the general run of their operations. The capital of neither of these was ever destroyed by the other, nor indeed is it known that either was ever fairly beleaguered. Invasions, it is true, occurred of each nation in turn, and the war, so to speak, was on occasions carried into Africa; nevertheless, for aught that appears in the manuscript, the cities of both would have stood to this day but for the long subsequent incursion by an entirely different race. It only pertains to this history, however, to say that neither was destroyed by the other, and if either or both afterwards succumbed to inevitable fate, and were driven from the face of the earth, some other historian must be held acountable for that information. It may have been in accordance with the decrees of Providence that the first races of people on the Pacific Coast of North America should be subdued by Mexican invaders, and that they in turn should be overrun by the inevitable American nation, but that concerns us not, nor does it belong to a story which, it must be remembered, relates to an earlier time and to entirely different events. Matters of modern date cannot be permitted to lumber up a history so old and authentic as this, and one which has come down to us in such a mysterious manner.

XLIV.

A PREDICTION.

MAN possesses but little ability to look into the future, and it is presumed, therefore, that Manuelo may have died in ignorance of the happenings which were to transpire in after ages on the very soil he was then familiar with, unless peradventure such information may have been obtained from the prophets of the Santos, of which there is some intimation. The future magnificence of the Roman Empire was clearly foretold at a period when there was no more reason for anticipating its greatness than existed in the case of California.

In a similar manner, says Justino, the Indians of the Pacific Coast were in the habit of listening to the oracular utterances of their prophets, and we have the combined authority of that good man and of Manuelo for the assertion that those seers did, in fact, look far into the future, and by the aid of disembodied spirits predict whatever of good or evil was to befall their people. In proof of this the author informs us that in a spirit of prophecy, a priest then foretold how in time there was coming an age of gold. But a difference he said one surely must draw between a golden age and the age that he saw; for while a golden age might with happiness flow, an age of gold would bring nothing but woe and distress to his people. He plainly set forth that men would pour in from the South and the North, from the East and the West, by land and by sea, all as vile and as wicked as men could well be; that his people would then to the mountains be driven, or so many at least as were not sent to Heaven. But this prophecy fell on ears too obtuse to comprehend what it meant, or foresee its use; as did also that other when the priest seemed to see that in time, in his country, a race there would be who swifter than birds would fly over the land, by a power that he said would be always at hand, and so convenient withal that every day his people, most happy, could ride without pay. But his ignorant hearers, Manuelo included, by the language then used were completely deluded; for they thought that the priest, by so strange a prediction, could not be sincere, but was dealing in fiction. The more credulous of them suggested such things as men made like angels and furnished with wings. But none could foresee what would afterwards be the condition of men in that land by the sea. Other things quite as strange were foretold by that seer, and some even now and to us seem as queer as at the time to his men they appeared; for the priest was much moved when he said that he feared that in four hundred years from that day a race from the ocean would enter the Bay, having tails from their heads, a numberless throng, bringing only a few of their women along, and would scatter about on every hand, and in a few years overrun the whole land, in turn driving out the people with wings. The prophet predicted so many such things that the faith of Manuelo in his story was shaken, and he thought that the priest must be surely mistaken. The consequence was that some true and some not were wholly ignored, and some were forgot. But the worst of them all to believe was the one that the men possessed queues, while the women had none.

The young priests of Evora found other similar prophecies in the old manuscript, but deeming them impious suppressed them. It is true they were of profane origin, and not in accordance with the ordinances of the church, but it is equally true that many books relating to the future, now extant, were written without inspiration, and it would have been not a whit more improper for the young Dominicans to have given a fair account of these predictions than it was for Friar Justino to record them. This much is said to the end that the blame for their omission may fall where it belongs, and not upon one who is only playing the part of an humble translator. If more had been given, we promise you it would have been furnished with fidelity; but the only thing left for us now is to share with the reader in the general disappointment.

XLV.
THE CAUSE OF THE WAR.

THE immediate occasion of the renewal of hostilities between these ancient enemies, the Santos and the Modens, may never be known with certainty, but a remote cause was undoubtedly the naval engagement of the year previous, in which Manuelo had received such a severe drubbing. His bruises were long since healed, it is true, but not so his feelings, for he ever cherished a mortal hatred towards the people by whom he had been so severely castigated. Mentally he continued to writhe under their blows, long after all traces of them had disappeared from his person; and cost what it would, he determined to have satisfaction sooner or later. To say that he intrigued to bring about a collision, might be too harsh an expression, but he himself could hardly object to the accusation of resorting to strategy in order to precipitate hostilities. The high priest had long since inferred from the oracles that some event of the kind was likely to occur. A message had been received by that functionary from the unknown in these words:—

> The Pines and the Oaks, like all other folks,
> Must needs crowd and encroach on each other;
> But in the great strife, which must be one for life,
> The Pines will the Oaks greatly bother.

This being somewhat indefinite and enigmatical withal would have led to no trouble but for another message received by Manuelo, as priest, from a similar source, not long afterwards, in these words, as nearly as they can be translated:—

> When the Pines and the Oaks deal each other strokes,
> All the plain with the slain will be strewn;
> But the most that are slain, and stretched on the plain,
> Not as Pines but as Oaks will be known.

This was alleged by the cunning Manuelo to be a message from the very highest supernatural authority, and was construed by him to be in the nature of a positive injunction from Heaven to the stalwart Santos to put on the war paint, a custom even then of great antiquity in that country. Their confidence in him as a prophet up to this time had not been impaired, however much it may have been shaken in his ability in other directions, and they immediately set about the requisite preparations for a campaign.

This determination arrived at in a general council of the head men was much against the will of the king, for obvious reasons, and he sought in various ways to prevent the result. He hesitated not to question the correctness of the interpretation as given to the message by Manuelo, nor scrupled he to express emphatic distrust of the authenticity of the communication, nor yet to impugn the right of Manuelo to apply for oracular advice upon the subject of war, he being but a stranger in the land and not interested like the rest of them in such weighty matters. But the king was the only one in all the assembly who had the assurance to interpose such objections, and his opposition was prompted, as all believed, by his dread of being compelled to take the lead of the forces to be gathered. All the other priests, including the chief prophet, concurred with Manuelo in the opinion that the message meant nothing short of war, and preparations were begun with great alacrity to carry it on.

XLVI.

A DILEMMA.

SMARTING still, as was said, under the flagellation suffered not many months before, at the hands of the revengeful Modens, Manuelo could but exhibit an unusual amount of zeal in pushing forward the conflict, and as a consequence he was left without excuse for remaining behind, while the war should be waged against the common enemy. His conduct very naturally led to the expectation that he would be not only ready but extremely willing to take an active part in the campaign. Strange to say, so blinded was he by a feeling of revenge that this untoward result had never occurred to his mind, though anyone else could have seen that it was the legitimate offspring of his dalliance with the oracles.

Finding affairs were taking this turn, he was considerably exercised, not to say distressed, over it, but not more so than was the beautiful Alola, who feared most lest her lover should never return from the war. In her vivid imagination she pictured to herself the bones of Manuelo whitening some far-off battle-field on the border, or what was almost as bad, in her distempered fancy she saw him a prisoner of war, languishing in servitude, a slave it might be to some rival of hers among the Modens, and she endeavored with great earnestness, and in various ways, to dissuade him from his purpose. And most gladly dissuaded would he have been, but no such happiness was reserved for either of them, and as a consequence her heart was nearly broken.

We have the authority of Manuelo for asserting, but the fact would have been known just as well had he remained silent upon the point, that Alola shed many tears over what she regarded as their hard fate. But under the circumstances, her weeping, like her protestations, was of no avail, since Manuelo had drafted himself, so to speak, into the service, and, with the rest of the men, must needs be in readiness for the expedition and take his chances. The brevity of this chapter, it will be observed, was unavoidable. Nothing more could be said. The dilemma itself enforced silence.

XLVII.

PREPARATIONS.

IN an incredibly short time every preparation for the war was perfected. A large army of brave and active young warriors was gathered from all the villages of the nation, each sending its quota. The whole command was ready to be put in motion, in three separate divisions of near a thousand men each. The faces of the soldiers were tastefully decorated with pigments of one kind and another, which were applied by the women, as more skillful in that branch of the arts, thus giving to the army altogether a marvelously picturesque appearance. But each division wore the paint after a style of its own, differing from the others, so that each could be readily distinguished. This was thought to be more appropriate, because of their different armaments. The first corps for their arms bore the javelin and the bow and quiver. The second, the bow and arrow and hatchet of stone, but no javelin; while the third division was armed with no bow, but with hatchet and javelin; so that each was prepared for a separate duty, it might be, or, if the emergency required it, for a general fight.

For food on the march they were supplied with fresh meat for the first few days, and with venison dried for the rest of the trip, and with nuts, in large store, in their leathern pouches. Their adornments, aside from the paint, consisted of the brushes of foxes and coons, and likewise of the tail of the deer, each division having only one kind; but feathers of the gayest colors were indiscriminately worn by them all, and each man, high up on the side of his head, wore the white wing of a bird, the national emblem of the swift Santos. The bird's wing, as the scholastic Justino remembered, was worn in the most ancient of times by the heathen god Mercury, as an emblem of speed; but by him it was placed on the heel, and not on the head, as these people saw fit to display it.

XLVIII.

THE MARCH AND BATTLE.

FULLY armed and equipped and prepared for the fray,
They took up their march to the east the first day,
Passing over some mountains that lay off that way,
From which they looked down upon the broad Bay,
And as well on the city from which they had come,
And each had a last look it might be of his home,
For each saw the danger there was in the strife,

And that it might end in the loss of his life,
A thing quite too common in wars, as we know,
But men must expect it who will to wars go.
A soldier must needs take his life in his hands,
When to kill and destroy he invades others' lands,
And if he should never his own again see,
A proper result of the war it would be.
This remark of Justino is thrown in this story
To benefit those who are seeking for glory,
But who are more likely to find, as he said,
Themselves either wounded, or crippled, or dead.
But eager for fighting and cheerful of heart,
They strove with each other to lead at the start.
And this strife they kept up the day nearly through,
And as long as the leading men thought it would do.
In a beautiful grove of evergreen trees
They camped the first night, and there took their ease.
When supper was ended, to their beds they retired,
For, most of all things, it was rest they required.
They posted no guard, for they feared no alarms,
Yet each, for security, slept on his arms.
The day had been warm, and the march had been long,
And it tested their metal, though each man was strong
They were used to fatigues, and all had before
Been on marches as tiresome as this one, or more;
And no one complained, but all were content,
And happy their dreams when to sleep they all went.
Having slept the night through, in the morning each man
Was astir when the lark its sweet music began.
On the first day from home, of the women a throng
Followed close to the warriors to cheer them along;
And among them Alola, bewitching and bland,
Was the first to encourage on every hand.
Her sweet, gentle voice was heard the day through,
Applauding the men, though she very well knew
How much danger there was to all in the move,
And that it might be the defeat of her love.
But brave girl that she was, she in God put her trust,
As the good Manuelo had told her she must.
The rules of their warfare at this time required

That the women should stop, though Alola desired
To go further. But she, like the rest, was compelled
To submit to the law, which long had been held
To be absolute; and she wrought up her mind
To the point of being left by her lover behind.
Manuelo embraced her and implanted a kiss,
First upon that cheek, and then upon this,
Then on her sweet lips he gave her another,
And consigned the poor girl to the care of her mother.
The army already was moving apace
When the two tore themselves from each other's embrace;
The one pushing forward, to catch those who were
Gone before, while the other remained in despair.
The women, with Alola, returned to the city,
But Alola, from sorrow, was an object of pity.
Her companions, as best they were able, consoled her
By saying the army was strong, and some told her
That all would return in a moon or two more,
That at furthest they could not be gone more than four
But all that was said no comfort could bring,
Such fearful forebodings oppressed the poor thing.

On the second day out they came near the mouth
Of a very large river which flowed from the South.
This barrier gave them of trouble some warning,
So they camped on its bank, and rested till morning.
It required all next day this wide river to cross,
But they effected the passage without any loss.
The men could all swim, and in that way got through,
But for baggage and blankets that way would not do.
So they made them some rafts from the timber near by,
And got their things over in order and dry.
From their camp the third night their second was seen,
For, in truth, there was only the river between.
Their course from that point to the northward was bent,
Sending runners ahead as onward they went,
So that any surprises they might thus prevent.
Crossing stream after stream, the army advanced,
And on the sixth day, about noon, as it chanced,
They came unexpectedly flat on the foe;
And further, just then, therefore could not go.

The Modens, by what means no one can now say,
Were informed of the war, and the march, day by day,
And for fighting their soldiers were fully prepared,
Nor did they appear in the least degree scared.
In numbers the Modens were more than their equal,
And likewise in arms, as appears in the sequel,
They were fully a match for the Pines,
Who at once formed themselves in three lines,
And in a short time a warm fight
Was begun on the left and the right.
The center soon joined in the battle,
And then was heard a most terrible rattle
Of tomahawks, and arrows, and spears,
Attended with shouts and with cheers,
As one or the other side faltered,
Or as the tide of the battle seemed altered.
The Oaks had the choice of the ground,
As the Pines to their sorrow soon found;
So back fell the Pines a short space,
And drew the Modens from their place
Of defense. The Modens coming out
Fully thought that a general rout
Of the Pines was about to take place,
And made ready to give them a chase.
But the movement was only a ruse,
As their king, had he not been deceived,
Might have seen. The two armies were then
On a footing nearly equal again,
And the battle, with desperate power,
Continued for more than an hour;
And the sky with the weapons was made
So dark that both fought in the shade,
As the Spartans had fought at Thermopylæ Pass,
Under lead of their captain, great Leonidas,
When attacked by the Persians, a numberless host,
Who with Xerxes came over from the opposite coast.
At that time we are told the Persians let fly
Of arrows so many as to darken the sky.
But now no Persians were engaged in the fray,
It was Greek meeting Greek in fearful array.

Bear-Slayer appeared in the front of the strife,
Contending, entirely regardless of life;
While Manuelo kept himself aloof from the foe,
For no weapons had he that were useful to throw.
His arms were only his pistols and sword,
And with these he concluded he could not afford
To expose and imperil his person too much
To the arrows and spears and to javelins and such
Weapons as were sent from afar by the Oaks,
Who if near would have felt his terrible strokes.
Standing back on a knoll by a tree,
Many plumes in the fight he could see
Waving high to and fro, as the men
To the charge rushed again and again.
At some points on the line a great yell
Would be raised, as whole ranks of men fell,
Cut down, not unlike as by reaping machine,
When driven through grain, as in later days seen.
The wounded, in numbers, were borne to the rear,
And their cries from the pain it was painful to hear.
But as bad luck would have it just then,
Of the Oaks more than five hundred men
Turned the flank of the Pines on the right,
Thus compelling Manuelo to fight.
The Modens before had not seen
Any man of such dress and such mien,
And his weapons to them were quite new;
As they viewed him, the larger he grew
To their sight. They were stricken with fear,
And kept aloof, for they durst not come near
Such a man. He advanced with sword out,
And in a moment he put them to rout.
How many he slew is not stated,
Though doubtless, had the fact been related
By another, we had heard that a score
Of the Oaks bit the dust, if not more.
The foe he pursued o'er the plain,
But to camp he returned not again
That night; for the day was far spent,
And he hardly knew whither he went;

But in the lines of the Oaks was betrayed
By pursuit, so the manuscript said.
But for him the whole fight had been lost,
And to the brave Santos at terrible cost.
Of this truth he was fully persuaded,
And the thought of it very much aided
His low spirits, and some courage inspired,
As with the Modens he slowly retired.
The friendly approach of the night
Put an end to that terrible fight;
But his friends he saw not again,
Nor knew he how many were slain,
Nor what number got off with their lives,
And in safety returned to their wives.
He hardly believed in their flight,
But supposed in the darkness of night
Their march to the South they had taken,
And in this he was by no means mistaken.

XLIX.

CAPTIVITY.

THE fact being plainly stated and without disguise or prevarication, the doughty Manuelo was a prisoner of war and had fallen into the hands of the very enemy upon whom he was seeking to wreak his vengeance. His case was a striking illustration of the predicament of a man spoken of in Spanish literature who went forth after wool and came back shorn, except that Manuelo could not get back, being kept in close custody by the blood-thirsty Modens. Perhaps a better elucidation of his condition at this unfortunate moment would be to say of him, in maritime phrase, with which he was himself familiar, that the very Old Nick was to pay. In less time than it takes to relate the circumstances, though not a moment were wasted in detail, he was deprived of his arms and likewise stripped of his bear-skin garments; for the enemy would be sure that he was not half bear and half man, as at first they feared.

Now, nearly naked and stricken with apprehension, he was bound hand and foot with thongs of strong rawhide. Fortunately for Manuelo, curiosity sometimes gets the better of man's as well as woman's judgment. He, being of an entirely different race from any they had ever known, was looked upon as an object of great wonder, else he might have been dispatched at once by his captors, as was their custom of treating prisoners of war when taken with arms in their hands. What struck them as most remarkable about his person was the peculiar style of his apparel, which, owing to his superior skill as a tailor, was far more complete than had been adopted by the rest of the Santos soldiers, and altogether different from any the Modens had ever before had an opportunity to inspect. This fortuitous circumstance inured to his advantage by causing sufficient delay in his punishment to allow him to bring into play his marvelous talents and to inaugurate a system of tactics which was to end in his deliverance, at least from the danger of immediate execution.

As upon his breast and arms, while a sailor, had been imprinted with India ink figures of one sort or another, so was impressed upon his memory indelibly a saying often heard at sea, to the effect that "the gods help them who help themselves." He was forcibly reminded of this now by the circumstance of his being in great peril. Taking in the situation in all its phases, he set himself, with great coolness, about the task of extricating himself from his present difficulties. In this he exhibited as much presence of mind as had ever been displayed by him on shipboard.

With a degree of shrewdness that has seldom been surpassed, he professed towards the Santos the bitterest animosity, and was most profuse in his denunciations of that people. He stigmatized them as base and cowardly beyond expression.

Could you have heard him you must have believed his late friends to have been the worst class of people upon earth. He represented truthfully enough that his coming amongst them was the result of an accident, and that he had long sought to leave the Santos, but had been prevented from doing so by their jealousy of the Modens, whom, above all people in the world, he had been desirous of visiting; that he had been compelled, much against his inclinations—another truth—to join the late expedition; and cited his reluctance in coming to the front of the fight as proof of his partiality towards the magnanimous Modens, as he now purposely termed them. With admirable tact he assured them his final assault was inspired by fear of the treacherous javelins of their enemies. In fine, his deprecations of the Santos were only equaled by his laudations of the Oaks, and so loud and persistent was he in both that on the following day the thongs were removed from his swollen limbs, and he was permitted once more to lift up his head, as he did at the same time his voice in his mother-tongue, in thankfulness toward Heaven for so much of freedom again. But he was yet a close prisoner, and was still looked upon with a measure of suspicion; for not only had he fought with effect in the late struggle upon the land, but his fight on the river was remembered by some of the men. His bear-skin blouse, which had served as a coat of mail on that memorable occasion, was the thing that betrayed him. He was pretty clearly recognized as the one who had been so fatally active in that encounter, and his conduct at that time was yet unexplained.

Fortunately for Manuelo assurance was a commodity in which he had largely dealt as a seaman, in his intercourse with other nations, and having a good stock of it always on hand, he found no difficulty in putting it in use as occasion required. With apparent cheerfulness he accompanied the Moden warriors back to their principal village at the mouth of that river, then, as afterwards, called the Uba.

He was not many days in learning whatever was peculiar about the laws and customs of the Modens, being aided in this by an experience drawn from visits to many ports of the world. He noted, in particular, such habits as did not accord with those of their more tropical neighbors, the Santos. He found that the government of the Modens was far more stringent than the other, and that the power of their king was more absolute than was that of Bear-Slayer. The leading men likewise were more austere, and the people at large less independent than any natives he had hitherto seen. Infinitely less goodwill and generosity were exhibited here than where he had formerly been, and he found it difficult, if not impossible, to ingratiate himself with the leading classes as he had in the city by the Bay. His efforts in that direction being abortive he indulged in some reflections, which Justino has had the goodness to transmit, and of which we give a very imperfect translation:

>Manuelo was wise and he very well knew
>As things were now drifting, what was left him to do.
>They had made him a slave and were treating him roughly,
>And the king most of all acted towards him quite gruffly.
>This insolence Manuelo could hardly endure,
>So he began to instruct and enlighten the poor.
>He taught them their rights and advised a rebellion;
>He told them their king was a regular hellion,
>And oppressed and annoyed them in every way,
>And made them unhappy by night and by day.
>He said that the king was himself only human,
>And, as they could see, was as weak as a woman;
>He argued that men of all ranks were the same,
>That the difference between them was only in name;
>That the slave was as strong as the king was, in body,
>And that royal pretensions were nothing but shoddy.
>By the mind he declared a man's power should be known,
>And speaking of mind, he referred to his own
>For the proof that his point was taken correct,
>And this proof was cited with the greatest effect.
>He told them that morals in the life of a king

Were truly a most indispensable thing ;
That his whole private conduct should be without blame,
Else the men of his kingdom might do just the same.
The life of this king was exceedingly bad,
Indeed, it was said by his men that he had
On many occasions his duty o'erstept,
And his promises made to them seldom were kept.
They knew that he fooled them whenever he could,
And, in short, that he would not, and could not, be good.
To Manuelo himself less respect was now shown
Than ever on land or at sea had he known.
His titles of Prince, and of Priest, and of Tailor,
To his boundless chagrin had departed together.
Base work of all sorts he was ordered to do,
To bear heavy burdens, or paddle canoe;
The skinning of beasts and the cleaning of salmon
Among other duties were far the most common.
To carry the game he was always required,
And to hurry along, though he might be so tired
That he hardly could walk, for the horrible Oaks
Would prod him along, but never would coax.
So severe were his trials and so hard was his lot
That he wished he might die, but die he could not.
Thus his life had become a sore burden to him,
Or, at least, very often a burden would seem.
No hope was in view, nor relief could he find,
When, at last, as was said, he made up his mind
To lead a rebellion against the old king,
Prepared as he was for some desperate thing.
His life was so wretched that little cared he
As to what, in the end, his own fate might be.
His plans were so good, and so well were they laid,
That two thousand men were prepared for his aid.
But for coming together a pretext was wanted,
And, as good luck would have it, such a pretext was granted.
Some huge grizzly bears now appeared in the valley,
And a signal it was for the people to rally,
To drive the beasts back; and while they were armed,
About Manuelo in forces they swarmed.
He exhorted them all to prepare for the fight,
Intending to lead them on the city that night.

An address he then made, in these words, very near,
And the slaves were delighted such counsel to hear.

" Throughout the whole world, and throughout all time,
The crime of oppression has prepared men for crime ;
Men treated like brutes like brutes will become ;
They will show it in public, and show it at home.
It is one of the laws of inevitable fate
That hatred towards others in others breeds hate.
If princes and kings this law would more heed,
There would be fewer jails, and of th' gallows less need.
Both subject and ruler more happy would be
If the one were more kind and the others more free.
The scepter of power in the hands of the strong
Should be wielded for justice, and never for wrong.
That rule is successful which is based upon right,
And the same sort of rule possesses most might;
For the king or the prince that dares be unjust
Can never with safety or confidence trust
In his subjects, for as he is their foe
The same disposition towards him will they show;
And certain it is, should the chance ever rise,
They will prove to the tyrant how much they despise,
In their hearts, such a man; and if ever
They can, his head from his body will sever."
Here ended the speech, and the crowd standing there
Were by it excited beyond all compare;
And if good Justino is himself not mistaken,
The earth thereabouts with their plaudits was shaken.
But the king and his chiefs, and the king's only son,
Had already been told what was then going on,
And were fully prepared for a lively defense
Whenever the rebels the fight should commence.
The serfs with much glee set out for the city,
And Manuelo exultingly declared it a pity
That the king was so blind, so deaf, and so dumb;
That the best he could do would be to succumb.
In this sort of strain they marched over the plain,
And back with quick step to the city again.
But the cowardly slaves, when they saw the king's men,
Were stricken with fear, and all of them ran.

One poor little squad, with Manuelo in lead,
Betook to the mountains, at the top of their speed,
And did not stop running that night nor next day,
For the mountains they sought were quite far away.
They lay to the west, but were plainly in sight,
And the men hoped by running to reach them that night.
That night they came to them, but, tired and footsore,
They lay down to rest, for they could not run more.
Some slaves it is said from the Romans once fled,
And were far in the mountains by Spartacus led;
And the case we are giving was a parallel case,
And differed from that but in name and in place.
The Spartacus here was Manuelo the brave,
Who, like the great Roman, his forces to save,
Went off to the mountains to hide himself there
Where he might live in peace and enjoy the free air.
But as Spartacus found his retreat was no fun,
So Manuelo's troubles were now just begun,
For, seeking his freedom, he found to his cost
That the further he went the more he was lost.
But he could not return, nor find his way out,
And all that was left was to wander about
In the mountains most wild, and through the dark wood,
And pick up a living in the best way he could.

L.

THE RETREAT.

PUSHING far to the west, to the ocean he came,
An ocean of which he knew not the name,
The one called Pacific he judged it might be,
But on its broad face not a sail could he see,
And his heart sank within him, as he stood on the shore,
And he feared that his home he would see never more;
The slaves that were with him became discontent,
And as he then thought on mischief were bent.
But he cheered them all up as best he was able,
And to inspire them with courage related a fable;
How once on a time when a boat was upset,
And the crew cast ashore all hungry and wet,

An angel came up from the depths of the sea,
And made them as happy as men could well be,
By giving them food and by lighting a fire,
And setting before them all their hearts could desire.
And he said when the crew, full of food, went to sleep,
The angel, standing guard, did safely them keep.
And when they awoke on the following day,
The angel, still there, pointed out the right way.
When he finished his story the Modens believed him,
For up to that time he had never deceived them,
And though they were all in a terrible strait,
He led them to hope that they need only wait
A little while longer, when an angel would come,
And not only feed them, but show the way home.

It was not what he meant, but it happened just then
That relief unexpected was found for his men.
Close by on the rocks some shell-fish he saw,
And so hungry were all that they ate them down raw.
Supplied with this food the slaves were content,
And believed Manuelo these shell-fish had meant.
Manuelo himself was filled with delight,
For just before then he was in a sad plight,
With a whole squad of men in a lonely retreat,
All hungry and cold and with nothing to eat,
And he as their leader was expected to find,
If not the best food, at least food of some kind.
The sun was now sinking, and as all had enough,
They concluded that night to sleep on the bluff;
But the next day thereafter, when breakfast was done,
They faced to the southward and marched one by one,
Keeping close by the sea as their base of supplies,
And to avoid any danger that might otherwise
Have arisen, as a bear, or a wolf, or a tiger,
Or it might be a lion, or it might be a cougar.
Their march they kept up for many a day,
But precisely how many we cannot now say,
For time was not made for those ignorant slaves.
Their object was always to keep near the waves,
Where clams they could find and their hunger appease,
And on the sea-beach in the sun take their ease.

CALIFORNIA

But we think we may say they followed the shore,
Going south all the while, some three weeks or more;
But how many leagues we are bound to confess,
If we were to state, it would be but a guess.
A hundred, we think, would not be too many,
And certain we are it was fifty, if any.
Here they came to a point where the shore ben's inland,
And the squad were at once forced to come to a stand.
Manuelo, the leader, knew not where to turn,
Nor was anyone present from whom he could learn;
Yet he did not make known, at the time, to his men,
The true state of facts and the fix he was in;
For all of the while he pretended to know
Just where he might be and where he would go,
And in this sort of way, as one may well see,
He kept discontent from his little army.
Taking in at this point of fresh clams a good store,
He boldly pushed inland, bearing off from the shore.
The Greeks under Xenophon were ten thousand men,
But the force on this march in all numbered ten.
The perils of both were the same very near;
In each case the soldiers were always in fear
Of surprise of some kind or a covert attack,
Which might stop their march and perhaps turn them back.
But the wisdom displayed on this expedition
Was greater because they subsisted by fishing,
And Xenophon's genius did by no means excel
That which was displayed by the great Manuel.
As the Greeks were compelled from their course to depart,
So these from the sea had to take a new start.
They marched over hills and through woods high and low;
Neither soldier nor leader knew whither to go;
But they kept right along nor stopped they to rest,
Till the sun was fast sinking far down in the west,
When they came to a spring from which they would drink,
But the water within it was blacker than ink.
It smelt strongly of sulphur and likewise was hot,
And when they would taste it they found they could not.
But they camped near the spring and rested that night,
And Manuelo in dreaming thought he saw a strange sight.
In the far-distant future he beheld on that ground

Large buildings erected and men all around;
And likewise of women and children a host,
But whether of boys or of girls there were most
He hardly could tell, and remained in some doubt
Till after a while their mothers came out,
When the girls all went in and the boys ran away.
The women he noticed were dressed very gay,
And he said they appeared all to him very pretty,
And in conversation were exceedingly witty.
The young men and maidens appeared to be flirting,
But which loved each other he was very uncertain.
He could not see why they had come to these springs,
But these things he saw and some other things.
This curious dream he could never explain
But he thought of it over and over again,
And that is the reason it is now related
Just as it is in the manuscript stated.
Whether true or not true no one can now know,
But as for myself I believe it is so.
The man could have had no motive in view
To relate such a story if the same were not true,
And it would have been wicked in him to deceive,
And therefore I say that the dream I believe.

After dreaming that dream at the Hot Sulphur Springs,
Manuelo and his men gathered up all their things
And set out, refreshed, on their journey once more,
As uncertain where it led as they had been before.
But such was their strait that they could not delay
Nor afford then to lose but a single half day.
So they climbed over mountains and threaded ravines,
Exhausting their strength and exhausting their means
Of subsistence. Through woods they meandered,
Over hill and through dale, still onward they wandered,
Until the fifth day about noon they espied
Far off to the south on a steep mountain-side
A large column of smoke in that quarter ascending,
And it lay in the way the lost ones were tending.
They saw it with hope and likewise with fear,
Or would have so viewed it if it had been near.
In a country so strange there was no way to know

If the fire had been kindled by friend or by foe,
But hunger compelled them to keep on their way,
And they traveled on towards it the rest of that day.

In the darkness of night and while the men slept,
Their leader, more bold, still on his way kept,
Intending to find if he could as a spy,
Who the people might be, or at all events try,
But he did not succeed, and he sought to get back,
But the night being dark he missed his own track
And was himself lost, or rather his men
Were all to him lost, for he never again
In all his life long at any time heard
Either from them or of them, so much as a word.
But he hunted and called for them early and late,
And was greatly concerned as to what was their fate.
Despairing at last his attention he turned
To the side of the mountain where once the fire burned;
But alas for the leader, and as he had feared,
The fire had gone out and the smoke disappeared!
Manuelo was now in a very bad way,
For, the truth being told, he could not well say
Just what he should do, or where he should go,
Ex-slave as he was and fugitive too.
No longer like Spartacus a leader was he,
Nor Xenophon-like could he march by the sea,
But more like Fred Douglas,* who flew from his master
To find and encounter some greater disaster.
At night the north star Manuelo could see,
But towards that star he wished not to flee;
In the other direction he rather would run,
And he took for his guide the full noonday sun.
He sped to the south and kept going ahead;
As a slave from his master so with vigor he fled.
At last when he came to a place on his route
Where signs were abundant that men were about,
Like a slave as he was, at a distance he hovered,

---

*This name is substituted for the one in the MS., which could not be made out very clearly, though it sounded something like this; but, being the name of a mere slave, it can make no difference.

And was in great fear lest he should be discovered.
While thus hiding and waiting and watching one morning,
A woman came on him without any warning.
His eyes, at the first, he could hardly believe,
And yet he was certain they could not deceive;
But looking he doubted and was troubled with fears,
For his orbs, the fact was, were fast filling with tears,
For the lady that came, do you think it could be
The gentle Noña? Oh, yes, it was she!
He was never so happy before in his life
As when he beheld his would-be young wife;
He rushed out to meet her, and would her embrace,
But she hurried away, and then he gave chase.
Such changes had servitude in his looks wrought
That she knew him not then, but the poor creature thought
That he was a Moden, as his dress indicated,
And how she was frightened after that she related.
He followed her closely, as close as he could,
And when at full speed they emerged from the wood,
"He saw by the smoke that so gracefully curled
    Among the green trees, that a village was near,
And he said if there's peace to be found in the world,
    The heart that is humble may hope for it here." *

LI.

SOME REHEARSALS.

IT is hard to descend from Pegasus, when once you are fairly astride; much harder in fact to dismount than it is to continue to ride. And so the young priests at Evora indulged pretty freely in rhyme, in giving Justino's strange story of what was told at the time he was living in old Acapulco, about a land to the north, far away; how a vessel they called the *Don Carlos* discovered and entered a Bay, and when from the length of her cruise she needed fresh water the more, she manned a small

---

* The utterance of these same ideas by Goldsmith was at first a mystery, but it is explained by assuming that the young priests of Evora were familiar with that English author.

boat with armed men, and sent them to find it ashore; how the crew of the boat were surprised as they ventured too far, and then ran; and all of them made their escape excepting a single young man, who was left by his friends on the ground, and was believed at the time to be dead, but who by the natives was bound and into captivity led. And since the young priests have seen fit to render the story in verse, I must needs, in translating, in like manner the story rehearse. Just as in their language they told it, in English I am bound to unfold it. Whatever in prose they narrated, in prose it is likewise translated; whatever in measure they gave us, in measure the same it is given, for I would not and could not, to save me, so faithless and willful have proven as to indulge in a style of my own, or in one which the priests had not shown to be suited to works of this kind. So he who reads further will find a most proper and truthful narration of all that Manuelo related concerning the Santos nation, and what likewise of others was stated.

Manuelo was left at the time of this little diversion in full pursuit of the Yono maid, but his utmost exertion to overtake her proved in vain. It should be remembered that the men of this tribe were swift as deer, and it is to be presumed that the women were equally agile. But the village was near at hand and there was an end of the race. The people, alarmed, hurried forth to see what the matter might be, and why the maiden was running. They supposed that a bear or some beast had caused her the fright, but just then emerging from the wood Manuelo himself hove in sight. So strange his appearance, and so unlooked for his coming, that not a person in all the tribe recognized the poor man at first view. The alarm caused by the event it would be hard to describe, if a single man could be said to alarm a whole tribe. But finding him out, as they did, there was quickly an end of their fears, and they greeted him again and again with their cheers. They first thought, as was said, that perhaps a bear it might be, a mistake not then great, for a lion indeed now was he.

The Yono women who had been so kind to him in former days did everything now in their power to make him as happy again. The men gathered around and loudly importuned him to tell, which he did, about his life with the Modens, and what had befallen him while a prisoner of war in the hands of that blood-thirsty nation; how they cruelly made him a slave, and with what unheard of vexation they compelled him to do work of every kind, bestowing upon him such treatment as slaves of the baser sort find; how he stood it as long as he could, till his life a burden became; how at last he was forced by his lot the minds of the serfs to inflame against the old king and his clique; and how he succeeded at last in exciting a rebellion. He spoke of his march on the city, which he expected to capture by night; of the slaves who, exultant at first, at the sight of the danger took fright. He told how he fled to the mountains, which lay far off to the west, a thing that he disliked to do, still he thought it might be for the best to be done for their safety, and as well for his own extrication from the burdens imposed upon him by the king of that horrible nation. Ten men, and no more, he informed them, were along on that perilous flight, and all, by running right swiftly, came up to the mountains next night. Seven days without food, he then stated, or just about seven, were passed, when out of the mountains emerging, they came to the ocean at last. He said they were dying of hunger, and his men he was sure meant him harm, when he told them a story of angels, and the story it worked like a charm. Just then a few clams were discovered, and the men ate them down without cooking. These were thought to be a godsend, as they came when no one was looking. He then went over the story about their long march by the strand, and how they came up to a bay, which forced them to turn thence inland, and keeping some time on that course, but how far and how long he knew not, they suddenly came upon springs, the waters of which were quite hot. And then he related his dream; but that it was no use to mention, since the natives, though listening throughout, had of it not the least comprehension. He next gave a statement in detail of the fact of his missing his men, and though he sought for them weary and long was unable to find them again.

The only thing further worth naming about which to them he then spoke was the fact of his seeing before him on the far mountain-side a large smoke; that while he was seeking his men the smoke disappeared from his view—and all the rest of the story he told them they very well knew.

LII.
AN APOLOGY.

IT may have been noticed, if not all the same, that Pegasus was weary or getting quite lame. Whether spavin it was, or the founder that ailed him, we cannot now say, but his wonted speed failed him. And why should it not? for far had he traveled, and a maze of events had thus been unraveled—from the city of Pines to the city of Oaks, in war and in peace and with all sorts of folks; from thence all around by the shore of the ocean, he had somehow kept up his ambling motion. Now, after all this, it was thought to be best to pull up a little and give him a rest. So from this time forward, almost to the close, this curious history will stalk on in prose, unless the poor beast should get over his lameness, and be able to avoid that intolerable sameness which has lately appeared, or unless he should take the bits in his teeth, and in that way should make a desperate effort to galop along, in which case by yielding we might not do wrong.*

---

*For some unexplained reason all the remainder of this chapter was omitted.

LIII.

WITH OLD FRIENDS AGAIN.

NOTHING had ever occurred to interfere seriously with the confidence reposed in Manuelo by the Yonos. However much such confidence may have been shaken in other quarters by events transpiring elsewhere, the causes of the same had not spread to this side of the Bay, and he was never the less an accepted guest among this simple people. His influence with them, established by those achievements with his pistols already described, remained unabated. It was, if possible, somewhat augmented by the heroism displayed during his captivity and flight. To them, at least, he was still prince and prophet, though with the disadvantage now of being poorly clad, the greedy Modens having, as he informed them, stripped him of his stylish apparel. Much to his disgust he had been invested with the homely costume of a serf, and even that, owing to the menial service required of him, no less than to the desperate emergencies of the flight, had become dilapidated. It was his early aim, therefore, to provide himself with new clothing, and in this task he had the willing assistance of the women of the village, who had by this time become as expert as himself in the use of the needle. Among the most active of these was the woman for whom he had conceived some regard on his former visit, and whose name, as already related, was kept to himself. This person he informs us possessed many accomplishments and not a few personal attractions. During his absence she had been married, in pursuance of the laws of the country, to the son of the first prophet of the village, who, as it happened, had ever been among the warmest friends and companions of Manuelo, and had shown him more kindness, if possible, than any other man of the tribe. He was believed, however, to have been the identical person who had inflicted the severest wound upon Manuelo at the time of his attempted escape with the crew to the *Don Carlos*. If that be so, the young man with great gallantry had since endeavored with much assiduity to repair the injury then inflicted. The warmest of friendships are sometimes sealed in this way; at all events these two were on the most intimate terms, and, as Justino thought, almost as inseparable as Damon and Pythias.

The partiality of this woman for Manuelo before her marriage, and likewise his attachment for her at that time, had been too conspicuous for concealment, and the fact was still remembered by some of her companions. All these things being considered, and also the fact of their now being thrown together again in the preparation of his new habits, it will not be very surprising that manifestations of her old partiality should be in some sort renewed. As before his departure so now her conduct grew to be the subject of remark in the village, and particularly among such women as are given to considerations of that nature. To the credit of Manuelo it should be stated that he exhibited the more circumspection of the two. As in duty bound he carefully avoided, as far as able, the least thing that might revive the unwarranted predilection of the woman for him. But notwithstanding his prudence, if we may believe his story, he was not a little annoyed by her demeanor; for in the simplicity of her innocence she bestowed upon him kindly gifts of wild flowers and beautiful ornaments of feathers. Had Manuelo been other than a true friend, the feelings of the husband might have been more speedily aroused against him; and as it was, the man could hardly look upon the conduct of his wife with absolute indifference. The husband grew cold at first, and eventually it was observed that unmistakable hostility on his part began to manifest itself towards the unfortunate Manuelo.

By the time his new garments were completed, the bodily strength of Manuelo was likewise restored, for be it known that in consequence of his horrible servitude, followed immediately by the hardships of his wearisome flight, his health had become impaired equally with his apparel, and it required almost as much exertion to restore the one as the other.

To increase the embarrassment—that embarrassment which seemed ever on the alert to overtake Manuelo—the gentle Noña, to whom, need I remind the reader, he had been unwillingly betrothed, now divested herself of her former shyness, and openly avowed that had she known or even suspected who it was she would never have fled from him in the woods. Her flight and her fright she insisted must be attributed solely to his strange garb and changed aspect, and by no means to her fear of the man. The poor creature having taken him for a Moden, or a veritable wild barbarian, did not even recognize his voice, though he called upon her again and again as loudly as he was able; but no wonder he failed to make himself heard, for was he not still hoarse from calling at the top of his voice, but in vain, after his ten lost slave companions?

LIV.

JEALOUSY.

INTERROGATED by the villagers upon the subject, Manuelo was obliged to confess that he had never been married; that neither when with the Santos, nor yet while a prisoner among the Modens, had he been furnished with a wife, and the hopes of Noña and of her friends were greatly stimulated by this information. The hopes of the prophet's son were in like manner duly excited by the same intelligence, for he was extremely anxious that his former friend should assume marital relations, in order to counteract the growing attachment of his imprudent wife, and he accordingly intrigued with his venerable father, and the other dignitaries of the village, to bring about that desirable end. In this conspiracy the young man had not only the tacit approval of the fair Noña herself, but he was happy also in the active co-operation of all the priesthood, and of many of the elderly women of the place.

The combined opposition to the movement embraced the unnamed woman, a few female friends, and of course the crafty Manuelo himself; but these were more than a match for the others, as the sequel will show.

Manuelo's aversion to marriage was based upon entirely different grounds from those entertained by his associates, in the work of resistance; but his real motives were carefully concealed from them, lest their zeal on his behalf should become slackened, as it doubtless would have been had they learned that his heart was fixed upon an object far away. He needed their cordial co-operation, and he was too wise to risk losing it by relating to them all that he knew about himself.

The simple-minded Yonos seemed never to have learned that there was danger in delays, and therefore, not suspecting his purpose, they listened with patience to one pretext and another brought forward either by, or on behalf of, the witsome Manuelo, for the postponement of his marriage with the timid village maiden.

In the contrivance of these excuses he had, of course, the aid of the young wife and her female companions. For the better accomplishment of his aims he would have consulted the oracles, as on a former occasion, and seriously contemplated doing so, until he chanced to learn that the priest had already communicated with them, and that an answer adverse to his views had been obtained.

This communication he could not expect now to overthrow, as he had that of the Santos, in reference to war, inasmuch as the loss of his fire-arms had deprived him of the means of creating either thunder or lightning. This privation was sorely felt, and he was put to his trumps, so to speak, to find a reason for again deserting the Yonos.

If the truth must be confessed, he was highly flattered by the attentions of the wife of his friend; but his heart was by no means captivated. We have his own assertion for the fact that his feelings towards this woman were those of commiseration only, and not of affection. Never for a moment had he forgotten, nor could he forget, the bright-eyed daughter of the king, the tearful and charming Alola, with whom he had parted with so much reluctance on going off to the war. Towards her his heart waxed warmer than ever now that he was almost as it were within the sound of her sweet voice, and his longing to meet her again overrode every other sentiment of his nature.

The intelligent reader who has floated along on the current of these events to this point, will hardly consider it reiteration to be told that all the Yonos, from the chief down, excepting the priest's son alone, but including particularly the females, were extremely reluctant, and now more than ever, to part with a person so distinguished in their eyes as Manuelo.

For reasons, some of which have already been disclosed and some not, they determined at a solemn council to retain him amongst them, and adopt him as one of their tribe. Numerous decrees of their priests pointed in the direction of their wishes, which Manuelo was unable to controvert without great danger of giving offense and at the same time of forfeiting his standing among them as a prophet.

The circumstances attending his early appearance in their country, his wounding included, and not forgetting the nursing received at their hands, were such as to justify this claim. They knew, almost as well as himself, that the country from which he had come in a great ship, must be reached again in the same manner, if at all. They argued with a shrewdness becoming a race of the highest intelligence, that his allegiance to them was more binding than to any other community with which they were acquainted. Moreover, the exceedingly distressed condition, more than half naked, and starved, which marked his second appearance among them, and the relief then afforded, were regarded as increasing manifold his obligations to them.

In all this, as Justino argued, they were right, for Manuelo was really indebted to these good Yonos to the extent of a life twice preserved, and for ten thousand acts of kindness besides. But his biographer might have remembered that a man is not always responsible for a roaming disposition. So far as born in him, his parents are chargeable with it, as they were in Manuelo's case; and most likely also for his having been early apprenticed to the sea, and acquiring thereby a bent, in addition to his natural tastes, for fresh scenes and pastures new. At all events it was utterly impossible just now to cast off this disposition; and all the fascinations thrown about him by the gentle Yonos could not overcome his predilection for the larger city.

Perfect freedom is the natural inheritance of man, and a child of nature as he was, he chafed under any restraint. Alluding to this disposition in the human family, Justino philosophically suggested that a person confined to the Old World would be likely, as in his own case, to pant for the New; and the good friar exultingly remarked that neither the Old nor the New could long retain him, since he would eventually reach that other and better world, where both himself and Manuelo had long since gone when the manuscript was discovered at Evora.

So intense had the dislike of the priest's son towards the unoffending Manuelo become on account of the strange infatuation of his young wife, that he would gladly have disposed of him, if not by marriage with Noña, then in some other way.

This the shrewd Manuelo understood full well; and with consummate wisdom resolved to avail himself of that hostility to aid in effecting his escape. How, or in what particular manner, he sought to make it available, will be disclosed to the reader presently.

On his leaving the Yono village the first time Manuelo had clearly held forth to the people the hope that he would some day return, and they had long continued to look for a fulfillment of his promise, wondering at his delay. Noña, whose betrothal to him ever stood in the way of her engagement to another, not only mourned his departure, but continued secretly to pine over his prolonged absence. In her sadness she was accustomed to seek consolation in solitude, and was actually wandering about in the woods, stricken with sorrow, at the very time she was so unceremoniously accosted by him. She had been quietly communing with the spirits before her surprise, and was afterwards convinced, as were also the priests of the tribe, that his coming in the manner he did and at that particular moment was providential, and it certainly bore that appearance. The good Father Justino was inclined to look upon it in the same light; and even the young friars of Evora, three hundred years later, could not contemplate the event without a great deal of astonishment, wondering that a kind Providence could show so much consideration for nothing but a poor heathen maiden. After much discussion the matter was finally left undetermined by the authorities of the church, and anyone is therefore now at liberty to form an opinion thereon for himself.

With the same degree of shrewdness that had marked the conduct of Manuelo on other occasions, he now turned this circumstance of his sudden appearance among the Yonos the second time to good account, by reminding them himself of his former promise, and assuring the people with utmost coolness that his parting words to them had never been forgotten. He deceitfully told them that his coming now was in pursuance of the promise made at the time of his departure before. Owing undoubtedly to the great distress of mind under which the poor man was laboring, in consequence of the unwarrantable restraint imposed upon him, he summoned courage to assure the thoughtless Yonos, that, but for that promise, he would never have abandoned the Modens as he did, nor undertaken that long and perilous journey by the sea and Hot Sulphur Springs to reach their village. He impressed upon these confiding people the idea that if he was ever compelled to leave their midst again, his absence would·be but temporary, and that any departure from them would be accompanied with the utmost reluctance on his part.

By this sort of strategy, these people were so far deluded as to yield in some degree their determination to prevent his departure, and from that hour he was hopeful of being able to extricate himself from the dilemma.

To the son of the high priest, who was all the more bitterly hostile toward Manuelo from having once been his warmest friend, he cautiously conveyed the impression that he was called away from their village on pressing business which might detain him a long time. All that was thus hinted to the young brave was strictly true except as to the matter of business, and even that was not without a shadow of foundation if we only consider an extremely serious case of love in that light. To Manuelo certainly it appeared to be business of the gravest concern; but it was at the same time of a nature not to be disclosed to the Yonos, on account of his constrained relations with one of their number.

LV.

STRATEGY.

THERE is a French proverb, also sometimes rendered in Spanish, which declares that "the unexpected is what usually happens," and the converse of this maxim, which would be, in effect, that "what is expected rarely occurs," is equally true. Both the proverb and its antithesis were amply verified in this part of our history.

Manuelo felt confident, from the impression produced upon

the minds of the leading men of the village by his fabricated account of the manner and object of his coming among them a second time, that he could, by the exercise of a due amount of prudence, easily effect his exit from their midst; but in this calculation he was reckoning without his host; he was surely mistaken, and in this was the converse of the proverb verified. The proverb itself was as well supported by the unexpected opposition he met with, not from the timid Noña herself, directly, but from her female relatives.

The anxiety of the poor girl, growing out of the suggested departure of Manuelo—for the rumor of his going had already spread like wild-fire—was, of course, greater than that of anyone else, and why not, since she was the party most deeply concerned in the matter? But her situation as an expectant bride forbade her to make much ado about it; not so, however, with her friends; they were under no such restraint, and their tongues, in the case, were let loose.

Being entirely free to express their opinions about the business, they indulged in that liberty to the fullest extent. With true feminine sagacity they had foreseen a determination on the part of Manuelo to evade his supposed duty towards their modest kinswoman, and they were duly indignant. This impression regarding his purpose was inflamed by their memory of his palpable evasiveness on a former occasion, and now again by his unaccountable coldness towards his betrothed, as was clearly manifested after the first few interviews on his second arrival in the village. Their conclusion that he wished to desert her, or, at least, to escape the performance of his duty, was strengthened by the well-known fact of his being the recipient of courtesies from the wife of his former friend.

Manuelo could not but notice the difference in sentiment between the immediate friends of the two women, and it puzzled him to account for the same. The kindred on the side of the demonstrative wife, flattered, it may have been, by the partiality of so distinguished a person, were full of expressions of sympathy and friendship for Manuelo, while those on the part of the proposed bride were boiling over with resentment.

Viewing the matter in the light of passing events, Manuelo concluded, and so informed Justino, that it was far more difficult to effect an abandonment of the one than it would have been to elope with the other, for the latter alternative was actually suggested, and aid tendered, should he feel inclined to undertake so desperate a step. But however deceitful Manuelo may have been in some things, he was not base enough to listen with equanimity to a proposition of this sort. It aroused within him a feeling of indignation which he could with difficulty suppress; but under the stress of circumstances he managed to pass over the suggestion in silence, regarding it merely as the emanation of a weak brain, or as a proposition coming from over-zealous friends.

These complications springing, as they did, mainly from the families of the parties, gave Manuelo more trouble than everything else that occurred during his stay with the Yonos. However cunningly he devised his schemes, and however successful he may have been in deluding the men, he found it quite impossible, by the use of similar means, to deceive the women. In affairs of the heart he observed they were capable of reading his very thoughts. Whether in the exercise of this faculty these Yono women depended upon supernatural assistance or not he remained in doubt to the end of his days. Owing to their remarkable shrewdness in such matters, it was in vain that he sought to suppress his fears lest he should be compelled at last to settle down among them and take upon himself all the duties imposed by their curious laws.

In this emergency he bethought himself, as a last resort, to intrust his cause to the generosity of his former friend, the high priest's son, who had already been furnished with the secret of his pretended business over the waters. Such an appeal to one's bitterest enemy was an experiment of doubtful nature, at best, but it was one for which Manuelo could discover no alternative.

With this determination in mind he sought the young man, and plainly and candidly laid before him his wishes, at the same time promising most faithfully that in the event of his getting safely away, nothing on earth would ever induce him to return.

The plan was well conceived, and the step wisely taken. It disclosed in its author a larger degree of intelligence than could have been supposed to belong to a person of his limited education. Although Manuelo's mind was not stored with knowledge in very great variety, his judgment was generally sound and his genius equal to any emergency. Learning does not always imply wisdom, nor ignorance of books the want of mental ability. Education is but the polish that is bestowed upon the marble, the labor of the sculptor being sometimes expended in vain upon the coarsest of granite, whilst the finest of stones may never have felt the artist's chisel.

A man, continued Justino, may be intellectual, and at the same time ignorant; he may be intelligent, and yet wofully wanting in wisdom.

Manuelo's proposition was as pleasing to the priest's son as its cordial acceptance by him was gratifying to Manuelo himself, and accordingly it was arranged between them that on the very first day of a favorable wind, the two would set out on a fishing excursion and take all the chances of being blown away in the direction of the Santos settlement. But the wind they desired did not soon arise, and their long-continued detention became terribly annoying to both.

It is declared to be an ill wind that blows nobody good, and the winds now prevailing were thought to be precisely of that character; not so, however, would they have been pronounced had the betrothed of the one, or the wife of the other, been consulted, either of whom, had she known what was transpiring behind her back, would have been more than delighted with the adverse breezes. Both women were resting in ignorance of the plot that was hatching on their account, though doubtless something would have been suspected had they but been familiar with the fable of the "Dog and the Wolf," which, as it is related, were seen traveling together to attack the sheep-fold; the moral of which is that "when old enemies are observed to go hand in hand, there is always some mischief between."

The mischief to be accomplished in this case was the abandonment forever, by Manuelo, of the Yono village, which it was known would prove as distasteful to the pretty spouse of the priest's son as to the modest Noña herself. But the enemies now, unlike the dog and the wolf, were seen but little in each other's society, and suspicion against them was not aroused.

LVI.
NEGLECT.

IT was clearly the duty of the sprightly priests of Evora to give the manuscript such rendition throughout as was intended by Father Justino, even though at the cost, to them, of a little more labor and trouble. Having voluntarily taken upon themselves the task of deciphering it, there could be no excuse for men of their leisure and scholarly attainments omitting from the scroll any feature which could have been preserved by diligent work, and yet it is undeniable that, though bound by their sacred calling to the faithful discharge of every obligation, they have, at times, in imitation of the rest of mankind, sought to glide over the labor before them in the easiest manner possible, and have actually neglected, for large spaces in the work, to follow the style of composition adopted in the original. But at this stage of the translation, conscience-stricken, it is presumed, they essayed to repair, as far as possible, the injustice inflicted upon Justino in departing from the manner of his writing.

It is not, however, charged upon the good monks that the injury to the author was intentional; on the contrary, their neglect is attributed to mere inadvertence in giving in plain prose what should have been transmitted in verse. But if they are successful in the future all should be willing to forgive them, and the charity of the reader is earnestly invoked in their behalf.

LVII.

PROLOGUE.

SO certain am I that 'tis best to be
Correct in what pertains to history,
That greatest pains to this time have been taken
In order that I might not be mistaken
In any of the more important facts
Relating to the thoughts, and words, and acts
Of the bold sailor boy, Manuelo,
When living, some three hundred years ago,
In that strange land which at a later day
Became so widely known as California.
For this I am entitled to some praise,
Since, beyond question, there were many ways
In which to have portrayed both thought and action,
And easier to have given satisfaction.
But that is not my way; I like much more
Than plaudits, truth, as I have said before.
To deal in fiction is a great mistake
For anyone in writing history to make,
But difference wide there is betwixt mere fiction
And what is in the nature of prediction ;
Sometimes, indeed, events have been foretold
By authors who have been a little bold,
And such events have proved to be as true
As anything that people ever knew.
Prognostications that have come about,

Or prophecies, so called, that have turned out
To be correct, and have been verified,
Have far more wonder caused than all beside.
These have astonished people more by far
Than what has written been of peace or war.
A taste there seems to be in man for that
Which is abstruse and hardest to get at,
Hence puzzles, such as thirteen, fifteen, fourteen,
And games of chess and twenty-one have been
Greatly in vogue, causing much waste of time
In every age, and almost every clime.
This strange propensity in man is my
Excuse, and is, perhaps, the reason why
I shall incorporate in this new book
A story which at first may seem to look
As if it had no base to stand upon,
Whereas it has, in fact, an excellent one.
This much I say at start, and now here goes,
But where the end will be no mortal knows.

While waiting for propitious winds to blow,
The man whose wife so loved Manuelo,
Proposed a trip inland in search of game;
And going far southwest at last they came
Close by a mountain which was very high,
And which the Indians called Mount Tamalpais.
Observing that their path upon it tended,
The hunters this tall mountain then ascended.
When to its lofty summit they did climb,
A sight at once broke on them most sublime.
Manuelo with the view was overcome,
The others with astonishment were dumb.
Mountains they saw that looked down on the Bay;
A hundred vales spread out before them lay.
A sight like this not one of them had seen,
For none had ever on that mountain been.
Oppressed, our prophet sank upon the ground,
Nor heed took he of anything around.
Just then there came up from the neighboring brake,

And near him coiled, a monstrous rattlesnake.*
Even this disturbed not his dream that day
For his prophetic thoughts were far away.

LVIII.

A DREAM.

IN the distant future, coming from the sea,
Great ships he saw, a thousand it might be;
All kinds there were, as sloop, and brig, and bark,
And some, he thought, as large as Noah's ark.
From different lands they came, and flags they bore;
Some spread all sails, and some the aft and fore.
What was remarkable, and strange did seem,
A few appeared to be propelled by steam;
At least from midships he could see arise
A cloud of smoke, ascending to the skies;
A wheel on either side was turning fast;
Their yards were small, as was, likewise, the mast;
They were without jib-boom; their hulls were long,
And, though trim built, they still were very strong.
Their bows straight up and down, were like a blade
Slender and sharp, to cut the water made;
Their sterns were like another ship, or brig,
But in all else they had a different rig;
Unlike the ships with which he was acquainted,
While those were white, these all quite black were painted.
Propelled by fire, or smoke, or power within—
For steamer at that time had not been seen—
Was to his vision something strange indeed.
He saw them move along with greater speed
Than ships with all sails set and wind astern;
And to their crews it was of no concern
Which way the tides might tend, or winds might blow,

---

*In the original Portuguese it is *enorme calebra venino*, which means an immense poisonous serpent. Availing myself of the license that clearly belongs to me, as translator, I have called it a "monstrous rattlesnake," and such, in very truth, it doubtless was, since no other poisonous serpents infest Mount Tamalpais. Future excursionists going there to verify the correctness of this narrative, are warned to be careful lest they should be bitten by these venomous reptiles.

For they against both tide and wind would go.
All other vessels they would leave behind,
Though sailing with a favorable wind,
And dashing through the ocean's troubled wave,
A line of long, white foam these ships would leave.
To him they seemed like some enormous creature
Of which he could not comprehend the nature.

When in the Bay the anchor was run out,
From all on board uprose a deafening shout,
So loud that all the hills for leagues around
The cheering heard, and echoed back the sound;
At the same time a bell on board was rung,
A bell as large as in cathedral hung;
And from midships, caused by a jet of steam,
Came forth a sound which was not quite a scream,
Nor whistle was it, but more like a screech,
And far and wide this fearful sound would reach.
To Manuelo this was all so new
That he was much in doubt what he should do;
Whether he should narrate or close his lips,
So far as it concerned this kind of ships.
He feared Justino might discredit all
On hearing what was so improbable;
For this strange dream, or vision, as you know,
Occurred three hundred years, and more, ago.
But happily for all he did not fear
To tell what then was strange, but now is clear.
The ships of every kind when coming in
He could but notice were all filled with men;
And those that seemed to be propelled by smoke,
From stern to stern were black with moving folk.
The other ships, besides the men on board,
Between decks had of tools and food a hoard;
Likewise some strange machines, formed like the crib
In which he had been rocked while yet a babe:
Though larger some were like a coffee mill,
And others not described were stranger still.
But not a plow, nor scythe, nor sickle bright,
Was there on board, nor anywhere in sight;
Nor was there wheel nor loom, nor fork nor rake

To gather grain, nor knives the flax to break.
No implements of any kind were there
To make what people need for use or wear.
The tools they had were bar, and pick, and spade,
And many others very oddly made.
The food provided them, and stored below,
It was of all the kinds that ever grow.
The greater part, if he was not mistaken,
Consisted of hard-tack, and beans, and bacon.
Codfish was also there, and apples dried,
And fruit in cans preserved, and jars beside.
There was provided, likewise, for their drink,
Most everything of which mankind could think;
But for some reason, none could tell just why,
There was a great preponderance of old rye;
But many of them thought it would be handy
To have along a little drop of brandy.
Of books, also, they had each man a few;
But most of these were novels, old or new;
For works of history they did not care,
And such, like poets' works, were very rare,
But, strange to say, among so many men
There was a Bible only now and then,
And as to books of psalms, and books of prayer,
And like religious works, not one was there.
But pictures each man had of friends at home;
Of cards, and such like things, each one had some.
While reading claimed but little their attention
I think, in passing, I may just make mention
That games of dice and chance they all would play,
And spend at these a good part of each day.

These people came from every land on earth,
From melting tropics, and from frozen North,
From Europe, and from South America,
From Mexico, and from far-off Cathay,
From Sandwich Islands, and from South Pacific,
From England, and from Ireland most prolific,
From Cuba, and from Africa they came,
And other places that he could not name;
But Sonoranians, I must not forget,

10

Nor those who were called Sidney-ducks, nor yet
The dark Chileno, who, not given to roam,
Among them acted as if coming home.
Among the throng were mixed both good and bad;
The many happy seemed, but some were sad,
As if they might have been weighed down with care;
But all were hopeful, and none in despair.
These men appeared to be all very young,
And some of them exceedingly high-strung.

There were of women 'mongst them almost none,
Or only now and then a single one;
But she was held in very great respect,
As gallant Manuel did recollect.
The men, in fact, all seemed to worship woman,
As if she might be something more than human.
Their adoration, praises, and affection
All seemed to center in that one direction.
Woman-worship, to his prophetic view,
Was the religion of each single crew—
Not as a goddess, as Diana was
Worshiped, in ancient times, but without cause
These women that he saw were thus revered—
A species of idolatry he feared.
But women, after all, he was compelled
To admit, in every land and age are held
In high esteem by men of real sense;
A brutal man alone will give offense
To gentle woman, nor is it profanation
To treat them as the best thing in creation.
To think them goddesses may not be well,
But angels they appeared to Manuel;
At least Alola so appeared to him,
And more than angel sometimes she did seem.
He did not worship her, but did adore,
And worshiping, in fact, is little more.
So when he blamed the men that came in ships,
He was himself condemned by his own lips.

Of children 'mongst them all not one was there,
No bright-eyed boy, or little maiden fair;

No infant at the breast, or in the arms
Of nurse, beguiled those present with the charms
Of its sweet prattle, or upon the throng
Bestowed its smiles, or with its chirpy song
Inspired the men with those kind sentiments
Which always flow towards those innocents.
How this amidst so large a crowd could be
Good Manuel could not exactly see;
But then this was, as you, kind reader, know,
Three hundred years and more than that ago,
That he was looking with prophetic eye
Not at what was, but would be by and by.

LIX.

THE PLAINS.

AS Moses from Mount Pisgah viewed the land,
So Manuelo, from his more lofty stand
On Tamalpais, next eastward bent his gaze,
And there a most inexplicable maze
Arose before his much astonished vision,
Which may be now described with much precision.
There lay stretched out a plain of vast extent,
On which his mind in prophecy was bent,
And in the distant future he could see,
Approaching, objects which first seemed to be
Like the small ants, which, moving in a row
From place to place, enlined, in order go,
Each on his work intent, and making haste,
Lest he should suffer of his time some waste.
While yet he gazed these objects larger grew,
And all before his sight came full in view.
He saw a force, a hundred thousand strong,
In fifties and in hundreds move along.
Of this great army there was none to lead,
Nor did they of each other take much heed.
There was no order in the march maintained,
And when one fell behind he there remained.
No care was there observed for one another;
Friend would neglect his friend, and brother, brother.

"The devil take the hindmost," was the law
With all that troop, which on the plains he saw.
The men were armed with pistols, guns, and knives,
As if they might be fearful of their lives.
They seemed to have no certain kind of dress;
Though Manuelo somehow did confess
That white felt hats, and pants and coat and vest
Of butternut, prevailed above the rest.
He thought he noticed also one thing more;
That hickory shirts most commonly they wore.
There may have been a few who did not wear
The hickory shirt, but they were very rare.
The only thing they wore that had been white
Was the slouch hat, and that was not so, quite.
They slept upon the ground, or dry, or wet,
And were, upon the whole, a filthy set
Of curs; but he could see they once had been
As clean as anybody he had seen.
Although they marched by day, and camped by night,
And were prepared at any time to fight,
And though well armed, as he could plainly see,
And all were men, it was not an army,
Except in numbers Their arms were for defense
Against some secret unseen foe, but whence
Such enemy might come did not appear,
For there was none in front and none in rear.
The line was fifteen hundred miles in length,
And if attacked it would have shown no strength.
While scattered as they were, so near and far,
He judged they could not be intending war.
Still on some object they appeared intent,
And vexed was he to know what it all meant.
Some were on mule-back, some on horses rode,
A few on asses mounted were, and many strode
Along on foot, and besides arms bore heavy packs,
And large enough almost to break their backs.
There were, besides all these, long wagon trains,
All covered in to shield them from the rains.
The covers were of whitest canvas made,
And when not moving looked like tents, he said.

Some wagons were by horses drawn, but most
By oxen, and of these there were a host.
Of trains of pack-mules there were likewise many,
And these were quickest on the march of any.
These trains would sometimes leave the rest behind;
But this the others did not seem to mind.
The wagons laden were with every kind
Of article of which the human mind
Could possibly conceive, to eat, or wear.
Salt pork, and beef, and flour, and beans were there;
All sorts of household goods, and beds and clothes,
And drinks of what description no one knows.
They were of kinds quite new to Justino,
When writing of them centuries ago;
No doubt their names familiar are at present,
As drinks that are to some so very pleasant.

Sometimes the teams were stalled by too much load,
And then the men would freely ply the goad,
And if in mire the wheels were sunk, would yell
And curse and swear like fiends let loose from *sheol*.
Then the poor oxen to their work would spring,
And from the mire the loaded wagons bring.

The rivers on the route were hard to cross,
And this resulted sometimes in the loss
Of wagons, horses, mules, and even men,
Borne down, were lost, and never seen again.
And mountains also had to be ascended,
As on their westward winding way they wended.
One range to him so full of rocks appeared
That looking at it long he greatly feared
That over it a pass might not be found,
And that the trains would have to turn around,
And from that point their weary steps retrace;
But through its rocky files they found a pass,
And onward a more crooked route did take,
Until they came down to a great salt lake.
Here to the army was a great surprise,
And they could not, at first, believe their eyes,
For men and many women found they here,
With customs and religion very queer.

It seemed each man was blessed with several wives,
A thing they had not seen in all their lives.
Prophet had these, but this was nothing new,
For Manuelo was a prophet too.
With plural wives, these men lived in seclusion,
In order that there might be less confusion.
Their children, were it not for some such care,
Might not know surely who their fathers were;
And hence it was a prudent step to take,
To come and settle by this great salt lake.
At this point then there was a village only,
And as to all the world it was quite lonely.
But Manuelo with prophetic view
Observed, while looking, that the village grew,
And, as it were, before his very eyes
He saw a city of great wealth arise,
Built by the people whom the army met,
And who, for aught now known, may be there yet.
They lived by farming and by cattle breeding,
Little getting from abroad, and little needing.
The men, and possibly the women too,
Contented were, until at last right through
Their settlement a road of iron was run
A thing which much against their wish was done.
This road of iron to Manuelo's view,
Like ships propelled by steam, was something new.
No explanation of it could he find,
And to the last it much perplexed his mind.
In modern times the wonder is dispelled;
But he three hundred years ago was held
Spell-bound, when, gazing with a prophet's eye,
He saw long trains of cars go whizzing by.
But what impressed him as most strange of all,
And was to him most unaccountable,
Was the great speed with which they seemed to glide
Over the plain, along the mountain-side,
Through deep ravines, along the tops of ridges,
Through tunnels in the hills, and over bridges.
They seemed, he said, to his prophetic eye,
To move as fast, at least, as birds could fly.

Not as the lazy gull, or sluggish crow,
But swift, indeed, as swiftest bird could go.
The sparrow-hawk unleashed and in full chase,
Of fleet-winged whip-poor-will, or when the race
Was with the dove, or with the purple pigeon,
Or when in hot pursuit of lark or widgeon,
Did not more swiftly cleave the ambient air
Than on this iron rail did speed the car.

In every coach could sixty people ride,
And if they chose some might hang on outside,
And as the cars in each train numbered ten,
There would be traveling full six hundred men.
So many men on these great trains were carried
That those at Salt Lake soon became less married:
And each was happy could he get but one
Woman for wife, and many could get none.

The army he was speaking of to-day,
At Salt Lake most of them made little stay.
They pushed on further towards the mighty West,
And as the trains appeared upon the crest
Of the Sierras, Manuelo could see
What kind of people in each train might be,
And where each company of men was from,
Or in what State was formerly their home.
Some were from York, and some from the Northwest;
Some came from Pike, but these were not the best;
Some from Missouri came, and those drove steers;
Some were from Michigan, well armed with spears;
Some were from New Jersey, known by their looks,
And some came from Cape Cod and brought fish-hooks;
A few from Maine, they called it "way down East,"
And these an average were, to say the least;
Among the rest that came were Yankees blue,
Who, from peculiar dialect, he knew.
Then Texans came, with pistols at their backs,
And then Kentuckians, riding on their jacks;
And Arkansaw was next, a thousand strong,
Each man armed with a knife ten inches long.
From 'way down South some came along at last,

Too much inflated these to travel fast.
He judged they might, from tone, and speech, and gait,
Be westward bound on business of the State;
Having their slaves along, some black, some brown:
They thus appeared to be men of renown;
But of this last he was not very sure,
As some of them appeared to be quite poor;
But what they lacked in wealth, I may here mention,
Was made up of conceit and of pretension.
In naming different people, it was th' intention
To speak of all then coming, and to mention
In particular the Pennsylvania Dutch,
For, scattered all along, were many such.
These for large horses were conspicuous,
But in some other things they were ridiculous.
I might have spoken of their wagons sooner;
They were boat-like, and called the prairie schooner.
It was observed that when they camped at night,
Such was their greed that everything in sight
Was seized and held, and for their use was kept,
And guard was always posted while they slept.
They seemed to be in constant dread and fear,
As if the Indians might be somewhere near.
All other people on the march would shun
These wily Dutchmen, and would from them run.
When other men to right or left would go
To shoot a deer, or hunt the buffalo,
These men, more cautious, close to camp would stay,
Content with salted meat, and never stray
From the plain road, unless to find good feed
For their fat stock, which seemed their greatest need.
Sometimes the wolves would come up, after dark,
And at their frighted horses howl and bark;
And in that case the men would everyone
Spring to his feet and quickly seize his gun;
A tumult loud they then would institute,
But never were they known a wolf to shoot.

It was not easy to discriminate
Twixt Suckers and men from the Buckeye State,
But if a nice distinction one would wish,

It will be found in that twixt pork and fish.
In jeans and homespuns both of these took pride,
And had ambition for not much beside.
But they were sprightly folk, and kind as well,
And everybody pleased with whom they fell.
Farmers they were by trade, and raising corn
Had been their chief business since they were born.
The Suckers were a little more inclined
To stay at home, and their own business mind
Than the Buckeyes, whose aims, and hopes, and wishes
Inclined them more to seek for loaves and fishes.
But if they fitness had for public places,
It was not indicated in their faces.
No wonder, though, for men of meanest looks
Sometimes know more of things and more of books
Than other men who look extremely well.
What a man knows, none from his looks can tell.

The men from Iowa were like the last;
And so from Wisconsin, though not so fast.
These all were pretty clever fellows thought,
And by others their company was sought.
In Manuel these did no wonder cause,
Since, as observed, it was among their laws
To keep on moving toward the setting sun,
As long as land was found to squat upon.
He might have stated more about these men
If it had not so happened that just then,
While he observing was their special actions,
And what appeared to be their chief attractions,
Some Indiana people came along.
These stalwart Hoosiers thought it nothing wrong
To seize a horse or mule when found astray,
And each man gained a number in that way.
Sometimes this practice would lead to a fight,
But Indianians held that might was right;
And stock thus seized was almost always kept,
Unless the owner got it while they slept.

The foremost people in this mighty tramp—
And 'mongst whom doubtless there was many a scamp—
Were from the Empire State, the western part.

With pack-mules these all came, and not a cart
Or wagon had, nor had they any tent.
On leading all the march, these men were bent;
They were amongst themselves a quarrelsome set,
And each of them was in a constant fret
Lest other trains should of them take the lead,
And use up all the drink and all the feed;
For on this march with all the chief desire
Was water, grass, and wood to make a fire;
These things were sought near which to pitch the camp,
Throughout the whole of that long, weary tramp;
And when the men at night lay down to rest,
Their dreams were always stretching further west.
Their thoughts when sleeping appeared all the while
To be concerning something called a "pile,"
But whether it was precious stones, or gold
They thought about, his dream did not unfold.
He was quite sure it was some sort of gain
They sought, but what kind entered not his brain.
Though these things all were clearly then descried
By Manuel, and many more beside,
What by it all was meant neither could he
Nor good Justino at that distance see,
And each of them, in turn, gave up the ghost
In ignorance for what that mighty host
Of men, by land and sea, were coming here—
A thing which seems to us now very queer.
But stranger things by prophets have been told—
I mean by those who spoke in times of old—
And people must not wonder, in our day,
At anything which a true prophet may
By inspiration have been led to say.

LX.

SAN FRANCISCO.

It was three hundred years ago and more—
A fact which has been stated twice before—
When from Mount Tamalpais, Manuelo

350 YEARS AGO.

Viewed with prophetic ken the land below,
And water, destined, at a later day,
To be well known as San Francisco Bay.
That country then was all *incognito*
To all white people but Manuelo.
I might, perhaps, except, also, the crew
Of the *Don Carlos*, for they had been there, too;
But all the crew of that good ship were gone;
And since of them none ever did return,
What I just stated must, I think, be so,—
The sole one living was Manuelo.
The land itself was picturesque and wild;
The climate was most charming, soft and mild,
And beautiful, just then, was all the face
Of nature, as beheld from that high place.

It has been stated how he was impressed,
And part of what from that tall mountain-crest
Broke on his view; how ships were coming in,
How vast the number of them must have been;
And how, by turning east, he saw strung out
A hundred thousand people, all en route
For the Pacific slope; and now we come
To something that he saw much nearer home.
Though what he viewed was not with natural eye,
To him it was as clear in reverie,
As he lay musing on the mountain-top.
Spread out there were before him, like a map,
A very great variety of things,
Which came up bold in his imaginings:
Some that appeared astonishing to him,
And some quite unaccountable did seem;
But still he kept on dreaming, where he lay,
From noon till end of that long summer day—
Nor did he weary in the contemplation
Of the affairs and men of that great nation,
Which at a future time was to control
All of America, from pole to pole.

In the good Book we are most plainly told
That what Isaiah saw, in days of old,

Was all to his prophetic vision clear,
And that if what he saw had been quite near
In point of time and space, he could not better
Have told what did take place; for to the letter
Did that great leader of the ancient seers
Predict what would occur in after years.
And Manuelo did in similar way
Foretell what is transpiring in our day;
And though three centuries ago he spake,
There is in all he said not one mistake.
It is, perhaps, worth while here to repeat,
In just one line, what then his eyes did greet.
First to the western sea his thoughts were bent,
Then eastward for a time he looked intent;
But gazing southward, now, across the Bay,
Just down before him, and not far away,
Lay a large city, stretching from the shore
Back westward, over hills and dales a score.
This city was to him a great surprise,
For until now it had escaped his eyes.
Perhaps a fog or smoke did intervene,
And thus prevent, at first, its being seen.
But that was not a matter of great weight,
Since all the city now was plain in sight,
So plain, indeed, that he seemed almost there,
And in his vision could see objects clear.
Some things were quite beyond his comprehension;
Of such he thought it best to make no mention;
Of others that by him were understood,
He spoke without reserve, just as he should.
Much that was seen was so entirely new
That his description may not seem quite true
In all particulars; but bear in mind
That everything which in this book you find
Is only the translation of a scroll
Found, lately, in a musty pigeon-hole
In the convent at Evora, and when
The manuscript was found it must have been
As old as three hundred and twenty years;
And I confess I entertain some fears
That it was not entirely genuine;

But this is certainly no fault of mine.
My simple duty to translate it is,
And faults in the original are his
Who penned the curious story at the start,
And framed this history with so much art.

But I must now return to that great town
Which afterwards acquired such just renown
Its wharves far out into the Bay extended;
Some were entirely new, and some were mended;
Others were broke, and needed much repair,
And he observed a few, he said, that were
Full of large holes through which men disappeared,
And nothing afterwards of them was heard.

A bulkhead stretched around the city front,
Upon which men in idleness were wont
To saunter, stand and muse, and sometimes ride,
Or hither come, intent on suicide.
And sometimes, though not often, women too
Would seek the city front with that in view.
But when a woman jumped into the water,
A man, he said, was always near and caught her;
But if a man it was plunged in the Bay,
The other men were all a league away;
Perhaps, at last, a few would come about,
And if reward was offered, fish him out.

Some streets appeared as smooth as any floor,
Others too rough too travel over more.
Some were well paved with stone, and some with wood;
The last were poor, the former very good;
That is, the first, when paved with blocks of stone,
And only when paved with that kind alone,
For there were other streets laid close with cobble,
And over these a horse could hardly hobble.
These cobble pavements were so very rough
The city soon obtained of them enough.
It would be difficult to pave a street
With substance more annoying to the feet,
And as the feet in this thing were consulted,

And not the head, it naturally resulted
In substituting stones, smooth on one side,
And over which men could with comfort ride.
The streets that were with wooden pavement laid,
And for which kind the people always paid
A good round price, would sometimes last a year
Or two, and perhaps three, but never near
So long as other kinds; but still some would
Persist in saying they were very good,
And good they were for just a little while;
But it took little time for wood to spoil;
A heavy rain would cause the blocks to swell,
And then the pavement was all gone to—well,
No matter; but the street would all appear
Thrown up in little hillocks, far and near,
And then no one along that street could drive
With any hope of getting through alive.

As many men have many different minds,
So of sidewalks there were as many kinds
As each saw fit to make fronting his door,
And some would have two kinds, and even more.
There was no uniformity whatever,
And so it never happened, or hardly ever,
That any two men could agree in making
The same sort of sidewalk, or undertaking
To make a walk that was at all worth having;
The end, as said, was many kinds of paving.
Some were of granite made, and some of flags,
And in these both most commonly were sags.
Some were of bricks, and some were laid with planks,
Which, so to speak, would cut up many pranks.
The planks would spring, and warp, and twist, and wind,
And never could be properly confined.
Some were of asphalt made with gravel mixed,
And this kind had to be quite often fixed;
The asphaltum would melt in the hot sun,
And quite, at times, over the stone curb run;
Or else, when level, get so soft, at last,
That women walking on it would stick fast.
And pretty girls, in going two and two,

Would, as it sometimes happened, lose a shoe,
Which at the time to her would seem shocking,
Since it exposed to public view a stocking;
But when some young man would the shoe restore,
She would appear as happy as before.
And walks were also made by mixing sand
With a cement; but none could understand
How this was done. It was a patent right,
And though performed by men in open sight
Of everyone, only a few could do
What to all people was exposed to view.
This kind of sidewalk was the very best,
And far excelled in smoothness all the rest;
But somehow only men whose wealth was ample
Indulged in it, and only then for sample.

Had he been looking with his natural eyes,
Reclining as he was on Tamalpais,
A waste of sand he would have had in view,
All over where the city after grew;
But in the future he was looking far:
To him a city was already there.
With mental vision casting o'er the place,
Long rows of buildings he could plainly trace.
These he observed with some degree of care,
And noticed features that to him were rare.
Some people on the sand their houses made,
But others, building, their foundation laid
In solid ground; and some built on the rocks,
And these could not be moved by earthquake shocks;
A few were built of stone, and more of brick,
But of these last the walls were never thick.
So thin, indeed, quite strange to say, were some
That when the least disturbed down they would come.
But houses most were built of wood called red,
And plastered on the side and overhead.
The windows, as a rule, were rather wide,
And from the house stood out on every side.
Long did he look, but never could conjecture
What style it was they had of architecture.
He noticed some oblong, and like a chest,

But these, he thought, were not among the best.
Immensely large to him some homes appeared,
But in the largest, he observed, were reared
Less children than in some mere hovels were,
Without a window, and with single door.
This waste of room, he thought, proved with mankind
That fortune fickle was, and likewise blind.
Some of these dwellings were palatial,
And in their grandeur rivaled the Querenial;
In these of works of art and bric-a-brac,
Selected with best taste, there was no lack.
All luxuries the world could then afford
Were there observed, and in the greatest hoard :
The statues and the paintings gathered there
Were by old masters made, and very rare.
Of tapestry and gems there was no end,
The cost of which no one could comprehend.
These dwellings mostly were built on a hill,
They called it Nob, and no one ever will
Or can well know how to Manuelo
These things appeared three hundred years ago.
The people that those houses occupied
Were genial folk, and some of them took pride
In kindly acts, and doing good to others,
And seemed to think that all mankind were brothers.
A few of them their boundless wealth enjoyed,
While others by their riches were annoyed,
And seemed to be in constant apprehension
Of breaches of the peace, or some contention
Among the other dwellers in the city;
Perhaps for lack of charity, or pity
Towards men of families that were in need,
For in that city some were poor indeed.

There is so much in prophecy revealed,
So many things that else would be concealed
In the dark womb of distant future years,
And about which poor mankind seldom hears—
Things, but for the good prophet's warning cry,
Would come like thunder-clap from a clear sky—
That man should heed what in this way is told,

And not confide too much in power of gold.
Justino, after making this reflection,
Turned his attention in a new direction.

LXI.

THE PEOPLE.

THE people that inhabited that city
Were, as a general thing, both wise and witty.
Their wisdom was in many things displayed,
Their wit was mostly seen in what they said.
Sometimes in action they would show some wit,
In failing to be active not a bit.
The thing in which they proved themselves most wise
Was in the most remarkably large size
Assumed by them for everything they had,
And all they hoped to get, and all they made.
Some might not see the wisdom of this trait
And think it was but to exaggerate;
But one should take of it a different view,
And one which seems to be to nature true,
That every man thereby improved his health,
And added likewise greatly to his wealth.
Another thing in which their wisdom shone
Was in a custom which was all their own:
This custom was to always look around,
And when, perchance, a thing of worth was found,
To try and turn it to their own account,
At least, if it was of some great amount.
This habit cultivated, grew so strong
That scarce a man among them thought it wrong
To take and keep whatever he could get,
Or to demand of anyone he met
A fair division of his surplus gains,
And on refusal to blow out his brains.
But rarely did this happen for that cause;
Nevertheless it was among their laws
That any man who might be called a thief,
And from the charge if he had no relief,
He could on his own hook hunt down the one

CALIFORNIA

Who slandered him, and this was often done.
The wisdom of such laws was clearly shown
In making men more careful of their own,
In making them more cautious how they talked,
And more particular, also, where they walked.
This good effect was noticed everywhere,
And breaches of these laws were very rare.
It did occur to him, however, then,
That 'mongst them all there might be a few men
Who would adhere to their determination
To break these laws, in spite of all creation;
Who might the laws of father-lands prefer,
And who were willing, therefore, to incur
The hot displeasure of those other men,
Who to each one of these would number ten.
This kind of conduct always raised a row,
But these few men, by management, somehow,
Would form themselves into a committee,
And take possession of the entire city.
And for a week or two, both night and day,
The very deuce would seem to be to pay.

The people were made up of different classes,
Some being wise, he said, but some were asses;
But then they came from many different places,
And were composed of several different races.
There was the man from Europe, with white skin;
And Southern men were there, with skins quite thin;
Then came the African, whose skin was black,
And some of these were striped on the back.
The South American came next, with features
That make it hard to tell what kind of creatures
His father and his mother may have been,
According to the teachings of Darwin.
Next came the India man, more brown than stout,
A race of men that seemed well-nigh run out.
Then English, Irish, Scotch, and French, and Dutch—
The number was unlimited of such.
Of Chinamen he thought there were a few,
And now and then a solitary Jew.
But in that city everything was made

By those supposed Chinese, and all the trade
Was carried on by Jews, if Jews they were,
And quite like Jews, to him, they did appear.

The people there had one infatuation
Which was peculiar to no other nation.
The men and women liked to be thought young,
Particularly when about half sprung.
They somehow seemed to think it a disgrace
To have white hair, or wrinkles on the face.
To make themselves look young the men would dye
Their hair a black, or brown, but by and by,
When it grew out, and sometimes all too soon,
It would assume a color called maroon.
Sometimes half white, and black the other half,
A man or woman's hair would cause a laugh.
The women, to look young, would paint their features,
And then regard themselves as charming creatures.
So thick would these sometimes apply the paint
That some of them appeared extremely quaint;
But still they would persist, both maids and mothers,
In self-delusion, trying to cheat others.
He really thought it was the strangest yet
That men and women should so far forget
That youth depends upon how one appears,
And not upon the number of his years.
Some are in very truth quite old at thirty,
While others are as young as boys at forty.
Those men who play the old boy in their youth
Are sure to be, while young, old boys in truth.
But those who temperate are in all their lives,
And those especially who have good wives,
Though many years may over them have rolled,
Will still be vigorous, and not grow old.
Some persons have been known at eighty-seven
To be apparently as far from Heaven
As others only twenty-five have been,
From being by the devil taken in.
While, in true youthfulness, there is some glory,
None is in being prematurely hoary:
And this may be with some the reason why

They use so frequently dark-colored dye;
And women may use paint with the same view;
But dye nor paint can make an old thing new.
Good habits better are than dye, or paint,
And these observed there need be no complaint.
Manuel thought the elixir of man's life
Was a good, loving, true, and faithful wife;
But what of women might be th' elixir
He could not guess, but thought perhaps for her
It might be well rich dresses to provide,
And jewelry, and many things beside.
But what he thought would most renew her strength,
And to her life add many years of length,
Was what appeared to him a simple thing,
That is, to give her tongue the fullest swing;
For women's lives, he thought, had been curtailed
By husbands who, most foolishly, had failed
To fully comprehend their greatest need,
Which was to talk, he said, and not to read.

LXII.
THE CITY.

MANUELO had been brought up in Spain,
And always hoped he might go back again.
As seaman he had traveled far and wide,
And visited a hundred ports beside
The one on which he now was looking down,
And on the shores of which he saw this town.
But in the ports and cities he had seen,
And through the busy streets of which had been,
Not one presented such a sight as here
Arose before his seer-like vision clear.
In other towns were carts and drays and hacks,
But here the carriages all ran on tracks.
A single horse would draw one very large,
And as capacious as a captain's barge.
But what was more surprising to him still,
Some of them would run up the highest hill
Without so much as single horse to pull,

And that, too, when they were chock brimming full
Of passengers. This surely magic was,
He thought, and contrary to all the laws
Of nature and of art. To save his soul
He could not tell what caused the wheels to roll;
But roll they would, and that, too, very swift,
And in some way would actually lift
Those riding in them up the steepest height,
And keep on doing so through day and night.

He saw, but could not tell exactly where,
Except it was on some great thoroughfare,
A single structure which, for style and size,
Surpassed by far all buildings that his eyes
Had ever rested on. Hotel it seemed,
But large enough it was for king, he deemed.
He doubted if there was a palace built
That for magnificence could hold a tilt
With this great building. It was so very high,
To see its top one had quite hard to try.
A court it had, rectangular in form,
Which was entirely shut in from the storm,
For it was covered with a roof of glass.
In beauty this fine structure did surpass
The Mosque of Omar, and the Vatican,
And every other building made by man.
A thousand people in it found a home,
And in its corridors a man might roam
For several days, and travel many a mile,
And something new and strange see all the while.
This structure by a banker was designed,
And owed its perfectness to the great mind
Of that one man, whose heart and noble soul
Shone forth in every part, throughout the whole.

In all the views that Manuelo took,
The only things that had familiar look
Were the cathedrals and the churches there,
And these were scattered almost everywhere.
Some churches that he saw were very small,
And some were large, with steeples very tall.

Some were surmounted with a cross of gold;
Some were quite poor, and others very old.
Those having crosses on he had no doubt
Were Catholic, and those that were without
Were Protestant. But this was nothing new,
For Manuelo, though a Catholic true,
Was quite familiar with this sort of thing,
For in his time Don Carlos V. was king,
And emperor as well of all the Germans,
And personally had listened to the sermons
Of Martin Luther, who sought to reform
The church, and who raised such a fearful storm
Throughout all Europe, and throughout the world,
By his bold threats against Pope Leo hurled.
So in these churches there was nothing odd,
Since all attendants worshiped the same God.
There were some places, though, Josh-houses named,
In which the God of Christians was defamed.
In these were idols worshiped by the people,
But then these houses had no bell, nor steeple,
And could not properly be churches called,
Though Christians, by them, were sometimes appalled.
In one of the best churches he saw there,
A man called Brother, someone, led in prayer.
This church was thought to be not orthodox,
Though it appeared to have been built on rocks.
In the largest cathedral that he saw
A bishop reverend laid down the law,—
The law by which the good should be directed,
And that likewise which vitally affected
The temporalities of all his flock;
And this church founded was upon a rock.

No standing army in that land appeared,
Nor outside enemy was ever feared.
The native born were peacefully inclined,
And most of them, it was observed, did mind
Their own business, and let their neighbors go.
A few, however, would kick up a row;
But these were not unto the manor born;
On the contrary, all of these were foreign

Men, who, as strangers, to that land had come
In search of food and for a better home.
These men were brought up under other rules,
And widely different laws, and different schools,
And could not quite take in the situation,
And therefore often caused great botheration
To such as had been born in that country,
And hoped there to enjoy prosperity.
These foreigners on Sunday afternoons
Would come together in squads and in platoons,
And on some sand lot listen to the blarney
Of one whose name he thought was Dennis Kearny.
This fellow, in reality, was clever,
And dosed his hearers with some good palaver.
He made them think they had been much abused,
And good men, in that town, this man accused
Of all the crimes found in the calendar,
And some that never had been written there.
At last this thing became distasteful to
A few, who said to him it would not do,
And that unless he stopped abuse right quick,
And better talked, that they would make him sick.
And just about this time, as history goes,
Began the serious troubles and the woes
Of this man Dennis, and his silly friends,
Who then did all they could to make amends
For the great injury they had thus caused;
And when, at last, and luckily, they paused,
And well considered all that they were doing,
And that their course would surely bring much ruing,
They promised in the future to do better,
And to obey the laws up to the letter.
The people, then, who had been so maligned,
But who were always very much inclined
To charity towards all other men,
And more particularly in cases when
They were misled by idle demagogues,
Who knew no more of human rights than swine—
These people, then, he said, their work suspended,
And all disturbance for the time was ended.

I said a standing army there was none,
Nevertheless, there was a sort of one.
This army called itself the police force,
And in the city they held sway, of course.
Their proper duty was to keep good order
Throughout the city, and along the border.
A star they wore, and dressed in uniform,
In order that themselves might do less harm.
These policemen were a good-looking set,
And behaved well enough to all they met;
But though their duty was to detect crimes,
They were most noted for their love of dimes;
And if one of them ever made arrest,
'Twas as likely to be one of the best
Of all the citizens, as of the worst.
It was remarked that not one of them durst
Take in his charge a person that was bad,
And persons caught by them were weak or sad.
By sad was meant they were oppressed by sorrow,
And wished some place to stay until the morrow;
If anyone could render this excuse
He would find lodgings in the calaboose.
If crime was perpetrated night or day,
The police force was sure to turn away.
To avoid trouble they were much inclined,
And each one his own business chose to mind.
Sometimes they would take in a girl or boy,
But full-grown men they seldom would annoy.
Like other armies this one had its fort,
And that, in this case, was the police court,
In which the police force was very strong;
And here they would pretend to punish wrong;
But wrong was not more punished there than right,
For the police would try with all their might
To get a fine imposed, or send to jail
The man, or woman either, who might fail
To pony up, whatever was demanded.
And in the jail the poor were always landed.

A common council in that city was
Called common, from the nature of the laws

Enacted by them, or, perhaps, because
They were an ordinary set of men,
And paid but little heed to duty when
Transacting business for the public good,
Or doing what in honesty they should.
These men would quarrel about little things,
But in all large ones were controlled by rings.
By rings are understood, some men combined
To carry out the scheme they have in mind.
The object of these men was always pelf,
And at the city crib each helped himself.

There was among the rest a water ring,
Which had an institution they called Spring
Valley. The object of it was to bring
Pure water to such people as were fond
Of it; but from a filthy, stagnant pond
The water for the citizens was brought;
Of which all were compelled to drink, or nought.

Another ring related to the light
With which the city was illumed by night.
Whatever this light was, they called it gas,
But when this dream occurred there was, alas!
No gas in all the world, or none by name,
Though something else may have been just the same;
But it was not then used for light at all;
If known it was to alchemists, that's all.
The lights in use in Manuelo's day
Were all produced in quite a different way.
The tallow candle was the main reliance;
But some had made so much advance in science
That lamps were used, in which was burned whale oil;
But these, for common use, were deemed too royal.
When Manuelo therefore heard so much
Loud talk about gas-light, his mind was such
That light thereon would have been well conferred,
To help him comprehend what then he heard.
But the first object of the great gas ring
From giving light was quite a different thing.
They sought to keep the public in the dark

Regarding their concern and all its work.
In just that way, that is, by means of stealth,
Immense amounts were added to their wealth.
Justino rather thought, but was not sure,
The practice of this ring towards the poor,
In wringing out of them their little gains,
To gather which had cost them so much pains,
Might be the reason why they were so named;
At all events, for wringing they were famed.
But then no matter how the term arose,
Or what we may concerning it suppose,
The fact will still remain, and ever be,
That ring the same is as monopoly;
And of monopolies in that fair land
There was no end. They were on every hand,
And controlled everything. If but a street
Was to be fixed you would be sure to meet
A band of hungry wights, hot for a job,
All ready to combine to steal and rob.

Another ring, the strongest one of all,
Was formed about a large new city hall
Which they were building on a sandy dune,
But which would not be finished very soon;
For when complete it would no longer give
The ring support, nor on it could they live.
Officials of the city, high and low,
Were members of this ring from the word go.
Some of them would get rich out of a job
Upon it, and others would try to rob
The city on some contract they would take,
Intending in that way large wealth to make.
A sort of sheep-shears was this city hall,
Which served to fleece the people, one and all;
And meek as lambs the people would submit
To whatsoever any ring saw fit
To do, or to impose upon the city;
And Manuelo thought it was a pity
That all the good men in the town did not
Arise and teach these combinations what

They ought to do, or rather what they should
Refrain from doing, unless it be for good.

The reader will remember the time when
That fight came off between four hundred men
On the one side, and on the other side
Some thirty bears, who, with mouths open wide,
Defied the men, and bravely stood their ground
Until the Santoese did them surround;
And how the men advanced with fearful yell,
And how the bears, affrighted, screeched as well,
And how the great tumult filled all the plain,
And from the hi'ls was echoed back again.
But this commotion could not be compared
To a tumult which Manuelo heard
In that city, in a great granite hall,
Built very strong, with steeple very tall.
About three hundred men were there assembled,
And in their conduct very much resembled
The men who were engaged in the bear fight;
But in loud yelling beat them out of sight.
He watched them closely, and tried to find out
What it all meant, and what they were about,
But it was of no use, there was no telling
What caused the men to keep up such a yelling.
In the great din he thought he could detect
That much of it was done just for effect;
And that the ones who made the greatest racket
Had much less cause than others had to make it.
As empty wagons make the loudest noise,
So loudest among these were empty boys.
He heard them saying something about stocks,
And sometimes one would speak of bottom rocks.
Much of their talk was about puts and fills,
And sometimes also about shafts and mills;
But to his understanding this was Greek,
And so to comprehend it d'd not seek.
Each man would have a pencil in his hand,
And now and then one of them would demand
Of the fat man, who sat above the crowd,
That he right there and then should be allowed

To bring some other fellow up to taw;
And then the fat man would pronounce the law.
Though all these men were full of demonstration—
For that among them all was all the fashion—
Not one was ever hit upon the nose,
Though many of them, as he did suppose,
Received black eyes, or were quite badly skinned,
And now and then someone would have the wind
Knocked out of him, and such would always then
Complain of aches about the abdomen.
Some of these men when chafed, like wolves would howl,
And others when close pressed like bears would growl;
So much like bears, at times, a part would act,
That others justly called them bears in fact.
Another set would bellow so like bulls
That they were termed, in spite of all the rules,
The bulls of that assembly; and this part
Would sometimes show in practice so much art
In puffing up what they might have in mind,
That good Manuelo was half inclined
To look upon them as sets of scamps,
And scarcely better than so many tramps.
About this granite hall, and on the street,
A stranger in the town would always meet
A crowd of hungry, seedy, anxious wights;
Where they were from, and where they slept o' nights,
A puzzle was, and mystery profound;
But some he judged must sleep upon the ground,
For they as filthy were, and looked as bad,
As if they board or lodgings never had.
Some hopeful were, and some were in despair,
As would appear from their disheveled hair.
Some from hard drink had faces very red,
And others from diseases were half dead.
These fellows, judging from their gentle ways,
May at some time have seen much better days,
But now their case was sorrowful enough,
And their prospect in life seemed pretty rough.
Each was beset with a strange sort of whim,
That some great fortune was awaiting him;

And this delusion would hang to each one
Until his course on earth at last was run.
Once in a while a woman would come there,
Though women in that crowd were rather rare;
But when one did appear she rushed along,
And would be hardly noticed by the throng.
If sensitive, the woman never failed,
In that locality, to keep closely veiled,
For women on that street were out of place,
And were quite apt to fall into disgrace
By going there too often, or by staying
Where those mad men their curious games were playing.

LXIII.

DRESS.

GOOD Manuelo in his youth had heard
That "finest feathers make the finest bird;"
Which words of wisdom he could not forget,
And that now brings us to the best part yet
Of this long dream. At least, I think it is,
And my opinion is the same as his
Who dreamed the dream. But then, nor he,
Nor yet myself, a proper judge may be.

By feathers here are meant quite different things
From those which grow upon the tails and wings
Of birds of various kinds. The things I mean
Are those which are so very often seen
In cities large, to wit, what women wear
When to the play they go, or when to prayer.
The dreamer wrapped in reverie profound,
In a great hall was borne, where all around
Were seated men and women, young and old,
In numbers greater than can well be told.
A theater it seemed, of vast extent,
And for the pleasure of the people meant.
Its form was circular, but from one side
A stage extended off, both far and wide.
The whole of this great hall was ornamented
With every figure that could be invented;

With angels in mid air, in nakedness,
Or with the least apology for dress.
Goblins likewise there were, with hideous forms,
Some having faces, necks, and breasts, and arms
Of lovely girls; but all the parts below
Of horrid beasts, of kinds no one may know.
Some were like fishes formed, with fins and tails,
Some bore the heads of men, but most females.
Of all these things no heed at all was taken,
Or none unless the dreamer was mistaken.
But mirrors large were set in many places,
In which reflected were the people's faces.
These mirrors objects were of much attention,
As if they might have been some new invention.
The women, he observed, would peer in these,
And some, in doing so, seemed ill at ease,
And anxiously adjusted what they wore,
Which Manuelo thought, in looking o'er
That vast assembly, might have been
A little more extensive than was seen,
For more than half of all the ladies there
Appeared with breast and neck and arms quite bare;
But then their dresses all, such as they had,
Were of the very finest fabrics made;
And gold and jewelry of every sort
Adorned the person where the dress was short.
Feathers, and likewise flowers, most gay, upon
Their heads they wore in the greatest profusion.
In this, he thought, he could most plainly see
They had a custom of the Santoee,
For all the maids and matrons of that nation
Adopted flowers and feathers as their fashion.
But from the Santoese they different were,
In that those in the hall wore golden hair;
And many of them were of light complexion,
Made so by paint, as was plain of detection.
Whereas the native women of his day,
Who then were living just across the Bay,
Had hair as black as any raven's wing,
And eyes as dark as any darker thing.
But paint was never used by dame or maid—

Though men themselves would paint when on a raid—
Their faces were as clear as amber bright,
And beautiful, though not exactly white.

The people in this theater assembled,
Which in arrangement very much resembled
The arenas by the Romans built in Spain,
But which for ages had in ruins lain,
Were waiting with impatience, all within,
For the evening's entertainment to begin.
At length, before them all, upon the stage
A man stalked forth, who seemed in towering rage;
He stormed and stamped and swore and beat about,
When, in a little while, two more came out,
And tried to cool his anger with soft speech;
But the first man replied in turn to each
Of the two men, denouncing them aloud,
With words severe, before the assembled crowd.
Just then a lady came upon the scene,
From a more distant place behind a screen.
This lady's dress was made of silks and fur,
And two bare-legged pages followed her,
Bearing her train, which was three varas long.
When near the front she soon began a song,
In which the men all three joined in, with notes
Quite loud enough to split their very throats.
With many demonstrations wild these four
Were singing, when in rushed a dozen more;
A troop of peasantry, fair maids, and men,
And women, young and old, and then
They all joined in the singing, and the noise
Was equaled only by that which boys
Upon a village green, on festive day,
Are wont to raise when foot-ball is the play.
The din continued half an hour or more,
When the first lady fell upon the floor,
And to appearances she lay there dead;
But still the play and singing onward sped.
The angry man then, kneeling by her side,
Showed by his actions that she was his bride,
For he with sorrow was quite overcome,

And anxious seemed to be to take her home.
But while yet there, and what to do uncertain,
And others still were singing, down came the curtain.
Then from the vast assemblage there uprose
Loudest applause. But this was not the close.
It was an interlude between the acts,
And Manuelo then observed these facts.

Foremost among the men, and near the stage,
Were many gentlemen advanced in age.
Some were adorned with wigs, but most were bald.
Though young some were, they all would old be called;
For while their years were few, they much had seen,
And their experience had quite various been.
These, in that town, were known as fast young men.
So fast indeed they were that never again
Could they be youthful, for their prime was passed,
And with much older men their lot was cast.
The old, bald-headed men, no doubt, drew near
In order that they might the better hear;
Or possibly their sight was dimmed by age,
And for this reason they sat near the stage,
In order that the better they might view
All that the actors on the boards might do.
It was observed when dancing girls came out
These old, and old young men, were close about
To see and hear all that was going on,
To cheer the actors, and enjoy the fun.
Of dancing girls there were in that same play
A score or more, and not for many a day
Had Manuelo seen a sight so fine,
Or anything, in fact, in that same line.
With hop, and skip, and sudden turns and whirls,
This troop of twenty beautiful young girls
Came vaulting on the stage, and briskly danced,
While each in turn on light tiptoe advanced
Quite to the front, so that the men might see
Which one of them best danceress might be.
All of these damsels had a sort of notion
That too much clothing might impede their motion,
And for that reason garments they had few,

350 YEARS AGO.

As few, in fact, as possibly would do.
In truth, it must be said to have had less
Would have been to be almost without dress.
Such clothes each had as modesty req ired,
And that was all the audience desired,
Particularly that portion near the stage,
Who have been mentioned as advanced in age.
These ladies danced with such transcendent skill,
And were applauded with so much good-will,
And all so smiled, and showed such winning ways,
That each in turn was showered with sweet bouquets.
But pleasures all must end, and so this play;
And the people went reluctantly away.

These things were seen some centuries ago,
And what is plain to us could not be so
To one accustomed to the different ways
Of people living in those ancient days.
'Tis nothing new to us to see men smoking;
But the good friar thought the dreamer joking,
When he related how he saw the men
Imbibing smoke, from something round, and then
Puffing it out again from mouth or nose,
When, as he said, the smoke in clouds arose,
And then the men would watch with anxious eyes,
To see how high the cloud thus made would rise.
He could not tell to save him what this meant,
But gave the fact, and with that was content.
He thought, however, it was childish sport,
And wondered that full-grown men could resort
To such a boyish practice as that seemed,
And one so foolish, too, as this was deemed.

Another thing that caused astonishment
Was, that men, young and old, were not content
To drink what their necessities require,
But were possessed with a most strange desire
To pour into their stomachs, all the while,
Some spirits strong, or some decoction vile,
Which they well knew would surely cause their death,
And while they lived, give them a horrid breath,

This common habit of intoxication
He thought the crowning curse of that great nation;
And so it was, for of their men the best
Were by it sent to their eternal rest.
But then he would not have it understood
That all the people drank; some were too good,
And some had too much pride to be seen drunk,
And rarely was one found who had so sunk
In his own estimation as to become
A common mendicant, without a home;
But such examples would sometimes occur,
Brought on by drink, as all such cases were.
By this account Justino's heart was moved
With pity great, for all mankind he loved.

Most people in that town were well inclined,
As good, he thought, in fact, as one could find.
Politeness and true goodness are the same,
The difference being only in the name.
Politeness marked the conduct of the many,
And of rude people there were hardly any.
But some there were disposed to foppishness,
Who counted overmuch upon their dress.
Even in this trait there was some wisdom shown,
And the distinction was not all their own;
For other men in other times have thought
That reputation with one's clothes is bought.
Say what you will, that is not all absurd
Which on this head we have so often heard:
Dress makes the man, the want of it the boor,
The ill-dressed man is always very poor.
Nine tailors, it is said, it doth require
To make a man; but we do not desire
To be unfair; one tailor surely can,
If a good one, make up a gentleman.
Why nine should be required to make the clothes
Of one is more than anybody knows.
But nine it may require to make a fit;
And should the fact be sought, that may be it.
The tailors as a class are much abused,
And payment of their bills sometimes refused:

By closest observation you will find
That they are benefactors of mankind.

Among the well-dressed men, it was observed,
Were those who in their health were best preserved.
The most of these in business were employed,
But some with business never were annoyed;
These mentioned last were mostly men of wealth,
But some of them appeared to live by stealth,
Their occupation could not well be seen,
And so he thought some of them might have been
Engaged in games, that is, I mean, with cards,
Or, which is much the same, in the stock-boards.
Most of the well-dressed men had lots of money,
While others as well clad were without any.
The impecunious ones were termed these last,
And they distinguished were for living fast.
A selfish sort of life some of them led,
And for all good they did might well be dead.
They had no wives nor children to support,
Nor would engage in business of that sort.
They were, in fact, a shiftless set of scamps,
And when they became seedy were called tramps.

Among the richest men it was a rarity
To find one much inclined to charity.
The man of wealth, who, with a generous heart,
Relieves the poor by giving up a part
Of the large gains which fortune has bestowed,
Does others some, but does himself most good.
That happiness which one may others cause
By operation of kind nature's laws,
Back to the generous man is sure to come,
By the same rule that curses roost at home.
If this wise law rich men could understand,
There would be less distress in every land.

In speaking of the laws good Manuel
Thought of the lawyers, and went on to tell
About this class of men as they appeared
In his long dream, but said he greatly feared
He might injustice do that curious class,

And half inclined he was to let them pass;
But, yielding to the friar's earnest prayer,
He then went on to say the lawyers were
By far the most deceitful, treacherous set
Of individuals he had ever met.
He said they would by cunning and deceit
Impose upon the people, and would cheat
The men by whom they were employed;
That in some cases men were more annoyed
By their own lawyers than by th' others'.
He said the lawyers called each other brothers,
And an association formed in which they would
Conspire together for their common good;
That they before the court would spout and spar,
And seem to be engaged in earnest war;
But when the court adjourned, and out they came,
They to each other would appear the same
As if they always had been best of friends,
And for discourteous words to make amends,
The two would step into the next saloon,
And all their quarrels were frogotten soon.
The two would there shake hands, and drink, and smoke,
And treat their quarrel as a pleasant joke.
They called themselves practitioners at the bar,
And such, he said, in fact they really were;
But then the bar that most attention claimed
From these good lawyers was the one just named,
Where whisky, gin, and wine were sold and bought,
And not the one where justice is dealt out.
The lawyers may in league be with the devil,
But then they are a necessary evil.
Regarding many things which there he saw,
Some men were needed to lay down the law,
And lawyers were employed that thing to do,
Though some of them had other ends in view.

And then the same precisely are the facts
In that profession where are found the quacks.
Some doctors faithful are and some are not;
Some are men of learning, and some have got
A mere smattering of the knowledge most in need

In that important calling to succeed.
Some to acquire that knowledge take great pains,
But never can succeed for want of brains.
"In such we see the bent of nature foiled,
A strong blacksmith or a good butcher spoiled."
Those doctors who lack power of diagnosis,
And give, hap-hazard, to their patients doses,
Are thought to be about the very worst
Of mortal men with whom the world is cursed.
The shyster may be cause of loss of gold,
In which event his client may be sold:
Such injury sustained is to his wealth,
But that caused by the quack relates to health,
And it may be extends to the man's life,
Or to depriving him of child or wife.
And yet there are who term themselves physicians,
And in their practice hold quite high positions,
Whose skill is all in humbug and pretense,
And who are lacking even common sense.
These, by their airy ways and solemn looks,
Lead to belief that they are learned in books;
Whereas, about their art they know much less
Than many persons who do not profess
To understand a thing about the ills
Of which mankind are cured by drams and pills.

In Barcelona, when he was a lad,
Manuelo's indulgent parents had
Sent him to school, to learn how to recite
His prayers; also, perhaps, to read and write,
And he could cipher just a little too;
But scholars in that country then could do
Not much beside. His teacher was a priest,
And worldly knowledge was deemed of the least
Importance, when compared with that which would
Result in the immensely greater good
Of being saved, when his career below
Was ended, and his soul at last should go
Up to its Maker, for its final sentence,
And proof demanded was of his repentance.
The schools, therefore, that in old Spain were kept,

And those now seen, while Manuelo slept,
So widely different were in all their aims
That they might well be called by different names.
Quite properly, he thought, some were termed schools,
While others were but nurseries for fools ;
But which the latter were he did not say,
And left us to determine as best we may.
But in the schools to which he, dreaming, went,
And not the one to which his parents sent
Him, a small lad, to learn to be a good
Young man, and to behave just as he should—
In these latter schools, seen in the vision,
And which he then observed with some precision,
The teachers were distinguished for their knowledge,
And had been graduated from some college;
That is, a college where the sciences and arts
Were taught. And some were from most distant parts
Of the world, and were men of the broadest learning,
And full instructions could impart concerning
The mysteries of nature, and those curious rules
Which govern the creation. These latter schools
Paid less attention to the future state,
But careful were about what might relate
To human conduct, and the life on earth;
Nor was much said about the second birth.
The mind, it was, received the most attention;
The soul was seldom thought worthy of mention.
All this to Manuelo seemed quite odd,
Since he instructed was to worship God;
And other learning was of little worth
Where he was taught, and where he had his birth.
But there were female teachers here as well;
And looking, as he dreamed, he could not tell
Which, for the work, might be the better fitted,
And on this point his judgment he omitted.
The females, he observed, received much praise
From all the pupils, for their winning ways,
And to impart instruction; these he deemed
Equal to the men; or so they seemed.
The scholars by their bright and sprightly looks

Showed that they were attentive to their books.
Not only could they read, and write, and spell,
But in the grammar and geography as well,
And in the higher branches, as the algebra,
And in philosophy, were taught each day.
The greatest aim in their instruction was
To make them understand and heed the laws
Of good society, and which relate
To the requirements of a prosperous state.

Few books were printed in Justino's time,
And none, I think, in that far-distant clime
Of Mexico. It is not strange, therefore,
That Manuelo's story was not more
Clearly understood, when he described the power-
Press, and assured Justino that in an hour
More than thirty thousand sheets of paper could
Be printed—much larger each of them than would
Be used to make a book. These paper sheets,
He said, were hawked about the city's streets,
And mornings early left at every door.
He thought there might a million be, or more,
Of these each day, which all the people read,
To find what might about themselves be said,
And learn the news concerning all mankind,
Which in these papers they were sure to find.
But how the news could be obtained each day
From places many thousand miles away,
Could not be comprehended by the friar,
And Manuel, he thought, must be a liar,
But did not tell him so, though both did laugh,
For neither thought about the telegraph.

In Manuelo's time book writers were
In numbers very few, and they were poor.
As want imparts to appetite a zest,
So, hungry authors, as a rule, are best.
The rich man, when he undertakes to write,
Lacks the great stimulus of an appetite.
The overpampered brain is never keen,
As in the rich man's writings may be seen.

An author never should be too well fed,
Since a full stomach makes an empty head.
The belly and the brain so sympathize
That when the first is full the last is otherwise.
The city Manuel saw while yet he dreamed
With writers and with authors fairly teemed;
They were of every sort and every grade,
And of as many kinds as could be made
Out of the poor materials then on hand
In that most fanciful and curious land.
Of those who wrote in measure there were many,
But real poets there were hardly any;
For wide the difference was, as he could see,
Betwixt mere rhyming and good poetry.
Poetic thoughts sometimes appear in prose,
And prose in rhymes, as everybody knows.
He found not even one in that vast throng
Who could compose a tolerable song,
And hence, he thought, 'mongst all the writers there
That real poets were extremely rare;
And he, in this, showed his superior wit
By holding that, *poeta nascitur, non fit.*
To be a poet he made no profession,
And the translator has the same discretion;
But history he thought was his strong suit,
And that distinction none can well dispute.

The writer would the reader not deceive,
Nor would he for the world have him believe
That he's in any way entitled to
The credit for what other men may do.
If in this story there is any merit
Or genius, such as author might inherit,
It all belongs to wise Manuelo,
Who really was a very clever fellow;
And if defects in composition are
. Observable, it is but just to say they were
Committed by the friar, and all respon-
sibility should be located on
His broad shoulders; for I now confess
That I had nought to do with the MS.

But it is proper that I here should mention
That when the manuscript first claimed attention,
Some thirty-five or forty years ago,
At the old convent in Alemtajo,
It was, as penned by Father Justino,
Writ in blank verse, just as, in ancient days,
Some authors would prepare for stage their plays ;
Or, as blind Homer did his story tell
About the valiant Greeks, and how Troy fell,
After a long siege, which in heroic deeds
All other written stories far exceeds,
Unless we should except this of the friar,
Who, like old Homer, thrummed the magic lyre.
But the poor foolish priests, who found the scroll
So snugly hidden in a pigeon-hole,
Were so obtuse and purblind at the time
That poetry for them must be in rhyme.
And so in prose they rendered most of it,
And in plain prose I have to now transmit
The greater part of this historic tale.
But the good reader will, I trust, not fail
To notice I have given all I could
In verse, and more, it may be, than I should ;
And more, perhaps, considering the kind,
Than persons of good taste will feel inclined
To justify in such a story as this one,
Which as a simple history was begun.
But then Justino lacked poetic fire,
And nothing in the story could inspire
A man like him, who from his childhood lacked
A taste for everything but naked fact,
While poetry is made up of invention,
And must be difficult of comprehension ;
It should be noted for obscurity ;
The more obscure the greater is its purity.
The fault with Virgil, and the men of old,
Is that their stories are too plainly told.
If they had been a little more abstruse,
There would have been a little more excuse
For handing down their works to modern times,

When they did not so much as write in rhymes,
And when their writings were so plain, indeed,
That anyone, in running, might them read.

LXIV.
THE RETURN.

AROUSED from his reverie late in the afternoon, Manuelo partook of such repast as had been provided, and at the dawn of the following day he and his companions set out on their return to the village of the Yonos, all refreshed and much pleased with what had been experienced. Manuelo himself lingered behind to take one last, long look, in the light of the rising sun, over the mighty expanse of delightful scenery with which he had been so completely entranced, and a sense of sadness crept over him, as he reflected that he was beholding for the last time from that inspiring elevation a land and sea which he verily believed were destined in future ages to become the busy scenes of a civilization entirely distinct from that of the people whose villages then dotted its shores, and whose canoes only occasionally disturbed its placid waters. Strongly impressed with the truthfulness of his vision, he at last tore himself away from the enchanted place, and with measured tread followed the priest's son and his companions on their winding way down from the summit of lofty Tamalpais. Returning, the hunters followed a new and devious path, much longer than the one they had pursued in coming, and the shades of night were fast falling, when, with weary steps, the little band filed into the Yono village, the manly form of Manuelo being the most conspicuous figure in the procession.

Their coming was greeted with various demonstrations of gladness, especially by the female portion of the population, some of whom, it may well be supposed, were most anxiously awaiting their return, and all joined in enlivening the event by the heartiest applause.

The expedition had not been eminently successful for the game that was taken, but far more had been accomplished than was anticipated by anyone, and far more than was understood, at that time, by the natives. Ascending the mountain was not among the things contemplated when they set out, and nothing was further from the mind of the hunters than the magnificent view which broke upon them from that towering height. The dream of Manuelo was something that pertained to himself alone; nor did he, when there, disclose what he saw to his companions; but on his way down he ceased not, nor afterwards, to revolve in his own mind the wonderful events that had passed in review before him, until they became so thoroughly impressed upon his memory that he was able to relate them, years afterwards, to Father Justino, with all the particularity with which they have been given.

Not many days were the conspirators compelled to abide in the village before a favorable wind arose, and they were encouraged to undertake their contemplated expedition upon the Bay. Accordingly the two set out in their boat alone, with a fair prospect of being driven in the direction they wished. So carefully was everything conducted that their purpose was not suspected even by the shrewdest of the Yonos, all of whom were accustomed to take a deep interest in every movement of Manuelo. It was with no little pain, as he subsequently acknowledged, that he embarked for a lasting absence, without being permitted, as he felt strongly inclined, to bid his cherished friends an affectionate *adios*. But his own prudence, united with the cooler judgment of the priest's son, forbade any demonstrations which might betray their purpose, and possibly defeat the end they had in mind. Until far away on the water he smothered, as best he was able, the reproaches of conscience, awakened, doubtless, at beholding the slender form of the confiding and hopeful Noña lingering upon the shore, and with sweetest smiles waving the fishermen good luck. Towards his companion's imprudent wife, who was also there, his feelings were different. Though Manuelo's sentiments towards her were those of extreme kindness, he had been so perplexed by her attentions that he left her now with less regret. The priest's son himself was the happiest person on that occasion, though he lacked not the discretion to conceal the cause of his merriment.

The boat and its occupants were soon out of sight on the broad expanse of the Bay, and, as had been anticipated, they were borne by the winds in the direction of the Santos settlement.

Landing near the city, late that evening, the long-absent Manuelo was greeted by all the people with every demonstration of joy, and by none of the men with more cordiality than by the old chief, and still more venerable high priest, both of whom had returned from the warlike expedition against the Modens alive, to be sure, but covered as it were with wounds. Their escape had been almost miraculous, for both were in the forefront of the fight at the time of the flank movement of the enemy, and both were compelled to cut their way out through the opposing lines, only finding safety in the darkness of the night, which, happily for them, was just then shutting down its curtain upon the earth. It was thought but for this circumstance, and the diversion fortunately caused by the sudden appearance of Manuelo upon the scene, utter annihilation must have been the fate of the Santos forces; and both these dignitaries were therefore ready to confess their indebtedness in some sense to the sturdy Manuelo for their return once more to their own kingdom. But as it was, many of their people were slain and left upon the bloody field; probably not more, however, on the one side than on the other; so that the treacherous Modens were compelled to render up a full equivalent for their victory. Among others who escaped from that terrible encounter was the stalwart young prince, Gosee, who had aforetime so disastrously worsted Manuelo in the wrestling match, and who, it will be remembered, was his rival for the hand of the princess Alola. This young man welcomed the return of Manuelo with some apparent good-will at first, but that was soon dispelled by his beholding the warmth with which the white man was greeted by the fair Alola herself.

Manuelo's coming was wholly unexpected, and the delight of the young woman on seeing him again could not be restrained; nor did she endeavor in the least to repress an exhibition of her feelings. Alternately she laughed and wept for joy, and, in the presence of them all, again and again kissed and embraced him. The engagement that had been made by the authorities between her and Gosee had in Manuelo's absence so far ripened by time that the marriage was to be consummated at the very next Feast of Flowers; but even this did not restrain her emotions. Her love had survived the lapse of time, and now, touched by the sudden appearance of her lover, whom she had been led to believe was dead, it blazed forth again without restraint. The perplexing situation into which affairs had drifted in his absence was soon made known to Manuelo from the lips of the maiden herself, and, as you may well know, caused a sorrow in his heart no less poignant than that which wrung her own; for during all his long absence, he had never ceased to think of her, nor to hope, with all the ardor of a true lover, that he might see her again. She alone of all the native women had captivated his affections, and he found it quite impossible to divest himself of the tender attachment, though he could plainly see that it was his duty to endeavor to do so. He might possibly have succeeded in repressing in some measure the warmth of his own passion had it not been for the almost insane infatuation of the poor creature for him. Her feelings were past all control. As may well be imagined by some of the readers, though not perhaps by others, the two were now terribly embarrassed by the situation, and utterly miserable.

Curiously enough we are left by Justino quite in the dark as to the length of time that had elapsed between the departure of Manuelo for the war, and his return, and it is mere conjecture on the part of those who discovered the manuscript when they set the period down at less than two years. A longer time it could hardly have been, since it would seem impossible for the flame of love to burn so brightly in the breasts of persons widely separated, for a longer period.

Though Manuelo could but admire many of the laws and customs of this strange people, he now became fearfully disgusted with those which related to matrimony. Different though these were from the practices of civilized people, and contrary to what had been familiar to him in his native country, nevertheless he might have been reconciled to them but for his own experience. We refer, of course, not more to his unwilling engagement with the Yonoese maiden than to his anticipated pleasure with the beautiful Alola, which was so liable to be interrupted by those laws. These two considerations led him to look upon them with the highest disfavor, and his deprecation of them to Father Justino was unmeasured.

Manuelo's re-appearance at the capital after so long an absence was to the people in general, as well as to his sweet Alola in particular, as joyous as it was unexpected. All had for some time been resting under the conviction that he had taken his everlasting departure to the land of shades; nevertheless, it was counted as ground for doubt on the part of a few, that the seers had been utterly unable to obtain any communication from him from that quarter. He was thought by most of the people to have perished in the battle, and none really expected ever to see him again. Alola had mourned him long and sorrowfully, and only after positive assurance from Gosee, and one or two others, equally mendacious, that his dead body had been seen stretched upon the plain, would she give up all hope of his returning.

The usual interruptions growing out of the excessive joy of the greeting being over, Manuelo, accompanied by a large retinue, was conducted to the dwelling of the great chief, where, being seated on a grizzly bear skin in the center of the principal apartment, he was required to give a detailed account of his movements during all his long and painful captivity. He began by relating to the eager crowd there assembled, with lips apart, how, in pursuit of the enemy, he had been led away from his friends, and after a desperate hand-to-hand encounter, in which were slain he knew not how many, he was overpowered by numbers, and made a prisoner of war. With all candor he told them how he had attempted to conciliate the angry Modens by pretending not too much friendship for the Santos, whom he assured his captors were neither of his own race nor in sympathy with him, and for whom he said he entertained no affection, in this instance forgetting Alola entirely. He next related how he was detected by his dress as the leader of the former naval engagement on the interior waters of the country, and he had no doubt his subsequent enslavement and the many indignities heaped upon him were attributable more to this one circumstance than to any other. In giving a particular account of the cruel treatment received by him at the hands of his heartless masters, it was observed that tears would often spring to the eyes of the sympathetic Alola, who listened to his story with more undivided attention, if possible, than anyone else. He then told how he had instructed the common people of the Modens touching their natural rights, and, in due time, incited an insurrection against their government; how an opportunity was providentially offered for getting them under arms and rallying them to his support; but that they failed him entirely when, like so many slaves, as they were, they came to facing their masters; how, accompanied by a handful of men, he had fled to the distant mountains off to the west, and finally, after much privation, reached the ocean.

His hearers were greatly amused with his account of the discontent of his followers, and his description of the manner in which they had been miraculously supplied with food, and how they subsisted upon shell-fish during all of their wanderings by the sea. They noted with interest what he said about coming to an arm of the ocean and being compelled to turn inland, and about his camping near some warm sulphur springs; but he prudently omitted relating to them, at that time, his dream at the springs, and he also forebore to speak, when he came to that point of his vision on Tamalpais, judging rightly that his hearers would fail to comprehend the events that were foreshadowed in them. When he came to tell how he had lost his ten Moden companions, and that he could not, by seeking and shouting, find hide nor hair of them, he could but observe that his listeners appeared to be especially delighted, and they more than expressed their gratification at the probable destruction of so many of that hated race. But when he related how, unexpectedly, he had come upon a Yonoese maiden whom he knew, and to whom he gave chase, but who did not know him, but fled with fear, a shout of laughter went up from all the assembly, with the exception of Alola alone, who did not seem to appreciate the joke.

The story ended, the night far advanced, and the fire in the great wigwam burning low, each hesitatingly retired to his home and to slumber. But there were two in that city who slept not soundly that night. Alola and her lover were overmuch concerned for their future welfare to rest in peace. The Festival of Flowers was fast approaching, and faster still, it seemed to them, the time for the marriage between her and Gosee, and unless something could be done to forestall that event, her happiness and that of Manuelo would be forever wrecked. Wakefully he thought of the matter the night through, and as he afterwards learned, Alola had been equally concerned, so that sleep visited not her drooping eyelids till the weary sun came peeping over the high eastern hills.

As for Manuelo, he asseverated that his embarrassment was not greater at any time during all his fearful round of captivity, than now, when his trials would seem, to an unsentimental observer, to have come to an end. As often happens to mankind, his anticipated quiet was turned into a sea of troubles. The goal of one's ambition, says Justino, in spite of the best calculations that can be made by mortal man, is frequently the threshold of events which, were they open to view, would never be approached. Man is seldom permitted to know in what direction his real pleasures lie; nevertheless, it is wisely provided by the Author of his being, that he should be deluded with the vainglorious belief that happiness is the reward of his own exertions. Were it not so, man might fall into habits of listlessness, and who can say to what depressions of the race foreknowledge might not lead? Whether this provision of nature be wise or otherwise, Manuelo was not disposed to criticise it, but, on the contrary, he strove to accept the situation with all the equanimity he could command. His great desire had been to reach the capital, confidently hoping the while for the best, and little anticipating that when there he would encounter troubles which must have crushed the spirits of anyone of less courage. The prospect of disappointed love was supplemented by dangers to the object of his adoration, which took hold of his sensitive nature with powerful effect, and caused him more real suffering than he had ever before experienced. The suddenness with which this burden was placed upon his shoulders rendered it the more oppressive, and it was not at all alleviated by the fact of its being shared by another. Love by one alone can be endured. In that form it is not a dangerous malady. The single-lighted fagot by itself alone will soon expire; but fagots in contact burn brightly, and are not so easily extinguished. So with the flame of love; when kindled between two such ardent, sympathizing souls as Manuelo and Alola, it burned with a consuming power. In truth

Manuelo was not aware until now how much he adored his sweetheart, and the danger of losing her by seeing her become the wife of the envious Gosee, would rush upon his mind at unguarded moments, and almost drive him to distraction. For the first few days after his return there seemed to be no circumstance to alleviate his distress, but on the contrary everything appeared to conspire to augment the trouble. The hated *Fiesta* of Flowers, which was to bring the hour of his calamity, was approaching apace, and preparations for the festivities, though not very near, were already in progress.

In the meantime also the devotion of Alola for her long-lost lover was increasing day by day. It had existed in large measure from the time of their first acquaintance, or, at all events, from the time of his becoming a leader of fashions in the city, and nothing had ever occurred to dampen its ardor in the slightest, until a positive assurance had come of his death, which false report had been forced upon her belief; and now, when he was restored to life as it were, the power of her passion became uncontrollable. It was greater under these circumstances than if it had been kept steadily ablaze from the start. By their forced separation there had been an accumulation of the materials upon which it could feed, and now all efforts to suppress it only tended to stir up the brands and cause them to burn the more brightly.

Ebullitions of feelings on the part of Alola were noticed with some concern by her father, the king, and at the same time by her venerable prospective father-in-law, the high priest. The women of the city, likewise, and particularly those about the chief's quarters, where Manuelo was again abiding, readily observed the renewed attachment. But the person of all others whose eyes were widest open to the conduct of the young woman was the stalwart Gosee, her intended husband. His jealousy was again aroused, and it was but natural that his partially suppressed hatred towards his more favored rival should occasionally manifest itself. He could not fail to notice that Alola sought the companionship of Manuelo more than was prudent for a person under an engagement of marriage to another. To allay suspicion as far as it might, the time was prudently employed on such occasions by Manuelo in relating to the girl, as he did over and over again, the story of his adventures with the Modens. She never grew tired of listening to the narration of his perils and hardships, and some of the more harrowing passages excited in her the warmest sympathy. To her alone, in the narration, he added an account of his dream at the Hot Sulphur Springs, and also ventured to give her in detail his vision on Tamalpais; both of which were related in a manner to excite in her the liveliest interest. The mystery of these communications to the listener was profound; but to Manuelo, whose experience in early life had been such as to give direction to lines of thought which might develop into such prophetic views, they were less mysterious. More particularly interested was Alola in what pertained to her own sex, and she was led to indulge in many inquiries concerning the apparel and appearance of so strange a people as were described in the dreams.

LXV.

A FLIGHT CONSIDERED.

MANUELO was fully admonished of the embarrassment that must certainly result from permitting matters to drift along in their present channel, until the opening of the approaching spring, when the long-existing engagement between those two prominent members of the Santos nation must, in due course, be consummated. This harrowing reflection seemed to produce less impression upon the mind of the girl, who was to be a party to the marriage, than upon Manuelo's. Like the rest of her race she was more given to fatalism than he, and consequently less heed was paid by her to the impending calamity.

It must not be inferred, however, that she was wholly oblivious of the distressing facts of the case; by no means. Even her present satisfaction in the society of Manuelo, though intense, was not of such a character as to obliterate from her mind all sense of the threatened danger. She was only a little less sensible of it than her ardent Spanish lover, that is all.

As for Manuelo, his soul was so thoroughly penetrated with the situation that he ceased not to contemplate the subject, and to devise plans for escape, first one and then another, out of the difficulty. Sometimes, and in spite of himself, his mind would recur to the suggestion of an elopement (made, as he remembered, before his expedition against the Modens) as a resort in case of emergency. After much serious reflection, this subject was broached anew, not this time by the maiden, but by Manuelo himself, and it was discussed between the lovers alone whenever an opportunity offered. But whither should they flee? that was the question. It was a most difficult point to decide, and the settlement of it gave them an infinite amount of trouble. There was one point of the compass, however, about which there was no hesitancy in arriving at a conclusion. That direction presented no attractions to Manuelo, at least; it was the direction of the Modens. He was quite content with his past experience in that quarter.

As a matter of actual fact, the lovers were not so very greatly restricted in point of time, in this case, since several changes of the moon must intervene before the *Florales* would arrive; nevertheless, time was flitting, and each day was one less for the business before them. Every departing sun but added its modicum to the already distressing suspense of the parties. If it added also to the hopes of the expectant bridegroom, the impatient Gosee, it is but natural, and without doubt he was as much annoyed by the tardiness of time as the real lovers were with its remarkable speed.

Manuelo in the meantime was duly active in obtaining information concerning the countries and peoples in other directions than the north, and was immensely gratified to learn that the native inhabitants to the southward were, and long had been, on friendly terms with the Santos. This doubtless was the more pleasing to him because of his disagreeable experience with the people at the opposite point of the compass.

It was really for the purpose of reconnoissance and observation, though ostensibly for game, that hunting excursions to the southward were set on foot. Some of these, at the instigation of Manuelo, were pushed quite beyond any limit theretofore attained by the warriors or hunters of the Santos nation. One in particular extended a great many leagues, and occupied many days in the performance. On this occasion they penetrated the territory of an unknown tribe, who lived beyond several ranges of mountains; but the adventurous hunters, with due caution, forebore to make known their presence to the people residing there, since all were in doubt as to the temper that might be displayed toward encroaching game seekers, and Manuelo, above all, was unwilling to run any risk of detention among them. The real object of this adventure was unsuspected by his companions, but the result was highly gratifying to Manuelo himself, and settled his purpose as to the course he should pursue in case of flight with his beloved Alola.

The disposition to inquietude which characterizes all persons brought up to the sea, had never been eradicated from the nature of our hero, and with him, therefore, there was less hesitancy about undertaking a movement like the one contemplated than otherwise would have been, and less than naturally belonged to Alola, who had seen but little of the world, and who could form but an inadequate conception of its vast extent. Her knowledge of geography was limited by the hills, the mountains, the Bay, and that little part of the ocean near her native home; and this seemed large enough for all purposes until the necessity for an elopement arose, when the world, as known to her, became at once exceedingly small. The fact being confessed, Manuelo was everything to her. Any place with him was large enough, and all the earth too small without him.

Casting this love affair aside, and Manuelo had may reasons to be content where he was. His associations with the Santos had been, as a general thing, of the most satisfactory character. The people had fairly overwhelmed him with kindness ever since his first appearance amongst them; and but for his relations towards Alola he would have remained there no one knows how long. But Alola was his guiding star. For her he was but too willing to make any sacrifice and incur any danger. Life itself was not too great a boon to lay at her feet. An elopement he knew was fraught with perils, and if undertaken would have to be conducted with the utmost caution, since a failure would be likely to prove fatal to both.

The Santos, though brave and generous, were at the same time, like all other uncivilized people, revengeful, and would be quite sure to visit any attempt at treachery with the severest penalties. He had no doubt that his own life, and he greatly feared the life of his fair companion, would depend upon the success of the enterprise. This opinion he was at great pains to impress upon the mind of the confiding Alola; but instead of softening her purpose, it only tended to strengthen her determination. She was no less resolute than himself in the determination to seek, by flight, that happiness which was denied her by the laws of her forefathers; and they deliberately resolved by themselves together to offer up their lives, if need be, upon the altar of love.

The usual perplexity to know just how the thing was to be successfully accomplished, weighed so heavily upon their minds that it was with difficulty they could conceal their purpose from others. Preparation for the journey could only be made in the most secret manner, and the initiation of the movement did not seem possible, without imminent danger of detection. But Manuelo's discretion forsook him not, and he calmly concluded that the first step, so to speak, should be accomplished by water. His familiarity with that element probably induced this idea, for it was very distinct from the plan proposed by Alola, who was willing to take the chances in a race, in case of pursuit, with so much of advantage in the start as could be gained in one night and the part of a day, as she hoped. Pursued they both knew they certainly would be in that case, and as they could take with them only a small stock of provisions, and of personal comforts but a limited supply, they must of necessity make themselves known on the route, after the first few days, to such people as might be living by the way. Hence it would not be difficult for the swift-footed Santos to ascertain their general course, and at last to overtake them. This was all pondered well by the cautious Manuelo, and his plan as finally concluded upon was to set out, some fine morning, a few days in advance of the feast, they two in a canoe alone, on a fishing excursion on the Bay, and after proceeding by such conveyance as far as was practicable, to abandon the canoe and pursue their journey by land. There was a well-grounded apprehension in his mind that suspicion would be aroused by the circumstance of their going together, and unaccompanied by anyone else, and here was the first obstacle to be surmounted. To allay apprehension growing out of this circumstance, a fishing expedition of the kind mentioned was made the subject of conversation not only between themselves but with other members of the tribe on divers occasions, and some time in advance of the contemplated departure, though, of course, no particular day was mentioned by either for the undertaking. This ruse was adopted in order that no considerable excitement should be aroused among their friends when their absence might be ascertained. And then they must needs make their calculations to go quietly away lest meddlesome persons should be inclined to accompany them, likewise, in canoes; and hence their purpose was to start early in the morning, before the people generally were aroused. Thus they hoped to avoid the liability of being followed by other fishing parties, and yet they would not start so early as to give the appearance of a sinister motive. It was Manuelo's design to leave the canoe, when they had done with it, afloat on the Bay, and he was hopeful that a favorable wind would drive it back in the direction of the city, to produce an impression on the minds of the people, when they should discover the empty craft, that its late occupants had found a watery grave.

The time of their departure was, for that reason, to be governed somewhat by the course of the winds and the tides. Another plan much considered was to so gauge the time of the flight that the canoe would float out to sea, when they had left it, and never be heard of more, in which case the people might conclude that its unhappy occupants had gone with it upon the boundless ocean and were lost. But this idea was not regarded so favorably as the first, since the people of the city, many of whom were shrewd men and women, would hardly believe that Manuelo could be so thoughtless as to be caught a second time on the fast-ebbing tides that rushed periodically from the mouth of the harbor. Those tides they knew were well understood by him, and consequently this second plan was dismissed from their minds.

Manuelo had now more than ever occasion to deplore the loss of his trusty sword and pistols, of which he had been deprived by the savage Modens. Armed with these he would have felt greater security in this perilous undertaking, but he was compelled to content himself with a spear, and with a bow and a few arrows, in the use of which, however, he had become, by constant practice, almost as expert as the natives.

After the plan was fully concluded upon between the anxious lovers, but some time before it was to be carried into effect, Manuelo pretended to have received, in his character as prophet, a communication from the land of spirits, which he hoped might, in an emergency, be of some avail to him in the flight; but he made no application of it either to himself or Alola. It ran as follows:—

> A man and a maiden a-fishing will go,
> But into what waters no person shall know.
> Many fish they will catch and many will fetch,
> If, in fishing for fish, no fish shall them catch.

Little was thought of this at the time, but both he and Alola were at some pains, by repeating it often, to impress it upon the minds of the people, in order that it might be remembered when they should fail to return from their contemplated fishing excursion. They would have it understood, when gone, that they had been attacked and devoured by some sea monster, and by such strategy avoid the danger of being pursued by their friends.

All preparations that were possible to make, surrounded as they were by a thousand sharp eyes, having been completed, the lovers only awaited the arrival of a favorable day for setting out on their long journey, a journey which by them was truly regarded, as all such journeys should be, as the journey of life, but which they fully comprehended might be, in case of mishap, a journey to their doom.

Heralds had already gone forth from the capital, in every direction, to notify the many villages of the nation of the time appointed for the Festival of Flowers, and to inform all that the principal occurrence to be celebrated on that joyous occasion was the marriage of the chief's beautiful daughter to the gallant son of the old ex-king and high priest. This expected event was likely to bring a far larger concourse of men and women together than usual. It had long been looked forward to by all the people of the city, and particularly by those about the larger central dwellings, with the greatest anxiety, and the fair Alola was congratulated every day, and every hour of the day, on the approaching happy event, as it was regarded.

Robes of the finest of white rabbit skins, and the skins of other small animals, were prepared most tastefully for the bride; and head ornaments of brilliant feathers and shining shells were constructed both for her and the expectant bridegroom, by the industrious women of the place. The most beautiful gifts of various sorts were fabricated in abundance in the city for wedding presents, and the people of all the country ruled over by her father were expected to bring in other gifts, equally attractive, to contribute to the wealth and happiness of the distinguished couple.

Little did anyone, except the astute Manuelo, imagine that these preparations, so far from adding to the enjoyment of the princess, only made her the more miserable, and it required the greatest exertion, as Manuelo could plainly perceive, on the part of the poor damsel to conceal her embarrassment, which became greater and greater as time rolled by and brought her nearer and nearer to her apparent fate. Unsophisticated as she was, with difficulty could she hide from general observation the anxiety that preyed upon her mind; but it was attributed by her female companions to an entirely different cause from the true one. By them her silent demeanor and many blushes were readily interpreted as indicating that maidenly sensibility which one must feel on the eve of exchanging her girlish estate for the responsible duties of womanhood; and, fortunately for her and Manuelo, the real cause of her disquietude was never so much as suspected by those about her.

LXVI.

THE ELOPEMENT.

UNFRIENDLY weather and adverse winds delayed the excursion until delay was no longer to be tolerated, and the lovers finally fixed upon a time, only three days in advance of the commencement of the festivities, as the period for setting out on their uncertain journey, be the weather what it might. Most fortunately for them, on the day appointed the winds were propitious, and the two friends met as it were by chance, in the usual way, early in the morning on the sandy beach, and without delay, but with some trepidation, embarked in their lonely canoe. The lazy morning sun arising from his slumbers discovered them several leagues away from the shore upon the watery expanse; but, so far as they could judge, no human being witnessed their departure, or knew of their going.

They were both skillful in the management of their tiny craft, and, not late in the afternoon, they effected a safe landing at precisely the point designated by Manuelo in advance, on the southwesterly side of the Bay, near the base of a mountain since then called San Bruno. The canoe was at once stripped of all its contents, and made to appear as if it had been emptied by capsizing. This accomplished it was set adrift, with a wind so blowing as to be likely to drive it back nearly in the direction it had come.

After congratulating each other upon the success of their movement thus far, the two, as a first duty, dispensed with everything that they deemed might impede their flight, carefully concealing from the view of possible pursuers all that was to be left behind. Taking with them only such robes and provisions as they could well carry, they assumed their line of march to the southward.

They were now traveling they knew not exactly whither, nor

did either much care, only so it might be to some quiet place in the wide world, where they could enjoy each other's society for all time without interruption. There was to be constant danger of encountering beasts of prey, but these were dreaded far less, at the outset, than creatures of their own kind; and their chief care during the balance of the first day was to observe any traces of humanity that might exist, and to avoid running upon some stray settlement of the natives.

They were less apprehensive of encountering hunting parties at this season of the year, knowing that the villagers thereabouts, if any there were, must be engaged in the preparations for the great feast at the capital, to which they would have to be starting in a day or two, at furthest, if they would be in time.

As a matter of caution the lovers kept away from the shore, and skirted the base of the mountains, making the best progress they could under that disadvantage; but it was a much more difficult route than one along the open plain would have been.

The pair were already as happy in each other's company as it was possible for fugitives to be, and each was heard to indulge in frequent expressions of solicitude for the other's safety.

Resting but little during the afternoon of that long, weary day, and only then to observe well their course, they passed a number of villages in the distance, the locations of some of which were already known to Manuelo, having been spied out by him in advance.

Just as sable night was letting fall her curtain upon the dark green earth, and all nature seemed in search of needed rest, the wanderers found themselves by the side of some bubbling mineral springs, located opposite to the head of the great Bay, in sight of which they had been traveling since noon, and here they concluded to rest for the night. It need not be told that they slept soundly, for Alola, unaccustomed to that sort of thing, was nearly exhausted by the long tramp of that day, and

Manuelo himself, but for the concern felt for his fair companion, would have been unable to proceed further without repose.

How far they had actually come may possibly be ascertained by geographers of later times, from the data here given, but the distance there was then no means of determining except from the extreme lassitude of the weaker partner in the flight, judging from which Manuelo thought it might be twenty leagues, and even more. But sleep restored the wonted vigor of both, and when, as Justino expressed it, the circling hours with rosy hands unbarred the gates of night, and Phœbus, with her shining face, came forth in chariot bright, they were awakened by the sweet music of the birds, which, in the overhanging foliage of the great tree under which they slept, were celebrating their own nuptials with songs.

The lovers, refreshed with their long repose, arose and prepared for a renewal of their journey. Their hour of starting was not so early as on the previous morning, nor was it beset with such intense anxiety as that had been. They were now under no necessity for slipping away surreptitiously to avoid the peeping eyes of men and women, as they had been but yesterday. The only observers of their present position were the merry feathered songsters, the innocent rabbit, and the soft-eyed antelope, and to these the gentle lovers paid little heed, as none of them were capable of exciting either fear or jealousy, and their presence was by no means unwelcome.

The conspicuous landmarks of the country thus far, such as bay, mountains, and hills, were tolerably well known to the fugitives, and particularly to Manuelo, who had taken special pains to inform himself about them, with a view to the use such knowledge might be to him on an occasion like the present. These being observed as they proceeded, the second day at its close found the happy couple in the unalloyed enjoyment of each other's society a little over the summit of a considerable range of mountains to the westward, and in plain view of the ocean, a sight that was always cheering to Manuelo.

But an incident occurred on this day's journey which must not be omitted, as it came as near as possible not to succeed in balking all their calculations. Ascending the mountain just mentioned, by a well-marked trail, they came almost upon, and would have met face to face, a large procession of people on their journey to the feast. There were men and women, young men and maidens, a hundred or more, wending their way towards the city by the Bay. The keen ear of Alola detected the merry laughter of the advance guard of young people just in time to enable herself and companion to secrete themselves in the convenient undergowth of the forest. The troop of pleasure-seekers passed on their course and were soon out of sight and hearing. As they filed by she could plainly hear them conversing merrily, but earnestly, about herself and Gosee, and for the first time she realized the great disappointment her absence must cause to the people on that festive occasion. Without regretting the step she had taken, she could but feel sorry, nevertheless, that there was no other way of securing happiness to herself and Manuelo, but by destroying so much of it in others.

The danger passed, the lovers came forth from their hiding-place and renewed their journey. This incident was a warning to observe greater caution in the future, for Alola was too well-known throughout the land to be disguised, and the appearance of Manuelo, as a man of a distinct race, was too conspicuous to be overlooked by anyone, in case they should unhappily be discovered. Their only safety lay in escaping detection by any human being until they could pass entirely beyond the kingdom of the Santos, and that, they judged, must require a diligent journey of many days; but how many neither could guess. They were convinced that numerous villages skirted the ocean, and danger in consequence must be lurking there; nevertheless, as they looked off upon its placid surface, they could not resist an inclination to approach it, and such accordingly was their determination for the following day.

Selecting a quiet, grassy nook on the steep mountain-slope, thickly bespangled with sweet-scented flowers, they encamped for the second night. A new world was now opening to the astonished vision of Alola. Hitherto she had formed no conception of the vastness of the creation of which she formed a part. The horizon here was many times farther away than she had ever observed it before, and the declining sun lighted up with the most brilliant colors the whole western sky. The sea shone with a luster only surpassed by that of the great orb of day, and reflected upon the intervening space between where she stood and the ocean, those peculiar tints only visible at the season of the year when nature first puts on her robes of green to greet the approach of summer. Though weary with the day's tramp, she could hardly persuade herself that she was not already in that Heaven of which she had heard so much from the lips of her Manuelo. On a bed of roses, so to speak, but without the thorns, here they slept and dreamed only of happiness for the future.

Their starting the next day was not early, for the fugitives chose to abide in this enchanted place to welcome the rising sun, which was slow to make his appearance above the mountain-crest. In the meantime Alola joined her gentle voice with the carols of the equally happy birds, and the whole place re-echoed with their music, while Manuelo made ready for the journey. Descending from the mountain was an easy task, and their resting-place on the evening of the third day was on the strand, where they were hushed to sleep by the waves breaking upon the shore.

The fourth day was mainly spent in reconnoissances by Manuelo, and in carefully circumventing several villages, which were discovered all in good time to be avoided, and less progress was made than on any day previously. Their course, in consequence of these dangerous obstacles, was exceedingly tortuous, and they were both distressed to think that so little real headway had been made since leaving camp in the morning. At the end of this day they were still by the sea and were comforted in their disappointment by its ceaseless music. To Manuelo the ocean was like an old friend. He was entranced by the ever-recurring motion of its billows, and he enjoyed, he said, the society of his beautiful companion by its side more, if possible, than when wandering in the solitude of the mountains. There was even danger of his being soothed by its grand old cadence into forgetfulness of the necessity of prosecuting their flight with the utmost vigor. The pensive quietude which is so apt to come over young persons when strolling on the smooth, sandy beach, seized hold of the romantic soul of Alola as well, and they lingered longer than was prudent. More progress they were conscious would have been made had they adhered to the base of the mountains instead of the shore, but they reasoned within themselves that jeopardy was in whichsoever way they went, and they therefore yielded the more readily to the fascinations of the breakers, preferring to take their chances where pleasures were most plentiful.

Speculations indulged in, however, upon what must then be transpiring at home, spurred them up to greater exertions, and their journey for the fifth day, as they could see from the position of certain mountain-peaks, was not altogether unsatisfactory. They rested for that night on the margin of a small river, a league it might have been back from the ocean, but still within sound of its breakers. During the course of this long day, they passed in sight of several villages, one of which they could see from an eminence was very large; and they narrowly escaped, more than once, coming in collision with parties of men, women, and children who were out on one expedition or another. They were actually seen from a distance by a company of half-grown boys and girls, but, hurrying along, made good their escape. So far as they could learn no alarm was created by this event, but their haste was increased thereby in order to get beyond the reach of possible pursuit.

The nations to the southward, for an indefinite distance, being on terms of peace with the Santos, it was the wish of the fugitives to go so far in that direction before indulging in any considerable halt, and before making themselves known, as to be entirely safe against invidious inquiries, and there to tarry for rest at least, and, perchance, for a permanent home. This was as far as their calculations extended; nor had they any more definite object in view. But the world was all before them where to choose a place of repose, and Providence their guide. They felt themselves excluded only from that little portion which had been left behind, but that at times appeared extremely large to the diminutive Alola.

The whole world, however, as Justino has informed us, was less to her than Manuelo. With him for a possession it mattered little whether what remained was small or great. Him she had now gained, and in her imagination there was not much beside worth living for. She preferred Manuelo with trials, trepidations, fears, and flight to the peace and abundance of a princess. She was better content to be a slave, if need be, with her lover, than a queen, as she was very likely to become, with Gosee, and her heart was light, however burdened her mind may have been with the cares and fears of the flight.

For greater security their time, while on the march, was spent mostly in silence, but when resting and at night the hours were beguiled by stories which Manuelo related of his own adventures, and stories that he had heard and read in his boyhood days.

The delightful tale of Abelard and Heloise was told with all
14

the embellishments, and the relation of it ran through more than one evening; but Alola was never tired of listening to stories from a lover whose attachment was even stronger than that of the unfortunate Abelard; for the love of Heloise, we are assured by Justino, was all surpassed by that of Alola for her instructor and companion in flight.

So little is said, and that so indefinitely, about the transactions of the sixth day, that it were as well, perhaps, to omit them entirely in the translation; and such was the intention until there was observed in the manuscript, written in the native tongue of Manuelo, the words, "El Monte," which, rendered in English, mean the grove, or the woods; and it was in a grove of pines and oaks, charmingly intermingled, that the lovers pitched their tent, figuratively speaking, but, in plain language, built their bower for the night of the sixth day. The place was but a short way, some three hundred varas as Justino expresses it, from a quiet nook of the ocean, and scarcely further to the eastward from a small rivulet that put into the sea at that point. Here Manuelo, before retiring for the night, at the earnest solicitation of the romantic Alola, finished up the story of Abelard and Heloise.

The first part of that strange, eventful history was so exactly similar, in many respects, to their own experience up to this time, so replete with love and devotion, which had their inception in the relations of teacher and pupil, but which were only promoted by absconding together, that when Manuelo came to relate the latter part of that saddest of stories, the poor Alola was stricken with fear, lest, peradventure, the parallelism might be continued in their own case, and the loves of herself and Manuelo encounter, at last, some insuperable obstacle. But Manuelo soothed the tender mind of the maiden by assuring her that though Abelard and Heloise were separated by cruel fate for years and years. nevertheless they came together afterwards, and were finally buried in the same grave.

In the morning everything about them appeared so ravishingly beautiful that the lovers agreed between themselves, then and there, that they could spend the balance of their days in contentment on that very spot were it not for the danger that some curious serpent would invade their terrestrial paradise. The deep-shaded atmosphere of the locality, at once resonant with the cheerful music of innumerable feathered songsters, and redolent with the most captivating odors of flowers, was entrancingly attractive to them. In very truth, all their senses were gratified to repletion in this most fascinating, this heavenly place, and they were charmed as never before. There being no words in the Spanish language to express their happiness, and none suitable found in the English, the subject, from sheer necessity, is turned over to the imagination of the gentle reader. But the moaning of the lazy morning zephyrs in the tall pines, mingled with the plaintive notes of a turtle-dove perched upon an oak nearly over their heads, reminded these children of nature that other matters than love should engage a part of their attention, and the two, tearing themselves away from the enchanted spot, hand in hand renewed their weary journey. Our first parents, thought Justino, left their Elysian home when commanded by the Almighty to sally forth into the troublesome world with scarcely more reluctance than did Manuelo and Alola leave this modern Eden on that interesting occasion.

On the seventh day they came to a point where the mountains abutted so abruptly upon the ocean that it was impossible for them to pursue their journey further along the beach, and they were compelled to retrace their steps for a while, and to strike inland before proceeding further southward. This necessity was particularly distressing from the fact that their stock of provisions was running low, and they had been able to eke out a supply from the different kinds of shell-fish found by the shore. They had no assurance whatever of finding any kind of food away from the sea, but Manuelo was skillful with the bow, and they hoped that in case of an emergency some sort of game might be taken. The seventh day, so far as progress on their journey was concerned, was as good as lost, and they were not yet beyond the borders of the Santos territory.

The experience of this day showed them very clearly that the country was not only to be traversed, but must also be explored for their future course, and their advance from that time onward might be slow. But every day, they estimated, would add a little to their security. It did not appear to them possible that anybody could trace their tortuous course thus far; and ere long, if they continued to make any progress whatever, they must be in a country where they would be unknown even if discovered.

Bending their journey inland the eighth day made up for the loss of the seventh, for at its close they were many leagues to the southward of their morning camping-place, and in a narrow valley shut in by high mountains on either hand. In fact, they had followed a well-defined trail pretty much the day through, and were under no little anxiety of mind to know whither it led. No village had been encountered since leaving the ocean, but the path they had been treading was one made, at least in part, by human beings, for they could see the evidences of that fact in broken bushes, and in fragments of baskets scattered by the way. The last persons passing along this trail had been going in the contrary direction, and as the number in that company was quite large, judging from the indications, Manuelo concluded they too must have been on their way to the great town on the Bay, to attend the spring festivities. He hardly had the courage to make known his suspicions to his fair companion, lest it might arouse some shadow of regrets in her sensitive bosom, at being the cause of disappointment to people traveling so far to attend the wedding of herself and Gosee. He feared this the more from the fact that their provisions were now almost exhausted, and they were compelled to lie down that night more or less oppressed with hunger, as well as by fatigue. To content her mind, a more than usually comfortable bower was prepared, and they would have slept well and soundly after the wearisome day's journey had not their camp been invaded before they were fairly locked in the arms of Morpheus, by two large bears. This threatening encroachment was with difficulty repelled by loud noises and many demonstrations on the part of the lovers, and only then by submitting to a robbery of all that remained of their scanty store of provisions. Nothing short of this would satisfy the greedy monsters; but the travelers were only too glad to be rid of their unwelcome visitors, even upon these harsh terms. Manuelo's experience with this species of animal, on a former occasion, had taught him the danger of an encounter with a single one, and he knew full well he would stand no chance of victory in a close contest with two, unarmed almost as he was. Moreover, the safety of the precious charge in his keeping, more than his own, admonished him to a course of prudence, which was by no means to excite the rage of the intruders. That the bears were hungry was evident, and his chief solicitude was that they should not satiate their appetites upon the tender limbs of his sweetheart. The night was passed without much sleep, and on the following morning hunger no less than fear impelled them to an early resumption of their tiresome journey.

Manuelo was as much surprised as pleased at the courage and confidence displayed by his young and frail *compañera*, nevertheless he failed not, as best he could, to incite in her a renewed determination to resist the hardships which were now coming thick and fast upon them. While extending to her now and then a helping hand, he would at the same time, by kindly words, hold out the hope that speedy relief from their perilous situation would come; but whence, had he been asked, he could not have told to save him. Owing to hunger and want of sleep they were constrained to move slowly, but Manuelo, if we may believe him, did not relax his vigilance and caution, which seemed the more necessary, since, later in the day, they came upon more than usual the signs of human beings. During the afternoon a rabbit and a pigeon were brought down with his arrows, and with these their hunger was partially appeased. By a brook, near which they pitched their camp, some tender plants were likewise found, and the lovers were not constrained to retire that night, as they feared they might be, altogether supperless.

The next day, which was the tenth, if we mistake not, of their flight, was entered upon in pretty good spirits, but it was destined to be the most eventful of all thus far.

Ascending a low mountain pass on their trail, they came in full view of an expansive and comparatively level country, beyond which the ocean appeared again. The prospect altogether was by nature most inspiring. This country was evidently inhabited by a numerous people, though the outward signs of it, from where the fugitives stood in the pass, were few. Manuelo was half in doubt whether this was a part of the Santos kingdom, or the land of some other nation; but as there was no way to satisfy his curiosity upon this important point, except by making his presence known to the inhabitants, he determined to run no risk of that kind, but to pass beyond it if possible, and thus render their escape from pursuit and capture the more certain. But food himself and companion must have, and to the obtaining of this he set his genius to work.

From their secure lookout, he discovered some leagues ahead on the plain below, the symptoms of a village, towards which in the afternoon they advanced as nearly as they could with entire safety, and made their camp for the night. From here Manuelo resolved, under cover of the approaching darkness, to reconnoiter the country, and spy out, if practicable, who the people might be. While contemplating this proposed raid, and just as the dull sun was hiding his ruby face behind the western horizon, Alola discovered at some distance a party of hunters returning to the village. Calling Manuelo's attention to this unexpected development, they were both half paralyzed with fear, thinking they saw the ominous bird's wing in the head ornamentation of the hunters. If true, this was an unquestionable sign of their belonging to the great Santos nation; but of this they were left in doubt by the distance that intervened, and as well by the fast-falling darkness.

The village, as usual with native villages, was on a knoll, close bordering upon a stream of clear water, and the plain about was interspersed, not thickly, with large oaks, so that as a hamlet it was really romantic and beautiful. The people were evidently as gay as the locality was cheering, for indications of merriment, on the part of old and young alike, were plainly observable from the cover of the fugitives. These were noticed with as much caution as the circumstances would admit of, and the lovers awaited with illy suppressed anxiety for the lengthening hours of the early evening to glide by.

Impelled by hunger and fatigue, and relying upon the long distance already come, the strangers might have been constrained to discover themselves to these people, running what risk there might be of recognition, but for the circumstance of their observing, as they supposed, the head-gear spoken of. This admonished them to forego the pleasure which they otherwise would have expected in a visit to such a delightful village, and to so merry a population as this appeared to be. Night came on, and with it silence, which grew profound as the evening waned.

About to part from his bride for the first time, he embraced her affectionately before sallying forth from their bower on his errand of discovery. So loth was she to part with him, even for a single hour, that she held his hand for a long time after he would have been on his way, and then with tears she bade him godspeed.

Observing first, carefully, the location of their camp, and marking out for himself and companion a line of retreat in case of pursuit by night, he cautiously advanced upon the village. Manuelo's eyes and ears were open to every moving thing, and not a bird or living creature, however small, escaped his attention as he silently felt his way towards the object of his investigation. Prudently hovering in the suburbs until all was still as the grave, he assumed all the courage at his command, and at the same time, as nearly as he could, the appearance of a native, then penetrated with noiseless tread to the very center of the village, where he discovered some venison, cut in long strips and hung on flakes to dry. To this he helped himself without ceremony, for it was just what himself and Alola needed, and then safely made his retreat, going in the direction of the brook until quite beyond the confines of the village. With hasty steps and less caution he now returned to the bower of his wakeful and anxiously waiting companion.

They were both overjoyed with the success of the venture, which, though in violation of the laws of civilized and savage countries alike, was justified by Manuelo on the ground, not of his own, but of the extreme hunger of the fairest creature living, as he said, and the act was not condemned by Father Justino, who was sure it would have been excused by the owners of the food themselves, had they been acquainted with the circumstances. But this was no time to tarry, even for a homily on the morality of the transaction, and so, refreshed, in the stillness of night, the two set out on their southward journey.

The rising sun discovered them many leagues away from the place of their last encampment; and henceforward their traveling was done under cover of the night, for in this country settlements were so frequent as to subject their progress by day to the imminent peril of discovery.

In scaling mountains they must needs follow passes which were threaded by trails on which people were frequently moving to and fro, some of whom they would be quite sure to meet in the day-time, but at night they were comparatively safe except from the assaults of wild animals, которые were numerous and ferocious in that country in those times.

On one occasion their progress was seriously interrupted by a hungry lioness, which, however, was dispatched by Manuelo's spear while its attention was diverted by the cunning of Alola, but not till its appetite had been gorged with nearly all that remained of their scanty supply of venison. This untoward event, though not so sad as it might have been, rendered it necessary soon afterwards to replenish their store, which it was believed could be done in the same manner as before. Although they had not yet gone nearly so far as they intended, they felt less dread of detection, since both concluded they must now be some distance beyond the dominions of Alola's old father. But as friendly relations existed between Bear-Slayer and all people to the southward, the lovers were apprehensive that information of their flight, should it be known, might find its way back to the country of the Santos, in which case their return or surrender would be demanded, and probably enforced by a war, if the demand was not speedily acceded to.

News of the elopement of so distinguished a person as the king's daughter they rightly judged would be likely to spread far and wide, and they were constrained to prosecute their flight for many days longer, and as far as absolute safety required. Their uncontrollable love for each other contributed immeasurably to their caution, and neither felt like resting in one place longer than a few hours.

About this period a large village was discovered on the well-shaded bank of a river, some little distance back from the sea, and here it was resolved by Manuelo to obtain a new supply of food if possible. The place seemed to afford peculiar inducements from the facilities with which it could be approached. In the rear it was beset with steep hills, and on the up-river side with a growth of large trees. From down the river the town was exposed to view, and in that direction looked off upon the not distant ocean. The situation was as eligible as ever could have been chosen for a village, and by its surroundings showed a great deal of intelligence and good taste on the part of its founder, whoever he may have been.

A secure hiding-place having been fixed upon by the fugitives at a convenient distance up the river, Manuelo made preparations to explore the place from that point for the means of subsistence.

In order to come without delay to the more important facts, for which the reader is impatiently waiting, it has been thought best to omit entirely from the translation the great solicitude felt by Alola for the safety of her lord, and likewise her earnest injunction given before starting on his perilous mission, to observe the utmost caution and to hurry back. Suffice it to say that the scene at this time, had it been witnessed by anyone, would have been nearly a repetition of what took place only a few nights before, but with this exception, that both were now infinitely more hopeful of success than they had been when inaugurating their first enterprise of the kind. This last observation called forth from the good friar the pious reflection that the best way to avoid disappointment is always to expect it. Had Manuelo and his innocent spouse observed this sensible rule, they would have escaped much disquietude to themselves and at the same time have enabled the author to proceed with this narrative with less embarrassment.

Practicing the same tactics very nearly as on his former raid, Manuelo penetrated this village in the dead of night, when all the inhabitants, as he supposed, were sound asleep. But finding no food exposed out-of-doors, as his former experience had led him to expect, he was constrained by adverse fate and too much daring to enter a dwelling to obtain what he so much needed. Guided more by his sense of smell than of sight, he was feeling about in the dark, when incautiously he stumbled upon one of the recumbent slumbering inmates. Instantly aroused, of course an alarm was raised. Manuelo fled and was pursued. Had he been as familiar as the people of the place with the locality, he could easily have escaped; but, alas! he ran in the wrong direction, and becoming entangled in some bushes, was captured. Here was a dilemma. The whole village was aroused, and he was at once surrounded by hundreds of people peering at him in the starlight and wondering what sort of a being it could be. So entirely unusual was his whole appearance that many of the wisest among the people were disposed to look upon him as a messenger directly from the infernal regions, and therefore entitled to respect, which they, one and all, in the darkness of the night freely showed him. Most of them, and the women and children in particular, kept quite aloof, and no injury was inflicted upon him by anyone. Had he been a veritable demon they could not have paid more deference to his person, but for all that, he was retained a close prisoner, under strong guard, until morning, when the fact was revealed to their astonished vision that he was human, and belonged to another, a distinct, and an unknown race of men.

The wonder of the people at now beholding for the first time, in the broad light of day, a white man, it would be difficult to describe, nor do we propose to undertake the task at this time. It is even doubtful if they expressed their astonishment in any words that could be written down; and why should Justino be expected to supply the deficiency? According to Manuelo's account of the affair, their exclamation of surprise resembled an expression often since heard in the Indian tongue, and sounded not unlike, "Woe! woe!"

Their language, in other respects, Manuelo could not well

understand, but he knew enough of the Indian character to make known by signs his wants, and in a measure to conciliate them. He gave them to understand that he came from the South instead of the North, and as soon as he was permitted, but under heavy escort, he sought out the hiding-place of his beautiful bride; but, alas! she was no longer there. The bird had flown, leaving only a few scattered feathers behind, and nothing to indicate in what direction she had taken her flight. Manuelo's distress was now unbounded. He called for Alola at the top of his voice, but could get no response. He judged rightly that she had heard the commotion in the village, caused by his detection, and had fled, and he greatly feared she would be entirely lost in her flight, or be destroyed by wild beasts. He felt almost certain she would not go far away without him, but he was none the less perplexed by her absence. He managed to make known, as speedily as possible, the fact of her existence, to his captors, and a search for her was generously undertaken by them all. It appears that the poor, affrighted creature, on hearing the terrible noise in the village, created by her husband's arrest, had approached with the noiseless, trembling tread of a kitten, to its very suburbs, and not seeing him, had fled in the direction of the ocean, believing that Manuelo, if he made his escape, would pursue the same course. There on the beach, running hither and thither, late in the afternoon, the poor thing was found by the natives, more dead than alive, and bemoaning aloud her hard fate, as only a young and tender creature like herself could be expected to do. She greatly feared her lover had been slain, and she was already contemplating self-destruction by plunging alone into the deep blue sea. Reluctantly she was brought by her captors to the village, and was there surprised and delighted to meet Manuelo again, and the two were happier then than they had ever been before in their lives. Captives though they were, all the pains of imprisonment were dispelled by the knowledge of each other's safety, and with ineffable ecstasy they recounted to each other every occurrence since their separation, only the night before.

LXVII.

THE BARBOS.*

THE people in whose hands they had now fallen, and who were called the Barbos, proved to be a distinct nation from the Santos, but there was no well-defined boundary separating the territories of the two countries. The people were known to each other, but no relations existed between them, or none of a diplomatic character, if I may use that expression, and this fact, when it became known, had a tendency to ease the minds of the fugitives, and to enable them to rest in peace long enough to recuperate their energies, which had been greatly exhausted by the long and tedious marches by night, as well as by day, without proper food most of the way, and part of the time without any. Though they were extremely solicitous to ascertain the relations existing between the Barbos and the Santos, the inquiry was conducted so cautiously as not to betray the fact that they were fugitives from the latter nation. On the contrary, both Manuelo and Alola studiously gave forth the impression, as the cautious Manuelo alone had done before, that they had come from the opposite direction; not, however, from the country immediately adjoining the Barbos on the

---

*SANTA BARBARA TRIBE.—When in 1769 [about 170 years after Manuelo was there], the Spanish explorers in their northward march came to the locality of the present Santa Barbara, they found there a large native village. The inhabitants were fishermen, who had fine boats, twenty-four feet long, made of pine boards. They also possessed considerable artistic skill, as exhibited in their wood-carvings, which were eagerly bought by the Spaniards, who in return gave glass beads to the natives. Some of the graves were opened recently, and the relics found in them were ascribed by many to prehistoric times, and to extinct races.—*Santa Barbara Independent.*

south, but from some far country in that quarter. This was the more readily believed, inasmuch as the Barbos had heard a vague rumor of a people resembling Manuelo, in some distant southern land.

As might have been expected, the sudden appearance of two such unusual characters in this village, not only created great excitement, as has been stated, but it also caused much gossiping comment, particularly amongst the women, who never ceased wondering how it was that such a pretty young woman as Alola could have been found in such limited company and under such strange circumstances. Much tattle about the affair was indulged in, and it sorely taxed the inventive genius of the happy couple to satisfy the numerous meddlesome inquiries made of them concerning the event. It may have been a weak pretense on the part of the strangers that they had become lost, and were wandering, they knew not whither, but it was the best explanation that could be offered, and the over-curious matrons and maidens had no alternative but to make the most of it. How much of this improbable story was really believed the happy pair could not know, but then, neither did they care, only so they were not betrayed by too bold an imposition upon the credulity of their listeners. Both Manuelo and Alola felt that it was little of the business of this people to know all about them, and that, at all events, their movements concerned themselves more, by far, than mere strangers; hence they scrupled not to mislead the prying Barbos women in any way they were able. To have told the whole truth, situated as they were, might have proved disastrous to their plans, and their deceptive course was fully justified by Father Justino, on the ground that, as husband and wife, they alone were entitled to their family secrets; unless, forsooth, such secrets might be demanded at the confessional, by a regular priest like himself, and who, in that case, would be bound to keep them in clerical confidence.

Aside from these meddlesome and annoying inquiries the

fugitives were treated with much kindness by the thrifty people of this Barbos village, and after the first few days of their stay, no restraint whatever was put upon their movements. They were at liberty to do whatsoever they would, and their sojourn, though begun as prisoners, was continued and ended more like a veritable honey-moon. Frequent excursions were made to the ocean beach, both for exploration and enjoyment, and for the first time in all their experience did the stream of their love appear to flow smoothly.

In the ceaseless roar of the ocean there is something so soothing to the senses of lovers that Manuelo made bold to recommend to all persons who might be compelled to run away, on account of their attachment for each other, to seek the sea-side by all means, and, if practicable, to resort to the coast of the Barbos, whose secluded vales and entrancing scenery, not to mention its unequaled climate, he thought presented unusual attractions for such romantic adventurers.

Fascinated by their pleasant surroundings in this beautiful land, Manuelo and his bride, too happy, remained as long as they dared, and longer, perhaps, than prudence would have allowed.

At last satisfied, though not wearied, with this genial locality, and with the attentions of its equally genial people, the lovers pretended anxiety to return to their home, and expressed to their new-found friends fears lest their long absence might create alarm. So much was true, but the alarm they were alluding to was in the opposite direction from the one they wished to go. Generously provided by the kind Barbos with all the comforts they would need upon their journey, the two, bidding their protectors an affectionate adieu, set out on their southward march, arm in arm at first, and always near to each other.

Manuelo had learned from these people that a powerful and warlike nation called the Anglos lay some five or six days' journey off in the direction they were bound, and before starting he determined to enter that territory boldly, and conceal from its inhabitants nothing except whence they came and the occasion of their coming.

It was Manuelo's intention to proceed still further in the direction of Mexico as soon as convenient, and perhaps to penetrate to the very settlements of the Spanish, which he knew must lay in that quarter.

The Barbos were not on the most friendly terms with the Anglos, and the security of the former from invasion, he could see, depended upon their isolation; for the part of the journey they were now about to make was more difficult and dangerous than any they had hitherto passed over. A succession of mountains and deserts intervened, and it was hard to say which of the two, whether desert or mountain, presented the greater obstacle to their progress.

The travelers were in constant danger of losing their way, or else of being destroyed by wild beasts, which abounded in the mountains, and they therefore felt constrained to make their camp each night on the open plain, or in the midst of some valley, though comforts there were fewer, in order to be away from the haunts of the bear, the lion, and other ferocious animals. There were few villages on the route, and only on the first night out were they favored with a lodgment in one. Thus far on their way the wanderers were accompanied by two stalwart braves of the Barbos, but the remainder of the journey had to be made in solitude and by themselves alone. Nevertheless they continued on their course with safety and by easy stages, no incident of importance occurring, or, if so, not related; until on the seventh day they came in sight of the capital of the Anglos. It was situated on the border of a magnificent plain interspersed with isolated groves of large trees, and not many leagues away from the ocean. The city was first seen from the crest of a mountain, not of great height, but precipitous, and the prospect, comprising as it did, plain, river, city, ocean, and all, was, next to that from Tamalpais the grandest he had ever beheld. Contemplating it long and earnestly, with Alola by his side, the two began at length to speculate upon the nature of the inhabitants, wondering what sort of people they must be who were living in such an inspiring region, and what kind of a reception they would probably meet with on the following day, for they were yet a great way off, and could not have hoped to reach the city that night, had they desired to do so. Resting there in the mountains they cogitated over what account they should give of themselves on arrival at the city the following day, and how they should make their *début* among that strange people. They still felt themselves under the necessity of concealing from public curiosity the cause of their journey, and their firm conclusion therefore was to evade answering too many inquiries at the first, and until they could be certain of giving a consistent and satisfactory explanation of their movements. But it was resolved in case nothing appeared in the way of such a statement, to say that Manuelo had been cast ashore far to the northward, some two years before, and with his fair companion, who had, with the consent of her parents, become his wife, was making his way back to his own country, which lay a hundred days' journey or more, it might be, to the southward. This was as near the truth as it was thought advisable to venture at the start. They would gladly have avoided making any misstatements or misrepresentation whatever, but such was deemed incompatible with safety. They had been compelled to enter upon a system of prevarication by the very unjust and arbitrary laws of the fiery Santos, and they were not yet far enough away from the influence of such laws to render entirely safe an abandonment of that policy, for one of candor and honesty.

It was the opinion of Father Justino, plainly expressed in the manuscript, that the laws of a country are responsible for many of the crimes committed in it, and that laws are sometimes so oppressive and unjust that they must needs be disregarded. Such is the case, he said, particularly where the happiness of the people is seriously impaired by the character of the institutions under which they are compelled to live, and where the lives of citizens are endangered by their operation. To be respected, laws, he added, ought to be equal and uniform, and bear upon all alike, upon the rich and the poor, the high and the low, and only such laws he thought could be conscientiously observed by everybody.

It was also said by Justino, but whether he was merely echoing the opinions of Manuelo, or giving utterance to his own sentiments, gathered from early observations in Portugal, cannot now be told, but he declared that unjust laws, by producing hunger, privation, and suffering, are the cause of a far greater number of premature and untimely deaths than wars, pestilence, and earthquakes combined; and he drew a comparison between different countries to show that the prosperity or otherwise of each depended almost entirely upon its government. Thousands, he said, yea, millions of innocent children each year, and of men and women not a few, whose early departure from this life was attributed, as the world goes, to blind chance and uncontrollable fate, were in truth murdered by oppressive laws; yes, absolutely murdered; sacrificed to appease the demands of unjust governments; and therefore it was, as he reasoned, that the infraction of the law was not always a crime, the criminality being oftener in the law itself than in its violation. He thought that if the palaces of the great could be turned into mausoleums to accommodate the victims of their tyrannical owners, they would be filled from base to turret with dead men's bones.

This good Dominican friar envied not any people the enjoyment of their crime-gotten gains; but, if we may believe him, was more content with his scanty allotment in the New

World than were the greatest of kings with all their possessions in the Old.

As evidence of the correctness of this conclusion, he referred again with powerful effect to the fact just then becoming known in America, that the great Charles V., though not yet old, had cast aside his glittering imperial crown, for the peace of mind which he hoped to find in the quiet of the cloister. In naming over at the time different kingdoms, some powerful and others weak, to prove that the condition of the one or the other depended almost exclusively upon the character of its institutions, good or bad, the strong nation possessing the good and the weak the bad, he was not content, but proceeded further to adduce a fact, well sustained in history, that the same country is at one period prosperous and at another otherwise; that the time of its prosperity was when blessed with wise rulers and just laws, and that degeneracy and decay were the inevitable results of corruption and injustice. Laws, he said, should be framed for the protection of the weak, and not the strong; for the poor, and not the rich; the powerful and wealthy, continued he, being able to provide for themselves, while the poor and the weak are at the mercy of others unless protected by law.

It sounds so much like a woman that we must believe that Alola herself was the real author of the sentiment, that the poor and unfortunate are the babes and sucklings of the government, and entitled to its first consideration. Not the lions, said the good woman, but the lambs; the hares, and not the bears, require protection, and yet the lions and bears of society have the benefit of nearly all legislative enactments, while the hares and the lambs, so to speak, are left to shift for themselves. The powerful and rich, who become so by the favor of the king, and use their bounty unmercifully, were declared to be the ravenous human hyenas of civil society, and more deserving of destruction than of the flattery which is so frequently bestowed upon them. If God is good and at the same time merciful, said the friar, the just lawgiver, who is too often condemned in this world, will be abundantly rewarded in the next; while the bad one, however pious he may seem to be, will fail of his aim to reach Heaven; for, said he, where laws are so oppressive and unjust that persons must from necessity violate them in order to obtain the necessaries of life, it is not the breakers of the laws, but the makers of them, that ought to be punished.

Justino observed, furthermore, that the character of the government of a country was always depicted in the countenances of its inhabitants. If the government be good, said he, happiness will prevail and will plainly appear in the faces of the people; but if harsh and oppressive, that, in like manner, will be shown in their dissatisfied and dejected expressions. He maintained that under just and equal laws a noble race of men and women would spring up in any country; while abject servility and degeneracy were sure to follow in the wake of an unjust and tyrannical government. This, he assured Manuelo, had been demonstrated in all ages and in all countries. The comely Greeks and noble Romans of ancient times had grown to their exalted state of perfection from much lower orders of humanity, under the influence of wise enactments; and as the result of oppressive government they had degenerated again, at times, to a deplorable extent. Addressing himself to Manuelo with much earnestness he added that even the manly and generous-souled Santos, if subjected to improper governmental influences, might, in the course of centuries, degenerate into an inferior race of beings, and their women, of whom Alola was a brilliant example, would be likely in time also to lose much of their beauty and comeliness. This sweeping assertion Manuelo was hardly prepared to believe, until reminded by the friar of the shameful conduct towards himself of the slavish Modens, when the great truth for the first time flashed across his mind that government has everything to do with the moral, mental, and physical condition of a people, a fact never afterwards questioned by him.

In the case of Manuelo and Alola, they were now fleeing from the operation of laws directly in conflict with a law of nature, and as Justino maintained, in opposition to the divine law of love; hence he was far from censuring the poor fugitives for resorting to so much of prevarication, as was deemed necessary to shield themselves from that vengeance which was liable to follow from the wicked practices of the Santos. The lovers had the entire sympathy of the good friar, as they have also of the translator, and doubtless will have of every honest reader of this history. Laws that are right and tend to promote human happiness are always readily obeyed, and are easily enforced; in fact, they enforce themselves by their own justness; hence, very little government is anywhere needed except to enforce oppressive laws.

LXVIII.
THE ANGLOS.

AWAKENED at early morn by the shrill, penetrating notes of a brown thrush piping its lays in answer to its mate, and refreshed by a night's rest in the pure mountain air of that elevated place, the doubting couple issued forth from their temporary bower, to find as clear a sky and as brilliant a prospect as ever mortal man had looked upon. The sun had not yet come forth from his hiding-place in the orient, and the two lingered where they were long enough to greet his appearance, and to plight anew, before the shining face of that great luminary, their mutual faith. Then and there, surrounded as they were by the untold beauties of nature, and fully inspired by the surpassing sublimity of the scenery, they vowed again most solemnly to love, honor, and cherish each other through all trials and temptations, through evil and good report, cleaving only one to the other so long as they both should live, and until death should them finally part.

They were now about to enter upon associations entirely new, the continuation of which was a thing of great uncertainty, and they deemed this a fitting occasion to pledge again their troth, and bind themselves more closely together. Should it be their fate to spend the balance of their days with the Anglos, they would leave nothing undone which might be needful to perpetuate the remembrance of their blissful union, and both, bending towards the east, earnestly called upon the rising sun to witness the sincerity of their affection.

This ceremony brought to a close by the sun entering upon his daily journey, the wanderers, cheered in heart, not more by the delightful scenery before them than by the consciousness of having discharged an important, but solemn duty, abandoned their resting-place, and were soon down on the plains, wending their way to the city, which, by diligent traveling, they reached before noon. Their approach had been observed from afar, and their unexpected advent in the place caused great commotion among the people. No herald or information of any kind had preceded their coming, and nearly the entire population assembled to express their wonder at so strange an event. They were able at first to converse but poorly with the gathering crowd, on account of a difference in dialect, and could therefore give but little account of themselves. They were regarded with amazement by all, but the authorities of the city were inclined to look upon them at the beginning, as nothing but spies. In consequence they were treated with coolness, and were kept under close surveillance for the time, but succeeded after a while in gaining the confidence of the great chief, and eventually, more liberty of action. This was accorded them with the more reluctance on account of the peculiarity of their costume, which clearly indicated that they were from some nation entirely unknown in those parts. Their dresses, though of skins, like those of the Anglos, were of fashions entirely different.

Manuelo himself was no less an object of curiosity here than in other places where he had been, and, notwithstanding his strenuous endeavors to appear and act like a native of the country, it was of little avail. It was impossible to divest himself of distinctive features, nor could he in any way deceive the shrewd Anglos. They detected in him at once something unusual and extraordinary. His fuller beard, his blue eyes, his brown hair, and his lighter skin, all betrayed him as belonging to an entirely different race from their own, and he was therefore contemplated with a great deal of suspicion, until his acquaintance with the people grew apace, and their friendship was ripened by time.

Towards the beautiful, dark-eyed Alola, whose general make-up, though superior to that of the rest of her race, was more in accordance with the accepted standard of the country in those days, they felt differently. Her gentle manners and winning ways soon gained for her the friendship of all. Particularly was this noticeable on the part of the women, but she was not wanting in attentions from any. The kind young people of her own sex took special delight in administering to her wants, and all the comforts that the city afforded were bounteously heaped upon her. The style of her garments, differing so radically from their own, interested this class of the population amazingly. They were really of a kind that had never before been seen nor dreamed of in that locality, and they seemed to promise as much of comfort on account of their pattern as of pleasure from being of a fashion entirely new. It was asserted that their delight with the dress of Alola was only excelled by their admiration for its wearer. Besides fitting her well, and showing off to the best advantage the graces of her person, it was profusely ornamented with fringes and feathers. To tell the simple truth, and we know no reason why we should not, it had been gotten up at her home, with the aid of the good Santos dames, in anticipation of her marriage with the gallant Gosee, as a sort of bridal attire, and it was lacking neither in good taste, nor in true regal style. That the genius of Manuelo was manifest in its general construction, there can be no question, but not with the expectation that his rival, the envious Gosee, would draw any pleasure therefrom. The head-dress of Alola was simple and tasty, and made of the finest of fur, but with few ornaments of any sort, as they were not at all needed to set off her comely features. Beauty unadorned is always the sweetest, and so in her case. No marvel, certainly, all these things considered, that the gay and festive Anglos maidens were well pleased with their unexpected female visitor.

The king and the principal prophets adopted costumes similar in fashion to Manuelo's, as soon as they could be prepared. In a spirit of true magnanimity the strangers rendered the Anglos of both sexes all the assistance they were able in fabricating garments after the style of their own. In this way, and by other kindly acts, Manuelo and his gentle bride ingratiated themselves with the people of the city, and of the neighboring villages, in an incredibly short space of time. In reality Manuelo acquired, according to the words of the manuscript, as much popularity with the Anglos as he had ever enjoyed with the Santos in his palmiest days, and it would have been known just as well, had the fact not been told us, that he was more than delighted this time to share his popularity with his charming young wife. They were hospitably provided with the best of quarters, in a great lodge near the dwellings of the head men of the nation, and there, securely ensconced, the loving pair were as happy as human beings could be under the most auspicious circumstances. It was a most fortunate thing for them at the beginning, that neither was able to converse freely in the tongue of this people, since they were thereby relieved from the necessity of entering upon an extended explanation of their sudden and most unlooked-for visit. But this duty was deferred only a short time, for the Anglos dialect was not difficult to acquire, and they were constrained after a while, by many importunities, to give an account of themselves, which they did, precisely in accordance with the plan as laid out in their last night's watch upon the mountain. These people, like the Barbos, were given to understand that the purpose of the wanderers was to continue their journey at some future day to the South, for reasons already detailed, but not necessary to be repeated here.

The Anglos differed not essentially from the other inhabitants of Upper California, at that remote period, in their habits and mode of living, but were regarded by Manuelo as a little shade less enlightened than the swift footed Santos; nor were they so numerous a nation. Their territory, likewise, was more circumscribed, but they were, nevertheless, a warlike people, and their chief, or king, exercised his rule with almost as much despotism as was exhibited by the old king of the Modens. He was more considerate, however, with his authority, and among the people at large was accustomed to require much less of servility than was exacted from the Oaks by their king. He was still a powerful man physically, though past the middle of life, and was generally foremost in war, in hunting, and in athletic sports.

The Barbos had not misrepresented the facts in saying that he was fond of war, and he was on terms of absolute friendship with none of the neighboring nations. His principal and most active enemy joined his territory on the south, and with these people, who were known as the Dagos, he was frequently in open hostility and with ever-varying results. In the last conflict the Anglos had been worsted, and the chief's proud spirit still writhed under the castigation then received, and he burned for an opportunity of revenge. In truth, he had been severely wounded in the head with a missile of some sort, sent by a Dago brave, and the wound was hardly yet healed when Manuelo and his female companion arrived in the country. He congratulated himself with having slain in that battle, with his own hands, several of the stalwart warriors of the Dagos, but their king was still spared, and it was against him in particular that Mosoto's enmity (for that was the name of the king of the Anglos) was particularly directed. The king of the Dagos, more than two years before, had captured and carried off the favorite wife of Mosoto, while she was out with others gathering berries near the border, an indignity to which the resolute Mosoto could never bring his mind to submit with any degree of composure. He had little hope of ever recovering his lost wife, but he was constantly thirsting for vengeance upon her captor, and for that reason, hostile incursions were undertaken into the country of his rival as often as the requisite preparations could be made.

The prowess of the enemy—the Dagos—who numbered many valiant warriors, deterred the Anglos people from these expeditions oftener than enforced by the angry king, but they were nevertheless quite sure to be set on foot as frequently as once a year, and sometimes more than once in the same season. Mosoto had it in purpose to try the fortunes of war with the Dagos again that summer, and he readily saw that he could turn the talents of Manuelo, if Manuelo was so disposed, to good account in fitting out this contemplated expedition. A great point he could perceive had been gained in the form of the clothing his people had been taught by the strangers to wear, and, besides, Manuelo had made some suggestions in regard to the shape and use of the weapons of warfare of the Anglos, which were regarded as highly advantageous. But it was in the management of the campagin itself from which Mosoto hoped to derive most advantage from the readily observed genius of his singular guest. When this fact became known, Manuelo contemplated with some dismay the use intended to be made of himself; and even the prospect of being invested with the dignity of commander-in-chief failed to dispel his apprehensions of danger in the movement. His exceedingly disastrous experience in the fight with the Modens had weaned him, so to speak, of the desire for military renown, and though he was quite willing to render what assistance he could in fitting out an expedition, he felt a great deal of reluctance about taking an active part in it; and what was worse, the very thought of his going off to war again was exceedingly distasteful to little Alola, who could not help picturing to herself a repetition of the painful servitude her husband had suffered while a prisoner with the cruel Modens; and even worse, for she greatly feared, from what she could learn about the formidable Dagos, that he might be slain outright.

On her account, therefore, more than on his own, he seriously contemplated an early desertion of the Anglos, and actually thought of making his way with his bride to the country of the Dagos, since it lay to the south. But this step he knew must be planned, and at the same time accomplished, surreptitiously, if at all, and that would be an undertaking fraught with, probably, as much danger to himself, and infinitely more to his wife, than to join heartily, and at once, in the campaign against the Dagos. By no means could he persuade himself to a step which would, more than any other, jeopardize the safety of the one he loved so tenderly. It was with apparent zest, therefore, that he took an active part from that moment in the preparations for the war, believing that he could thus, in a measure, control the movement for his own purposes, judging wisely that his return to Alola would depend thereupon, and that her happiness forever afterwards would hang upon the success of the campaign.

According to Justino's account of the affair, Manuelo, with

all his fears, betrayed a little streak of vanity, such as many another embryo general had felt before him, and as some may possibly since have felt, at a prospect of promotion, and he was less reluctant to enter into the war on that account. He confessed to some gratification springing out of the great confidence reposed in him by the king, in voluntarily offering him the management of this delicate and dangerous business.

The matter having been fully considered in every point by Manuelo and Alola, and the work of the campaign laid out, so far as it could be, in all its diversified particulars, it was reluctantly entered upon, though with all apparent good-will, Manuelo not betraying to anyone, except to his fair bride, his real sentiments.

Most diligent exertions for several weeks were required to equip and prepare the Anglos warriors as he directed. Each man was to be clad in close-fitting garments instead of a blanket of skins, as theretofore, and the more vital parts of each soldier's person were to be partially protected from the arrows and javelins of the enemy by patches of the thick hide of the bear, or of some other large animal, sewed into the garment. The soldiers were shod with more substantial moccasins than had been their custom to wear, so that they could clamber over sharp rocks, and even trample upon the prickly cactus, with impunity. Each warrior's head was adorned with a helmet, fashioned out of the firmest leather that could be made in that country, and these were ornamented with the tails of wolverines, foxes, and other wild creatures. Each helmet was crested with an abundance of the longest feathers that could be procured, much after the manner of civilized nations; and with these they presented a remarkably martial appearance. No very radical change could be made by Manuelo in the construction of their weapons, owing to the scarcity of implements at hand for their manufacture; but, as a compensation for this disadvantage, each soldier was able to arm himself with a greater number of weapons, by reason of his having fewer incumbrances of other kinds. In addition to the protection their uniforms afforded, one whole division of the army was furnished with shields, or bucklers, usually of more than one thickness of skins, stretched upon a strong hoop of wood, and always of more than one thickness, unless of the heaviest kind. By much practice this division became remarkably expert in receiving weapons cast towards them, upon these bucklers, and turning such weapons aside.

Instead of burdening each man with his own stock of provisions, as had been the custom from time immemorial with the Anglos, a commissary department, so to speak, was provided, and men less fitted for battle were detailed to carry the food. The organization of this corps, so very unusual among them, cost the general an infinite amount of trouble and annoyance, the tendency of the individuals in that department being always towards a too hasty consumption of the supplies. But by the severest discipline they were brought to a perfect discharge of their duty, before the campaign began. Manuelo was a native of Barcelona, and had seen enough of military maneuvering in the land of his birth when a boy, to enable him to put his army through a sort of drill each day, for several weeks in succession, before setting out on the expedition.

His own military dress was carefully prepared by the assistance of Alola, with special reference to the safety of its wearer. He selected the very best of the skins for himself, and it is doubtful if arrow or dart, or even a javelin, could have penetrated any portion of his uniform with fatal effect, when it was completed; while he relied upon his shield for the protection of his face, in the event of his being exposed to the missiles of the adversary, which, by the way, he hoped, as commander-in-chief, to avoid, as was customary with all well-regulated armies.

His forces were prudently divided into several different corps

—how many was not stated in the manuscript—and a competent officer was designated to take charge of each, while Manuelo was to be in command of the whole, to direct the movements of all. At the head of the principal division, and the one that was to be in the lead, was the formidable king himself, whose giant frame, surtopped with the tallest of plumes, was the most conspicuous figure in the whole army. If Manuelo was proud of his command, it is needless to say that Mosoto was still more proud of his share of the same, and he chafed at the little delay that was deemed necessary by the real commander to make ready for an entirely successful campaign.

In view of the pageant, in which her husband was the leading spirit, Alola's objections to the enterprise gradually grew less, and it is no discourtesy to say that her admiration for the general overcame in some degree her early scruples about his engaging in a war in which he had really no concern, and against a people that had never done either him or her any harm, no, not even the slightest. But it is not the first instance, said Father Justino, where military glamor has obliterated the sense of justice, and blinded the eyes of men, and women too, to the horrors of bloody war. It has been a common thing in all ages for people to become so dazzled by the glory and splendor of military movements, as to forget all the dire consequences.

LXIX.

WAR WITH THE DAGOS

PERFECTLY equipped and disciplined, as they now were, and well supplied with provisions, this Anglos army of scarcely a thousand fighting men, bearing arms, and not more than fifteen hundred of all ranks, and including camp followers, filed out of the city, by the principal southern exit, and took up their line of march towards the country of the Dagos. As they moved off in a long extended column, in perfect order, they might be likened—if great things may be compared to small—to a large flock of wild geese going South, as the advancing season invites their return from the high Arctic regions, where they have spent the summer in multiplying, and recruiting their energies, upon the fresher products of the North. So the Anglos army, with long, waving line, their leader a little in advance, but with rear-guard somewhat disorganized, bore away to the southward, on that beautiful midsummer morning.

In less than a week these exulting forces were in the heart of the enemy's country. But the wary Dagos, ever on the alert for their foes, had observed their approach; and the progress of the Anglos, day by day, had been reported by heralds to the king of that nation, who, with the utmost alacrity, gathered together his forces also, and made ready to meet and give battle to his hereditary foe. With the utmost confidence on either side the two armies proudly approached each other, both eager for the fray.

The Dagos outnumbered the Anglos more than two to one; but this fact was not unknown to Manuelo, who, like a skillful general as he was, took account of it by drawing up his forces on the right bank of a small river, just where it debouches into the ocean, so that his right wing rested upon the sea, leaving no opportunity for the enemy to pass between him and the water. His left wing, in like manner, rested upon a high bluff, rendering it as impossible for the Dagos to turn that flank; and in this situation he was aware that the fight must be a square face to face contest, in which case he judged his own men would possess greatly the advantage, by reason of their superior armorial defenses. To choose this favorable position he was admonished by his sad experience at the time of the bloody fight between the Santos and the Modens, in which, it will be remembered, the battle and his own liberty, at the same time, were lost, as the result of a flank movement. It was not so much for his own safety as out of regard for the loving Alola, that Manuelo selected for himself the securest place in the whole line, or, rather, in the rear of the line, where he could spur on his warriors to greater exertions, in case the tide of battle might require it. It was no slight evidence of his prowess as a commander, that he was able to inspire all his men, from Mosoto down, with confidence, and even with enthusiasm.

Posted as we have seen, Manuelo and his gallant army calmly awaited the approach of the bloody Dagos, who in vastly superior numbers came up, at the expected hour, in hot haste and with shouts that almost made Manuelo's hair stand on end, as he said; but the inveterate Anglos, nothing daunted, received the first discharge of arrows from the other side upon their bucklers, almost without harm, and then returned the fire with terrible effect. The fight at once became general and desperate, but Manuelo's brave men held their ground, dealing blow for blow with most fatal results, to the astonished Dagos. Urged on by their desperate leaders, the enemy now advanced across the shallow stream separating the two armies, and coming upon the lines of the Anglos at several points at the same moment, the battle was fast assuming the form of a hand-to-hand contest. Just then, foremost in the fight, on the Anglos side, was observed the herculean frame of the fierce Mosoto, moving to and fro in the line, protected by his huge armor, and striking to the right and the left, slaughtering his opponents in great numbers, but receiving little or no harm in return. Manuelo, noticing the advantage thus gained, could not restrain his own fiery disposition—general though he was— to take an active part in the fray, and his weapons did good execution. Encouraged by these noble examples of individual bravery, the men advanced, with loud cries of exultation, and not only checked, but drove back the Dagos again, across the narrow river. The Anglos had been taught that their security from hostile weapons lay in keeping their faces to the foe, for their backs had been purposely left unprotected in order to discourage retreat. In flight, Manuelo, not being over-swift of foot, would have stood a poor chance of escape, and this fact had been shrewdly taken into account by him in the preparation of his army. The Dagos were completely surprised by the new and strange accouterments of their old enemies, and being stricken with dismay at their apparent imperturbability, a rout ensued. The triumphant Anglos followed up their victory sharply, and the consternation of the enemy increased at every step. In compact order and under good command, but with terrific and repeated yells, the pursuit was continued the balance of the day, and until, weary with the chase, a halt was called by Manuelo, for the night, in a secure place by the sea.

The Anglos were elated beyond expression by their success, and now felt themselves invincible. Their casualties had been few and their wounded were easily provided for. These were, by order of the commander-in-chief, put in charge of the commissary department, and, to say the least, they were well fed Manuelo was now a hero indeed, and every tongue was loud in his praise. No one was more ready to do him honor than Mosoto himself, who was really overjoyed with the victory. When fairly in camp, and supper over, a council of war was called by the chief, and it was resolved on the morrow to continue the pursuit.

The king of the Dagos, a most desperate character, was afforded sufficient time during the night to rally his shattered forces, and, without consulting his chiefs or his prophets, he determined to make a stand on the following day, and to renew the conflict. This time he had the selection of his own ground, and choosing a pass in the mountain through which the retreat had to be made, he there drew up his crippled army for a last desperate struggle.

This advantage of the enemy was noticed at once by Manuelo as he proceeded on the next day, and in so great doubt was he as to his ability to surmount the difficulty before him, that he called a halt, and, at the same time, another council of war, and took the advice of his corps commanders as to whether they should undertake it or not. Elated by their victory of the day before, which was certainly glorious enough, they were unanimous in the wish to prosecute the war with vigor, and consequently, without much delay, an assault was made, by a select body of the Anglos with Mosoto at their head, upon the strong position of the Dagos. The assaulting party was supported by the entire force of Manuelo, which rushed forward when the word was given, with an impetuosity that would have done credit, as was said, to the very best soldiers of the great King Charles. There was no withstanding the onslaught, though the stubborn Dagos, who were now fighting, not for glory merely, but for their homes, their families, and their firesides, resisted with the most unaccountable determination. The fight was persisted in for some time with unexampled energy, before the pass was finally made, but the enemy were compelled to yield to the better equipments of the Anglos, and were driven again in great confusion towards their capital.

This second battle with the Dagos was won about the middle of the day, and before sundown the heroic little army, under the brave Manuelo, with hasty steps marched into the principal city of their discomfited enemies. They were preceded, of course, by the dismayed and flying soldiers of the Dago king, and their approach being known, the women and children of that nation, old and young, fled precipitately to the mountains, in the greatest consternation. A few only remained behind, but among these was the stolen and long-absent wife of Mosoto; and here we are compelled to relate, or rather translate, an event most sorrowful. Gladly would the translator avoid the narration of it entirely if he could with propriety, and the mind of the sensitive reader should not be harrowed up by an account of the occurrence, could he be permitted to have his own way, but the truth of history demands, imperatively, at his hands, a performance of the task, however disagreeable.

This poor woman, not greeting Mosoto, her former husband, with as much cordiality as he thought it was his right to expect, possibly not recognizing him in his new and strange uniform, was cruelly slaughtered by him in cold blood, then and there. This horrible event, in the mind of the good Manuelo, detracted vastly from the glory of the campaign, and he could never think of it without actual regrets that he had undertaken the war at all, for so heartless and revengeful a person. He could not to his own satisfaction account for the motives that induced such a blood-thirsty act, and least of all could he forgive it. The thought of it always brought tears to his eyes, and when the sad event was related by him to Alola, as it was in pathetic terms, she too wept bitterly. There had been no chance for Manuelo to interfere, or even to expostulate with the cruel king before the bloody deed was accomplished, so hasty was it. But Manuelo's anger was thoroughly aroused at the time against the author of it, and, as he acknowledged, he would have slain Mosoto on the spot, and in the presence of his victim, had he been armed, as he wished he had been, with his sword and pistols.

In discussing the matter afterwards, Manuelo was of the opinion that this dreadful tragedy might be attributable, in part at least, to the wicked passions of Mosoto, whose love for the poor, gentle Red Berry having been once very great, as everybody knew, was suddenly converted, by the magic power of jealousy, into uncontrollable hate, on beholding her the wife of another. The less sentimental Dominican friar, turning the matter over in his own mind, suggested that the fell deed may have been the result of sheer habit; that Mosoto, having been so vigorously employed for the last two days in slaughtering people, may have actually killed poor Red Berry without much thinking. But the more probable opinion is the one entertained by Manuelo and concurred in by Alola, that Mosoto's enmity towards the king of the Dagos was at the bottom of the whole thing, and that he could not bear to behold the slender person of his *inamorata*, embellished as it was, with raven locks, with ruby lips, and teeth of pearl, in the possession of another, and that one to him the most detested being on earth. These views of Manuelo were fortified by an allusion to the Moor of Venezia, and the fair Desdemona, the tragic story of whom was often repeated throughout the Spanish world in those days. Had there been some miserable Iago in the army, to excite, by false insinuations against the meek-eyed Red Berry, the fiery temper of Mosoto, Alola would have had no doubt as to the motives which led to the untimely death of the poor, defenseless woman.

It is needless to say that this affair wrought a complete change in the feelings of Manuelo towards the king. But they were yet in the captured city of the enemy, and there was no opportunity now to show his indignation, surrounded as they were on every hand by a people greatly superior to the Anglos in numbers, and capable, to say the least, of giving them much annoyance. Without bestowing protracted consideration upon the subject just then, Manuelo posted a strong guard at every entrance to the city, and the conquerors rested in the enemy's stronghold that night, but not before observations first made as to a proper line of retreat to a place of greater safety, in case of a night attack.

The Dagos, however, were too seriously disconcerted to disturb his repose, and on the following morning, by the peep of day, the Anglos battalions were on their line of march towards their own homes, taking with them such booty as they desired, and leading captive a few prisoners of war. After the first day their march was by easy stages, and in less than a week their return was greeted with the most unbounded demonstrations of joy, by all the people of the Anglos nation assembled in the capital for that purpose. The heart of the fascinating Alola overflowed with delight at the safe return of her gallant husband, and the pleasure she enjoyed in a rehearsal by himself of the events of the campaign was only alloyed by the tragic occurrence already alluded to, but which is altogether too sorrowful for recapitulation.

LXX.
TROUBLE WITH MOSOTO.

WE have now reached a point in this eventful narrative where some embarrassment is liable to occur, and for the following reason : all the remainder of the manuscript—the outside portion of the same—being more or less nibbled away by the mice, it was impossible to decipher some of the words, and occasionlly a sentence was so obscured as to render its interpretation exceedingly difficult. As a consequence, the ambitious young priests of Evora who had this literary treasure in their keeping, were unable to give it, in all respects, a construction absolutely literal, and candor compels the acknowledgment that now and then a word, and, possibly, the fragment of an idea, was supplied by them in order to give the story an intelligible rendering. All the remainder of this history, therefore, will be justly obnoxious to the suspicion of being in some small degree problematical ; nevertheless, it will be quite as reliable as histories in general, and much more so, we promise, than many of the writings of the most renowned historiographers of these times, who, it is well understood, seldom permit facts, particularly if they happen to be of an unwholesome nature, to stand in the way of an agreeable narration.

Writers of profane history—called profane on account of an irreverence for truth—are as likely to indulge in prevarication as other people, and much more likely than good, pious monks, who rarely do anything wrong, and who in this instance, at least, did all in their power to get at the exact meaning of the scroll, or rather at the ideas of Justino, the real author of the same, Manuelo himself, from whom was obtained the facts, being only an humble actor in the drama. To that kindhearted Dominican the world will be indebted from this time on for all that is known concerning Upper California at that remote period, though some little gratitude may possibly be due the humble translator for preparing so speedily this valuable volume for the printer. Its rendition in English, and good English at that, has been no mean task, and the duty has been interrupted by many serious misgivings. Hence, the world will never know the risk it has run of being left in the dark touching the events recorded.

Should this apology be satisfactory, we will proceed, without further delay, to narrate how exceedingly popular Manuelo found himself on his return with his little army of heroes from the war with the arrogant Dagos, and how, eventually, but unexpectedly, he became king of the Anglos in consequence. That he was inspired to both these movements—we mean the one against the Dagos, and the other towards the throne—more by his love for Alola than by any ambition of his own, there can be no question, for we have his personal authority for the statement that he was always controlled by the loftiest motives—a fact which has never been controverted. The authority in this case is precisely the same as that upon which rests the fame of Julius Cæsar, who also gave an account of his own exploits—and the one authority is certainly as good as the other. It may have been observed already that the expedition of our hero against the barbarous Dagos bears a striking similitude to that of the great Julius against the Helvetians, and this parallelism in the careers of the two personages is not by any means lost in subsequent events, though, of course, there can be no pretense that the rude Anglos were the equals of the enlightened Romans, nor that the political power of the one commander bore any comparison to that of the other. The chief difference springs from the circumstance of the one people being well acquainted with use of metals, while the other was wholly ignorant of their use; and, besides, there was some difference betwixt them in point of numbers, as candor compels us to admit, and in the extent of territory of the two nations also, though this is less certain. But that they were all human beings equally brave and inspired by similar motives, will always remain true, in spite of any apparent discrepancies that may be found in the histories of the two men and the two peoples.

The glory of Manuelo, as in the case of Cæsar, was shared by his wife, who was the recipient of almost as many congratulations from the grateful Anglos as were bestowed upon her noble husband. A princess herself by birth, it must be presumed that she enjoyed to the fullest extent the distinction so worthily won by Manuelo in the army, and if she was incited by a feeling of ambition, it ought not to be wondered at. These congratulations so worthily bestowed came not from her own sex alone, they were united in by the men as well, and men of all ranks and classes. The greetings of the bravest of the soldiers were so cordial as to amount almost to adoration, and though she was anxious to do so, for obvious reasons, hereafter to be mentioned, she could illy conceal her blushes. Possessing all the acumen of a true woman, Alola was not slow to perceive that the attentions shown to herself and Manuelo began to excite in the breast of the king a feeling of envy. His cruel treatment of his former wife, the inoffensive Red Berry, in the capital of the enemy, was regarded with horror by all of his good subjects (as well as by his guests), and very naturally led to a perceptible coldness on their part towards him, which he falsely attributed to their new-born esteem for Manuelo.

To make matters still worse, tyrant that he was, he became smitten with the beauty of the dark-eyed Alola, and conceived in his heart a purpose, most foul and wicked, of possessing her for his own. This fact, of course, first became known to the princess herself, and caused in her great trouble and trepidation of spirit. When reluctantly, at last, the cause of her sorrow was conveyed to her gallant husband, his indignation was aroused towards its author to the highest pitch, and his resentment was unbounded, or if bounded at all, it was by prudence. His first inclination was to leave, without delay, the dominions of so unjust a king, but the war with the Dagos, whose territory lay in that direction, forbade his continuing his journey to the southward, else he must have left, at once, with his beloved wife, the kind-hearted Anglos, and sought some more peaceful land, where would be less danger to their happiness, and where they could enjoy that domestic tranquillity to which they were so justly entitled. But there was now no escape for the lovers, except to retrace their steps towards the country from which they had fled, and that would be no less dangerous to their peace of mind than to remain where they were. Therefore they reluctantly chose the latter alternative, resolving to make the most of the situation. It required much exertion on the part of Manuelo to conceal his real feelings towards the wicked king, but he was put upon his guard, knowing that Mosoto would like nothing so well as a personal encounter, and realizing that, in all probability, he would seek to accomplish his nefarious designs by first depriving Alola of her husband, in some way or other. The king could see, as well as anybody, the strong attachment which existed between the wanderers, and he knew full well that it must be broken in some manner before he could accomplish anything. But he was reckoning without his guests, for Manuelo was an obstacle not easily to be removed, unless by violence, and both Manuelo and Alola were duly cautious not to give him an opportunity.

While a captive with the Modens, Manuelo had, as we know, some experience in setting on foot a public insurrection, and that experience stood him in excellent part at this time. Like Cæsar before him, he kept control of his military organization by the practice of drilling and exercising them almost daily. With great shrewdness he courted the favor of the army, by pleasant suggestions of one sort and another, until, as he believed, every man would have died for him had there been any real necessity for it.

In the meantime there was no neglect on his own part, or that of Alola and her intimate friends, to keep vividly before the minds of as many people as could safely be approached, a picture of the dreadful slaughter by the king of his lost wife. The matter was whispered throughout the city by thousands of trembling lips, and no one was found to justify the deed. This vindictive act of the revengeful tyrant was portrayed by Alola in all its repulsive enormity, and her womanly eloquence gathered tenfold more fire from the danger in her own situation, from this same identical person. She could but reflect that, as the poor unfortunate Red Berry had been, while with the Dagos, so she herself now was in a strange city, and how was she to know that the poor woman had not been held there by some attachment no less powerful than that which bound herself to Manuelo. This idea was strengthened in the mind of the thoughtful Alola by her reflection upon the fiendish character of Mosoto, who, she firmly believed, was never entitled to the affections of any good woman, and least of all to the love of Red Berry, who, she was assured, was a person of most gentle and loving disposition. Alola even suspected, though she was careful to express her misgivings to Manuelo alone, that the sorrowful Red Berry had not been captured by the Dagos at all, but had simply fled with some lover, and taken refuge from the anger of Mosoto, by resorting to the land of his enemies. Why otherwise, reasoned Alola, should he have killed her? Why otherwise should he have expressed no remorse? And how, she continued, could it be possible for him, if he were not a thoroughly bad man, to show such a fiendish disposition as to seek to destroy the domestic happiness of herself and Manuelo?

Father Justino, though not over-partial to the other sex, with a degree of candor that did himself infinite credit, conceded the force of Alola's argument, although, as he said, by way of vindication of his own disposition, it had no better support than the naked suspicion of a woman.

This bloody transaction engrossed the attention of the female portion of the Anglos population more than all the other occurrences of the war, and frequently bathed in tears were those who knew Mosoto's victim the best. As often as it was safe, maledictions were heaped upon the head of her destroyer, not only by Alola but by others of her friends. As a matter of course, these things were conducted in secret, and the chief, suspecting no evil, gradually grew bolder in his attentions to Alola, until, at last, his conduct became unbearable. If it was annoying to Alola, it was still more so to her faithful husband, who could illy brook any indignity shown to his loving wife.

But Mosoto being, as already recorded, a powerful man in battle, and possessed of great physical strength, Manuelo was no match for him in that regard, and this the king well knew. Relying then on his herculean power, he sought on more than one occasion to provoke a personal conflict, but Manuelo knew his despotic purpose too well to accede hastily to his wishes. It was with much difficulty sometimes, however, that Manuelo could restrain himself from gratifying his rival in just the manner he desired. He was, in fact, so strongly incited to a personal encounter that he was only dissuaded from it by the incessant prayers and tears of his tender bride, who was at times fairly overcome with fear lest his impetuous nature, which she well understood, should lead her husband into a rash conflict with his royal adversary. His anger fairly rendered Manuelo regardless of consequences, so far as himself was concerned, but from his better judgment warning came that in case of disaster the result would be fearful, indeed, to her whom he loved, and the conflict in his mind between the two passions of affection and revenge was something terrific.

As a matter of fact, the life of Alola was so entirely wrapped up in his own that were he to be slain she would at once have committed suicide. This Manuelo was given plainly to understand, and it had a controlling influence upon his conduct under these most trying circumstances.

Thus deterred, not by his own fears, but by the fears and importunities of another, he was constrained to listen to advice, which he knew was more to be relied upon than would have been that of a person not in sympathy with him.

In this he was more fortunate than most men similarly situated, for counsel in such cases usually comes from persons who would see another's honor vindicated at the cost of his life, and who scruple not thus in their zeal to heap injury upon insult. Manuelo believed, as he said to Justino, that he could have compassed the death of his adversary in a quiet manner, since others were ready to aid him, but he disdained a resort to so unmanly a method of relieving himself from annoyance, and it made no difference in his determination that he could not count upon equal magnanimity on the part of his rival.

Both himself and Alola were in perpetual fear lest some undue advantage should be taken of him by the king, for they knew full well his treacherous and blood-thirsty nature, and there was abundant reason to apprehend an exhibition of it at any unguarded moment.

Manuelo remembered some examples in history of similar arrogance on the part of great men, which he ventured to relate to his wife, and notably that of the renowned Henry

VIII., king of Great Britain and Ireland, who still at that time may have been upon the throne, and enjoying the society of a wife of one of his murdered subjects. By much contemplation of these matters the peace of mind of Manuelo, as well as that of Alola, was eventually wholly destroyed. They were fast becoming convinced that affairs were approaching a crisis when delay would be entirely incompatible with safety. They wisely concluded that something must be done, and that speedily, or worse would follow. Manuelo himself was too good a general to be caught napping, and a better subaltern adviser no commander ever had than the bright-eyed and keen-witted Alóla.

During all the time we have been speaking about, Manuelo was diligently drilling his compact little army, with the ostensible purpose of undertaking another foreign war, and it was observed that, on several occasions, jealousy cropped out on the part of the king in reference to the chief command on future expeditions. This feeling Manuelo was at no pains to quiet; on the contrary, it was rather encouraged by him. He even sought an occasion for an open *emeute*, which was not long in coming.

The national forces, well armed and equipped, were purposely led out on the plain one autumn day by the doughty Manuelo, when the arrogant Mosoto, presuming upon his civil rank, sought to take charge of them, and to give forth his commands. This movement of the king was promptly resisted by Manuelo, and a difficulty at once arose on the field. Mosoto, incited by a terrible rage, advanced with some haste upon Manuelo, and would have stricken him down on the spot, or at least made the attempt, had not Manuelo, observing his actions, with great presence of mind appealed to his faithful soldiers for protection, who sprang to his rescue like so many lions, and the king was by force resisted.

A counter appeal was then made to the men by the angry

Mosoto, but all in vain. Manuelo, with military promptness, now rallied the army in a short speech, and almost to a man they sided with him. Inspired by the personal courage of a general who had led them to victory against the formidable Dagos, they no longer feared their king, powerful in person though he was, but would then and there, in large numbers, have set upon him with their ready weapons, and put an end to his miserable existence, had they been permitted to do so. But the generous Manuelo restrained them by his words, and kept their impetuosity in abeyance until their indignation had time to subside, for he was now no longer in fear of his rival, and did not wish to subject himself to the ungracious charge of regicide.

The stalwart king, or rather Mosoto, for he was from that hour no longer king, seeing himself deserted by his soldiers, and alone, turned upon his heel and fled towards the mountains. He was brave by nature, none more so, but conscience had made a coward of him, and he took himself away as fast as his legs would carry him. Pursued by the jeers and derision of his late subjects, he relaxed not his pace until his giant figure was reduced by distance to the dimensions of a mere pigmy.

The triumph of Manuelo was most marked, and in about half the time it takes to relate the circumstance, he was proclaimed king by the shouts of his gallant little army. Theretofore it had been his custom to march his men, but this time they marched him back into the city, and it would have puzzled any mere spectator to say whether the victory that had been achieved belonged the more to Manuelo or to his followers. The truth may be, and probably was, that it pertained to both, and in just about equal proportions to each. The one was rid of a rival, and the others of a tyrant, and their congratulations were mutual.

The news of the elevation of Manuelo spread with wonderful

rapidity throughout all the country of the Anglos, and so happy were the people to be rid of the despotic Mosoto that a great feast was proclaimed and presently inaugurated in honor of the event. In a week's time nearly all the residents of the several tribes and villages of the nation were gathered in at the capital to give expression to their joy. Such a man as Manuelo before him had never been seen in that country, and one and all looked upon him as a being sent from Heaven to rule over them. Lacking positive information on the point, Justino was half inclined to the belief that the proud Manuelo made no effort whatever to dispel that delusion, and that he continued to reign, in the opinion of his subjects, by right divine.

Never was monarch more popular with his people, and never was one more deservedly so. But what shall we say of Alola? Here we are compelled again to abandon the subject to the imagination of the reader, for language is wholly inadequate to depict her happiness. Her affection for Manuelo had been fully vindicated. A poor fugitive from her home and native country, and a renegade from her distinguished relatives, she had been transformed by the prowess of her chosen lord into the most prominent person in the land.

Queen was she now of the Anglos, a people at that day given to all manner of kindness, and possessing a country unexampled in beauty. It is a mild expression to say that she was fairly worshiped by all the vast assemblage at that great feast. Woman-like, her first impulse was to make known her good fortune to those from whom she had fled, but that was not practicable just then; however, the fact became known to them, without her agency, all too soon for her happiness, as will be seen further along in this history.

Alola contented herself for the present by redoubling her demonstrations of love towards Manuelo, who as cordially reciprocated the same. He did not forget that he owed his elevation indirectly to the fascinations of his charming wife, and the greatest pleasure he found was in her adoration.

LXXI.
MANUELO AS KING.

IT seems very remarkable that so observing a person as Manuelo, who was now fairly installed as king of the Anglos, and who had been successful in wars, at least with the Dagos, and who doubtless was equally so in other respects, should have failed to give an extended insight into his civil administration, or even to describe with any degree of accuracy his public policy. Yet such is the fact. He neglected to do it, unless, indeed, the fault be Justino's, for the manuscript contained almost no account of his management of the affairs of state, so to speak, while presiding over the destinies of that splendid people. It is barely possible there may have been design in all this, and that the course pursued by them was the subject of deliberation. It is not altogether unlikely that both Manuelo and Justino realized that it was the uniform practice of historians, both ancient and modern, to speak only of wars, contentions, conquests, and the like, and to leave civil government and the piping times of peace to take care of themselves, or to be taken care of by the writers of fiction alone.

If such be the solution of this apparent negligence, they certainly had the example before them of the great Julius himself, who, while both actor and narrator of the stirring events of his time, confined his history to wars and conquests, to the neglect of his civil administration, which some might contend was no less glorious. Peace, it has been said, hath its triumphs no less renowned than war; but if such belonged to the peaceful portion of Manuelo's government, they are now irretrievably lost to the world. We may nevertheless congratulate ourselves that all is not lost. Much pertaining to that distinguished character and his remarkable people we certainly have left us. Thanks to the far-seeing young priests of Evora, some of the salient points of King Manuelo's rule have been preserved—rescued as it were from the lethean shades—and among these is considerable that related to his foreign troubles, which, as the world goes, are after all the most interesting. About these, therefore, we proceed to speak, but in the modest terms transmitted through this Portuguese channel.

The festivities consequent upon the enthronement of the white man and his interesting bride lasted several days, and until the hilarious Anglos were fairly exhausted with merry-making. Feasting and dancing and all sorts of games were indulged in to excess, and the newly-endowed royal personages were heartily glad, at last, to see an end of the dissipation. Attention was now to be turned to more serious matters. The public business must be looked after with care. The new chief felt the full responsibility of his exalted position, and he was not the man to be found derelict in duty. Gratitude was one of the liveliest sentiments of his nature, and he resolved from the first to render, in his public acts, a full equivalent to this generous people for their kindness to himself and Alola.

In that country then, as later, there was almost perpetual summer, and not much necessity therefore existed for that providence which has to be exercised in more rigorous climates, but Manuelo, nevertheless, required his people to keep always on hand an ample supply of wholesome food, as they might need; and, likewise, an abundant store of peltry for clothing. To accomplish these desirable ends the necessity was involved of frequent hunting and fishing excursions by the people.

Distant expeditions, also, to the mountains and hills in quest of wild fruits, berries, and nuts of various kinds, in their season, were frequently set on foot. In this way the people were always prepared against a possible drought, and there was never the least fear of a famine among them. In case of a war, in like manner, they would be ready to march on short notice, and be able to avoid the accustomed delay on occasions of the kind.

Everything that Manuelo needed for his own convenience, or that of his household, was gratuitously supplied in large quantity by his devoted subjects, and his principal occupation, when engaged at all, related to foreign affairs. There was no longer, on his part, nor on the part of his people, any fear of the troublesome Dagos, for they had been thoroughly quelled in the last campaign. But off to the eastward a nation existed, more distant by far than the Dagos. Though not particularly hostile, these people were in the constant habit, and had been for years, of encroaching upon the dominions of the good Anglos, for the purpose of hunting and foraging. A sort of predatory tribe they were, from a wide desert country that lay in the direction mentioned, no one knew exactly how far away. From the description given of these people they must have partaken largely of the nature of Arabs; but they were called the Movos. Little could be learned concerning them from captives, since their language differed radically from that of the Anglos and the other nations to the north. Besides, they appeared to be, on the whole, a sullen, silent set of scamps, and disdained when interrogated, as prisoners were, to enlighten Manuelo as to their strength, or as to the extent of their territory.

LXXII.

AGAINST THE MOVOS.

AFTER suffering no inconsiderable annoyance from these inhabitants of the desert, as they were supposed to be, Manuelo determined at last to chastise them, in a military sense, and, possibly, to subjugate them to his rule. His well-disciplined army of veterans had long been unemployed and naturally thirsted for conquest, so that when an expedition against these Arabs of the desert, as they might be termed, was first suggested to the soldiers it was met with a ready response, and preparations for war were made after the manner of those times, but without the accustomed delay. At Manuelo's suggestion Alola was to be left in possession of the government at home during his absence, an arrangement that was quite as satisfactory to the people as to herself.

Not calculating on a lengthy campaign, or one of much difficulty, little ceremony was observed on the setting out of the army, but they were admirably equipped and provided, and were all in most excellent spirits. The forces thus ready, in every respect, and numbering some eight hundred effective men, their commander-in-chief, the gallant Manuelo, one clear morning in early summer, while the larks were yet singing, led them forth from the city and proudly took up his line of march towards the country of the predatory Movos.

The march was uninterrupted and eventless, so far as reported, until they came upon the broad desert, but there Manuelo unexpectedly encountered, in the barren waste itself, a more formidable adversary than any number of fighting men could have been, but he was by no means discouraged, nor did he suffer his men to become so.

The tiresome tramp, through sand and dust, sand under foot and dust in the air, was continued for weeks without finding any other enemy than the parched waste, and until their stock of provisions began to run low. The general-in-chief realized to the fullest extent the necessity of finding an enemy upon whom to forage for supplies, and he courageously kept on his course. About this time, and when almost in despair, the little army, begrimed with dust, foot-sore, and hungry, came up to a large river, along the borders of which many villages were observed to be strewn, and the evidences were abundant of a large population. These villages had been recently deserted, and not a human being was to be seen moving in any one of them.

But upon the opposite bank of the stream numerous warriors, decked in bright martial paint and with waving plumes, were assembled, prepared, as it appeared, to dispute the passage. These things were viewed from the bluffs a little way back from the river by Manuelo, with mingled feelings of satisfaction and consternation—satisfaction at seeing a prospect of appeasing the hunger of his brave men, and consternation at beholding the evidences of a probable controversy over the gratification of their appetites. His forces, all told, had been no more than eight hundred men at the start, but the number of efficient soldiers was now considerably reduced by the long march through a barren country, and even those who were still able to keep their places in the ranks were greatly diminished in strength and efficiency by continued hunger and thirst. The warriors of Scipio, after a long forced march over the hot sands of Africa, were in a better condition than Manuelo's at this moment, and the Carthagenians were much more accessible to the Romans than were the Movos to the Anglos.

Without delay, and impelled by their necessities, the latter eagerly rushed down into the vacated villages on the hither side of the stream, hoping to find wherewithal to satisfy their appetites; but the cunning Movos had taken the precaution, on the approach of the invader, to destroy, or remove to the opposite shore, everything that could in the least supply their wants, and the disappointment of Manuelo and his men can better be imagined than described. They were in such a dilemma as had never beset them before. The enemy on the further bank outnumbered them apparently by thousands, but this disparity in numbers perplexed them less than how they should cross the wide and rapidly flowing river. There was some wasting of arrows on both sides, for firing across was at too long a range to be effectual, and Manuelo, in his strait, essayed negotiations, but in vain. His men had already given too many demonstrations of a hostile purpose to deceive the wary Movos, who felt secure in the advantage of their position, and kept close watch over the movements of the enemy. It was presently seen by the sagacious Manuelo that he must somehow or other make the passage of the stream, otherwise many of his noble warriors would miserably perish, and long before they could retrace their weary steps across the wide desert. He therefore determined to attempt the transit at all hazards. He felt most unbounded confidence in the new and superior armament of his men, and still more in their bravery and skill.

Hungry and exhausted as they were, he believed they could hold their own and make headway, too, against any number of the timorous foe, could they but once set foot on the opposite shore. Casting about in this emergency, he observed in the village already in his possession, and scattered along the river bottom, above and below, an abundance of timber of the cotton-wood species, and he determined, as soon as the night should shut down its curtain, to construct as many rafts as the time would allow, and on these to cross the river, if possible, before the break of day. This plan was made known to his men, but all signs of the contemplated movement were carefully concealed from the overconfident enemy. Accordingly, when darkness had completely covered the earth, and the Movos, as was supposed, had retired to rest for the night, the little army of heroes, as one man, silently and cautiously, and for the time forgetting their hunger and hardships, set about the construction of rafts, working in squads of fives and sixes upon each craft.

Some time before the dawn of day, all being in readiness, at a given signal the rafts were pushed into the rapidly moving current, and, loaded with men, were hopefully pulled in line for the opposite bank of the river. A landing was effected on the other side some distance below the principal camp of the Movos, but not without annoyance, for the alarm was given while they were yet in the middle of the stream, and the enemy, in vast numbers, came rushing down to repel the advance. But the place of landing had been well chosen, and Manuelo and his men, protected by their shields, sprang ashore and stood their ground with heroic firmness.

The battle on the strand was waged with terrible fury, until the morning light showing the way, an advance was ordered by the general, and the vast forces of the Movos were put to rout with great slaughter. The desperate Anglos followed up their victory with rapid steps, and soon had possession of the enemy's camp, with all his stores.

The casualties of this hard-fought field on either side are not given, but they were infinitely greater on the part of the Movos than on the Anglos' side, not to mention the loss sustained by the former of their villages and all their supplies. The Movos had not calculated upon the passage of the river as among the things possible, and had taken no pains to remove their stores and munitions of war back from the water's edge. Even their women and children were left reposing in conscious security on that side, but the good Manuelo, anticipating all this, had given the strictest command to his soldiers not to visit revenge upon these helpless classes, but to turn their weapons against the men alone.

Most of the cowardly and predatory warriors of the Movos, when they found themselves beaten, fled precipitately to the hills, for they could make no stand against their better armed, more stalwart, and more skillfully commanded antagonists.

Manuelo without unnecessary delay brought over, in the boats of the enemy, which he found moored in numbers on the left bank of the river, his hungry reserves and likewise the enfeebled, who had been left in charge of his own camp.

Notwithstanding the efforts of the Movos to escape, many prisoners were taken with arms in their hands, and these were put to work at once in burying the dead and caring for the wounded. Owing to their reduced and weakened condition, no less than to the desperation of the Movos, who were contending for their homes and firesides, quite a number of the brave invaders were made to bite the dust.*

Keeping possession of their principal villages, and retaining in his custody many of their women and children as hostages, for greater security against a secret attack of these barbarians, Manuelo recruited his attenuated forces as rapidly as he possibly could, preparatory to a return to his own country. The campaign had been much more difficult and disastrous than had been anticipated by anyone, and it adds another to the many warnings to ambitious monarchs, to undertake no war without adequate provocation, nor to pursue a people for the mere purpose of gratifying a thirst for conquest. The best disciplined of armies, under the most skillful of leaders, is liable to fall into dangers, particularly when it has to contend against the forces of nature, which, when arrayed against man, are a more unrelenting enemy than his fellow-creatures can possibly be. Deserts, forests, rivers, and storms have before now broken the spirit of the proudest military organizations, and subdued generals whose genius rendered them invincible to arms. It so happens in human affairs that a sense of justice, which nature herself is very apt to display, often comes to the aid of the weak against the strong, and overwhelms the arrogant oppressor. Mankind is thus admonished, and on most unexpected occasions, says Justino, to avoid the perpetration of wrong, for it was the firm belief of that good friar that any injustice, by whomsoever committed, will be visited, sooner or later, with merited punishment; if not in this world, certainly in the next.

---

*Precisely what is meant by this expression so often used by other historians, or how it arose, we are unable to say; but as it appears in the narrative, so we are constrained to give it in the translation. But as for Manuelo's men, they had been eating nothing but dust for days past.

LXXIII.

RETURNING HOME.

BUT the disaster to Manuelo and his gallant little army on this occasion was not so very great but that in a few days they were sufficiently recruited to set out on their homeward march, and it was resolved by the commander, for reasons that need not be explained, to return by some other route than the one by which they had come. Taking in an ample supply of provisions and carrying along with him a few men and women, still as hostages, Manuelo dropped down the river with his command, some in boats, but most marching by land near the water, intending to make a more southerly and circuitous route back to his home. But the treacherous Movos getting wind of his intentions, posted themselves in secure places on the bluffs along the line of his march, and harassed his men with their arrows and javelins almost every step of the way. As the Anglos advanced, the number of the enemy increased every day, for the Movos had sent information of the invasion to the Macops, the Umos, and other friendly tribes further down the river, and they too were gathering in front in overwhelming numbers to intercept Manuelo and cut off his retreat. Seeing this danger, the wily leader of the Anglos, on the fourth or fifth day, crossed over all his forces to the right bank, abandoned his boats, and struck off to the westward. The route now lay just to the south, but near the margin of a salt lake many leagues in extent, but which recent geographers have been utterly unable to find. That it must have existed at that time there can be no doubt, else how can its mention be accounted for? Barring so much of the route as lay by this lake, and after abandoning the same, their course was over a desert country, even more repellant, if possible, than that which had been traversed on their outward march. Still the enemy, now recruited to an immense force, hung upon their flanks and rear like a swarm of enraged bees fresh from a disturbed hive. Being of a predatory nature, they were more at home on the desert, and annoyed the Anglos in every possible way, but could not be brought by any device to give battle. This uncomfortable worry was kept up with unabated zeal by the combined foe, giving the retreating army no rest night or day, until at last, happily, a range of mountains was reached, where, selecting a secure locality and fortifying their camp, Manuelo and his men rested in comparative quiet for three days. But the Movos prisoners, in the long and hurried retreat, had all made their escape, and the Anglos, thus deprived of their only trophies, and less accustomed to being pursued than to pursuing, were somewhat crest-fallen if not dispirited. They had been delighted, however, to see the enemy diminishing in numbers, day by day, as they receded from their homes, and when the mountains were finally reached, the pursuers presented more the appearance of straggling parties than of a well-organized army.

It was evident that the strength of the Movos, and of their allies, was not in their personal prowess at all, but in the barren and desolate character of the country they occupied, and their method of warfare was to annoy and harass an enemy by raids and dashes and by night attacks. They were no match for the well-armed and thoroughly disciplined troops of Manuelo, in an open and manly warfare, and, fortunately for themselves, they were too shrewd to risk a battle with him.

But a new and unexpected danger now confronted the Anglos. They were again in the country of their ancient enemy, the Dagos. These mountains, or rather the desert that lay at the foot of them, constituted the eastern boundary of the Dagos territory, and the little army of the Anglos was liable to encounter their opposition at any moment. Manuelo half suspected that the wide-awake Dago chiefs, having seen the immense advantage of the new and superior armament of the Anglos, would fall to imitating the same and be able to meet him on another occasion on more equal terms. He was therefore exceedingly anxious to avoid a collision with them at this time, and at all events until his men could recover from their late disasters. Accordingly he wasted no time in leading his army through the passes of the mountains in a northwesterly direction, where, as best he could calculate, lay their homes, and where he had left his loved and loving Alola, whom he had long been most anxious to see. But he had not miscalculated the danger of the situation. Swift runners of the Movos, or of their nearer neighbors, the Umos, had borne intelligence of his movements to the sleepless Dago king, and he, hastily gathering an army of his faithful subjects, was moving with alacrity to intercept Manuelo's retreat. The last camp of the Anglos before emerging from the territory of the Dagos, was pitched at night in a narrow valley near some warm springs, shut in by high and impassable mountains on either side. Here they rested in security, as they supposed, and were apparently in a fair way of reaching their homes within the next three or four days. But alas for the foresight of man! How little did they know what was before them! Awaking right early on the following morning they were more than surprised—they were horrified—to behold in their front, ready to dispute their further passage, a large army of the dreaded Dagos, evidently much better prepared for a fight than they ever had been before. Retreat was not practicable for the Anglos, in fact they were retreating from the Movos and their allies at this very time, and, besides, they were too anxious to reach their homes to think of turning back. Manuelo took the situation in at a glance and determined upon his course. In a stirring speech he rallied his men with the hope of soon seeing their homes and again greeting their wives and children, and then, drawing them up in order of battle, prepared for the desperate charge. Before the forward movement was ordered, he reminded them of their previous triumphs over this same treacherous foe, and assured them that they had only to stand firmly by each other, and preserve their ranks unbroken, to achieve a victory, no less glorious than the former one, over that same hated race. So forcible and eloquent was his appeal that the men even rejoiced that they had once again an enemy before them whom they could meet face to face, the only opportunity, in fact, of the kind they had enjoyed in the whole campaign, unless we except the fight in the night on the strand. Manuelo's forces being now inspired with unwonted courage, he watched, with eagle eye, the arrival of a favorable opportunity, and then, with one tremendous whoop, in which all the army joined, he ordered a charge. The Dagos, relying too much upon their greatly superior numbers, and being less skillfully commanded than their adversaries, were taken a little at unawares by the impetuosity of the attack, but they were most surprised by the unexampled daring of so small a force.

Manuelo and his intrepid warriors, in solid phalanx and with long-continued yells, pressed forward like a band of heroes, as they were, and presently struck the center of the enemy's line with consternation. Seeing the middle and strongest part give back, each wing of the Dagos forces, in succession, yielded likewise, and a rout ensued. The affair may be compared to a band of wolves attacking a large herd of sheep and scattering them helpless in every direction, filling even their shepherd with dismay. No victory was ever more complete or gallantly won. The celebrated charge of the Hebrews upon the Philistines could not have excelled it in bravery. It was the crowning event of the whole campaign, which would have been none too brilliant without it, but which now shone with transcendent luster. If the general of the Anglos had lost, in any degree, his standing with his troops by reason of what had transpired of a disagreeable nature, since they left their homes, it was now entirely recovered. He was never so much of a hero as at this time. Again was he worshiped by his soldiers, and his praises were upon every tongue. Not waiting for further laudations, nor wishing to enjoy them alone, Manuelo continued his march without more interruption, and on the fourth day after the battle of the Warm Springs, the little army, weary and worn with the toils of war, but full of courage, entered the city of the Anglos, where they were greeted with the joyous acclaims of all the people.

LXXIV.

MOSOTO'S WAR.

THE arrival of Manuelo at home was not a moment too soon, for the wicked and desperate Mosoto, when driven from his own country, had gone to the North among the Barbos, and there, by the most foul misrepresentations, had stirred up a feeling against his former subjects, and particularly against his successor. Having treacherously won his way into the confidence of that people, he had armed and disciplined them after the exact manner taught him by Manuelo, and, with the approval of all the Barbos chiefs, was actually leading an army of that nation against the Anglos. Information of this movement had reached the ears of Alola while in possession of the government, and ruling alone, and caused her the greatest imaginable distress of mind. She hoped and prayed for the return of her long-absent husband in time to avert, if possible, the impending danger, but the worst results were feared. Brave woman that she was, and being at the head of affairs in the absence of Manuelo, she set about with the utmost diligence the business of arming, equipping, and disciplining all the men, young and old, yet remaining in the land; and when Manuelo returned from his Eastern expedition he found an army, a sort of home guard, already well organized, and much stronger, in point of numbers, than the one he had led against the Movos. With this force, so fortunately and with so much forethought provided in his absence by the fair young queen, added to his own little army of veterans, he had not much fear of the meddlesome Barbos, though led by so powerful an enemy as Mosoto himself. In fact the ex-king was most to be dreaded for his individual prowess, and it was on account of that, mainly, that he had won the confidence of his new allies. He had, moreover, represented to them Manuelo in the worst possible light, describing him as a traitor, an ingrate, usurper, and as altogether a most dangerous man. He concealed from them the fact of his own unholy passion for Alola, but assured the suspicious Barbos that Manuelo and his wife had been among them as spies, to find out their weak points, intending to subjugate, and, if need be, to annihilate them; that Manuelo was planning and preparing a military expedition against their country, and that the only way to head him off was to carry the war into Africa, so to speak. With apparent magnanimity he proffered his own powerful services to crush out so dangerous a neighbor, and the simple Barbos were but too glad to accept his offer.

Alola, with remarkable sagacity, had kept informed, by means of scouts and heralds, of the movements of her dreaded enemy, and had fully made up her mind, though nothing but a tender woman, to take personal command of her improvised army, meet Mosoto in some mountain pass, and hold him at bay, or possibly drive him back. She well understood that his principal object was to gain possession of her person—a thing that she more abhorred than any other earthly calamity that could happen.

Much time had elapsed since her royal husband had set out on his campaign against the people of the desert, and not hearing from him, she greatly feared some dire calamity might have befallen his little army, himself included, and she firmly resolved, in her own mind, to repel the advance of her tormentor, or perish in the attempt. The plans of the brave little woman were all laid with care, and she was preparing with diligence to execute them, when she was happily interrupted by the sudden appearance at the capital of her husband. Justino, the considerate author, almost regretted, he said, that Manuelo had not remained away a little longer, in order that the world might have had one more instance added to the many examples of female heroism recorded in history. The good friar was certain that had she been permitted to go ahead, as she intended, Alola would have put to rout and driven back the wicked Mosoto, and would thus have acquired another, and most brilliant gem, with which to adorn the crown of her many virtues.

He remembered the history, not long then past, of the wonderfully inspired Joan of Arc, and he doubted little that the marvelous heroism of that young French woman would have found a parallel in that of the equally youthful Alola. But he trembled when he reflected that her fate might possibly have been that of the more renowned Queen of Palmyra, who was led away captive and made to grace the triumphal procession of her cruel enemy. The case of the royal Zenobia, to be sure, as compared with Alola's, was, strictly speaking, hypothetical, nevertheless the kind-hearted friar could but observe the remarkable similarity in the careers of the two persons, at least up to this time, and his apprehensions for the future of Alola were most naturally aroused. Turning the matter over in his own mind, there arose before his distempered vision, the history, then unwritten, of his own noble queen, the great Isabella of Castile—for he was now in a Spanish province—and he was, at times, enthusiastic enough to believe that as Isabella, by her incomparable genius, united under one crown the two kingdoms of Aragon and Castile, so Alola, had there been no interruption, might have joined under her single scepter the kingdoms of the Anglos and the Barbos. But something may have to be set down, in this free translation, to the monkish partiality of this Dominican friar. In his overwrought view of the affair, it is probable that womankind, as represented in the character of Alola, was enveloped with some sort of a halo, and that possibly her brilliancy, like that of the stars, was augmented by distance. It is not to be denied, however, that women, under certain circumstances, display even more real resolution than is exhibited by those who are called the sterner sex; but, as well remarked by Justino, it is in their own, and not in manly virtues, as a general rule, that women excel.

While congratulations on account of the return of Manuelo and his army from the east were being freely exchanged in the city, matters were rapidly approaching a crisis at the north. Mosoto, already within the territory of the Anglos with his well-ordered army, showed no disposition to await the convenience of either Manuelo or his royal wife, but was advancing by regular marches towards their capital. To avoid the desert country he was coming by a route nearer the sea, and through a region exceedingly mountainous and broken, so that his progress, with the numerous army under his command, was almost as slow as could have been desired by Manuelo; nevertheless, Mosoto would be, in a few days longer, should he not be intercepted, in a position to menace some of the largest towns and cities of the Anglos. Another object of the wary Mosoto in adhering to the mountainous country was, doubtless, to avoid the danger of a surprise, and perchance to enable himself the better to protect his soldiers, and his own person, in case of disaster.

It is thought to have been impossible that he could have known anything whatever about the invasion of Italy by Hannibal, but his tactics were the same in every particular as those put in practice by the great Carthagenian general, when approaching the imperial city.

The mountains and hills among which Mosoto was now hovering constituted an endless succession of strong natural fortifications, some of which were actually impregnable. From these, even with a much inferior force, he could, like Hannibal, sally forth at pleasure, and annoy his enemy beyond endurance. As Hannibal before him threatened Rome from his mountain fastnesses, so Mosoto was already threatening the capital of the Anglos, over which he had once been the unrestrained sovereign.

The mutilated manuscript also contained something in this connection about Coriolanus, a Roman general of distinction, who, having been banished from his native city, went off and joined his old enemies, the Volci, and revengefully led an army of them against his ungrateful countrymen, beleaguering Rome and compelling its inhabitants to sue for peace. But the remainder stated in the scroll about this character could not be made out with sufficient distinctness, and was omitted by the young Portuguese priests, as not particularly illustrative of the present case, inasmuch as it is related that both the wife and the mother of Coriolanus successfully joined their importunities with those of other citizens of Rome, for him to spare the city, whereas nothing of this kind could possibly have occurred in the case of Mosoto, who was not only motherless, but whose wife disliked him intensely.

Delaying but a few days to recruit his veteran soldiery, for there was little time now to devote to that purpose, Manuelo gathered all his forces together, from every part of the kingdom, and set out, with his best warriors in the advance, to meet this new adversary. He selected a route more inland than the one by which the Barbos were approaching, with a view to getting in their rear, or at least upon their flank, and so force from the bloody Mosoto a battle. The Anglos had been out but four days when suddenly the advance guard came upon a scouting party of the enemy, and at once drove them back. The pursuit was eager, but the enemy, retreating, were soon securely ensconced in the fastnesses of the mountains, and Manuelo's men were compelled to desist. What the general of the Anglos most desired was to bring on a battle without delay, but the cunning Mosoto knew too well the power of his opponent as a military commander to risk an engagement upon anything like equal terms, and he adhered with his usual tenacity to the mountains. He was ever on the lookout to take his antagonist at some disadvantage; but Manuelo was too shrewd a general to be caught napping by one whom he hated with so much cordiality as he did his predecessor in office and rival.

Occasionally parties of the Barbos would sally out to harass and bother their enemies, but on all such raids they were made glad to hunt their retreat, as wolves are glad to seek their holes when pursued by a pack of blood-hounds. In this manner valuable time was being wasted, while simultaneously, the patience of Manuelo's men, who had seen too much of war of late to be content without fighting, was becoming seriously impaired, and he saw plainly the necessity of bringing things to a crisis without much further delay. But how to do this was the question.

To force a general engagement, under the circumstances, required the exercise of some sort of strategy, as he could distinctly see, and his genius, as ever, was equal to the emergency. Selecting out from his army the oldest and youngest, the most inefficient portion of his men, he put them under the command of his most trustworthy subordinate, one Warno by name, and directed him to take possession of and guard the mountain passes in front of Mosoto. Warno was instructed to obstruct and resist in every possible manner the progress of Mosoto towards the Anglos country, should he attempt to continue on his course in that direction, but by all means to keep open a safe line of retreat for his command, in case the formidable Mosoto should prove too powerful for him. Warno thus admonished and directed, Manuelo, with the main body and better portion of the Anglos army, took up his line of march directly back upon the track of the Barbos, as if he would invade their country, but marched slowly. Seeing, from their lofty places of lookout, this threatening movement of the larger part of the Anglos forces, the Barbos soldiers, as Manuelo had anticipated, became alarmed for their homes, and clamored to be led back to the defense of their families and firesides. The ruse had the desired effect; Mosoto could not resist the demand of his men, and, in some disorder, they followed upon the heels of the Anglos, moving towards their own country. At a favorable point, while the simple Barbos, with the sulky Mosoto in their midst, were crossing a valley of some little extent, Manuelo, like a lion pursued, looking back over his shoulders at his pursuers, suddenly turned upon them and forced an engagement, when the Barbos were least expecting it. The commanders of the two armies, Mosoto and Manuelo, now rallied their forces respectively in short but energetic speeches, and in a few moments the fight became general. There was no particular advantage of ground for either, but, if any, it was on the side of the Anglos, who had a little the more elevated position. Both parties contended with stubborn bravery, and for a time the issue seemed doubtful, as the Barbos were much the superior in point of numbers. Their missiles, for they were well armed, filled the air, falling like hail upon the shields and bucklers of the noble Anglos, and were by them returned with fearful execution. The battle had not progressed long before it became apparent that the strength of the Barbos was mainly in their tall and stalwart leader, who was making terrible havoc among his former subjects, most of whom were known to him, and who (that is, Mosoto) presently manifested a clear determination to force a personal conflict with his hated rival. Manuelo, seeing this purpose, would gladly have avoided the encounter, for he was no match for him in physical strength;

but to avoid it was no longer possible. Well armed himself, and supported by a little squad of his best-equipped followers, Manuelo coolly awaited the onslaught of his exasperated foe, who was coming down upon him with dreadful impetuosity. When Mosoto was at a convenient distance, but still rushing on with uplifted spear, conscious of his own prowess, and fearing no danger, or not fearing it much, Manuelo, with the speed of thought, hurled his well-poised javelin full in his face, the weapon taking effect in the left eye of Mosoto, causing him suddenly to halt; and, spinning about twice on his right heel, he fell to the ground with a terrible thud. So heavy was the fall, declared Manuelo, with some apparent seriousness, that had the cause of the tremor not been known, it might have been mistaken for the slight shock of an earthquake. Seeing this great giant prostrate, Manuelo's men bravely rushed upon him, and, with uplifted spears and stone hatchets, speedily put an end to what little remained of his miserable existence.

Manuelo, the victor, like David before him, stood proudly erect, and would magnanimously have restrained his men from mutilating a fallen foe had it been possible; but time did not suffice, for sooner than one could think about the matter the thing was done, and the poor slaughtered wife of the wicked Mosoto was avenged.

Observing the complete vanquishment of their leader, the Barbos, stricken with dismay, precipitately fled. The pursuit was not long continued, but the affrighted enemy halted not in their flight unless to rest for the night, until they had entered their distant homes.

The indignation of the kind Anglos, and of Manuelo, was less roused against these simple Barbos than it had been towards the author of the war, the cruel Mosoto, and he being now out of the way they would gladly have buried the hatchet with his dupes, had they but asked for a performance of that ceremony.

The damage resulting from the invasion extended to the sacking of some small fishing settlements of the Anglos in a remote part of the kingdom. The victorious portion of the army, joined by the reserves under Warno, now all again under the lead of Manuelo, made their way back by easy marches to the capital, where again he and his soldiers received expressions of the profoundest gratitude from all the populace.

Manuelo's renown as a great military leader, and likewise his fame as a just king, spread beyond his own borders, and his reputation was such as to insure peace for his own dominions with all who heard of his mighty achievements. His great successes up to this time, as a prince, a prophet, and a warrior, had been far in advance of any hope or expectation entertained of him, but his talents were now, for the immediate future, to be put to the severer test of conducting with equal success the peaceful affairs of his people. The good fortune that had presided over his destinies hitherto was not disposed, as we shall see, to jilt him now, when at the top of his fame, as it might have done a person of less natural parts.

Genius, whatever that may be, thought the matter-of-fact Justinn, is the offspring of courage and application. It is not, said he, a gift at all; it is an achievement. If it were among the bounties of Providence, there would be no merit in it, and in that case the man of genius would be entitled to no special praise for whatever he might accomplish. The fact, he argued, that mankind are disposed to bestow their laudations upon the possessor of true genius is proof conclusive that in their estimation, at least, the accomplishments of the great men of the world are the result of labor and perseverance, and not in the mere hap-hazard of the original making up of the individual. He held, moreover, that the display of extraordinary talents in any particular line of action, depended less upon opportunity than upon the force of will in the person. As may be concluded from this dissertation, Manuelo lost none of the credit to which he was entitled, by the inane sentimentality of his historian. On the contrary, Justino awarded him all the commendation, which, from his native goodness and laudable ambition, justly belonged to him. But fame is usually the growth, not of the present, but of subsequent generations, and so with Manuelo's. His name, though revered by his Anglos subjects, was little known throughout the world in his time, and his great deeds all lay buried in the musty tomb of uncertainty till dragged to the light, as it were, by the appreciative monks of Evora three hundred years after the hero of them had retired to rest with his fathers.

It is possible, without any great stretch of the imagination, to account for the triumphs of Manuelo as a military chieftain from the fact that he dated his nativity at Barcelona, a city that was actually founded by Hamilcar, the father of the great Hannibal, whose blood, for aught we can know at this day, may have coursed in Manuelo's own veins; and with whose history, at all events, Manuelo must be presumed to have been familiar. When a lad, strolling forth for an evening's walk upon the famous *rambla* of his native town, his thoughts may have reached out beyond the Old World, a notion that finds encouragement in the statement somewhere found, that it was at his own special request that he was apprenticed a seaman, to the end that he might escape the dull routine of a life in Catalonia.

Living there in the city of Hamilcar, with the citadel of Mount Jove ever looking down upon him, how was it possible for his youthful mind to avoid the thoughts of war, and how could he fail to become inspired with that ambition which cropped out so distinctly in his future career?

But the place above all others where a person is without distinction is in his own home and among his neighbors and friends. There his faults and not his virtues attract the more attention. In other lands his foibles, being unknown, stand not in the way of his advancement. Our divine Master has told us that a prophet is not without honor except in his own country, and his own brief and sad life was a most complete illustration of the truth of the announcement.

Manuelo, with his transcendent talents, enjoyed in Spain no higher reputation than that of a sprightly sailor boy, but in another country he arose, by chance, as some might say, but really by the force of his own character, to the highest dignity. His elevation, as pious Justino would have us believe, was in accordance with inevitable destiny, but it was also, doubtless, in order that the saying above referred to might be fulfilled, for Manuelo, it will be remembered, was himself a prophet.

This good Dominican priest was not only in his life a most commendable example of Christian excellence, but he was also a close observer of the ways of Providence, and this, no doubt, led him to give a much more extended and specific history of the worthy Manuelo than otherwise would have been written. As a consequence, also, the world is now blessed with the knowledge of a people who were themselves without books, or written language, and who, but for Justino's wise forethought, must have sunk into that great gulf of oblivion which now and forever effectually conceals from mortal view tens of thousands of nations similarly situated,—nations whose records were once plainly written along the sandy shores of time, but which have long since been washed entirely away by the breakers that keep rolling in from the ocean of eternity.

LXXV.

THE ANGLOS DESCRIBED.

IT was mentioned as a matter of regret by the young priests of Evora, that Manuelo, who was not overmuch distinguished for his piety, should have neglected to give the world more light touching the religious character of the people over whom he was called to exercise government; but regrets in the case are now unavailing. We only know that they were beset with heathenish superstitions, in many respects similar to those entertained by the inhabitants of that country in after ages. If there was any difference between them and other contemporaneous peoples, the Anglos were a little more careful to maintain perpetually burning a fire upon the altar of the high priest, and they were, as we glean from the record, like the Santos, unmistakably worshipers of the sun. The sun they regarded as the source not only of light, but of all life also. The rising sun was ever greeted by them with demonstrations of joy, and the setting of the same was the signal for expressions of sorrow and sadness.

The inconstant moon was looked up to as an inferior deity, and its propitiation was never sought, except in times of great trouble. The stars were attentively watched by the priests at night, and the motions of the planets seemed to be understood by them. They were fond of the ocean and believed that its ceaseless waves uttered intelligent sounds, but they never ventured far out upon the broad bosom of its waters.

Towards their children they were very affectionate, and their respect for aged women, and sometimes for venerable men, amounted almost to adoration. There were no insane or idiotic persons among them, nor was there intemperance of any sort. Schools they had none, but every household was a place of instruction for the young, and they were fully taught in all the virtues, in goodness, and in charity.

By hunting and fishing, and in the spontaneous growth of fruits, berries, and nuts, all their needs were supplied, and they cared for nothing beyond these natural resources.

In peace they were happy, and in times of war not greatly otherwise, for they were little in fear of death, believing that the spirits of the departed could return to the earth as often as they would, and that the life hereafter was fraught with infinitely more happiness than the one in this world, besides being eternal, while the one below was only temporary, as everybody knew.

Manuelo said little or nothing on the subject, but Justino was thoroughly convinced, and so stated, that the gentle Anglos only needed a knowledge of the true faith to make them as contented and happy as any people in the wide world, and the good man yearned to be the agency of conveying to them knowledge of that religion by which their souls could be saved. If we may rely upon the manuscript, he ceased not to deplore, in the most pathetic terms, the loss of a people so little deserving of that perdition to which all pagan nations are inevitably consigned.*

As may be inferred from what has already appeared, the Anglos were not a numerous people, but they made up in bravery and in shrewdness what they lacked in numbers. Their strength had been greatly augmented by the teachings of Manuelo since he came amongst them, but, like a good king, he was never satisfied with their advancement, and could not content himself as long as there was more glory to achieve in the line of improving his people.

His greatest adversary, the wicked Mosoto, having been disposed of, he turned his attention earnestly to the instruction of his subjects in so many of the useful arts as could be inculcated with the limited means at his command. He felt very sorely the need of iron implements, and though he tried the experiment in various ways, he could never succeed in supplying the place of iron with gold, the only metal in a pure state that the country afforded. Gold, he presently discovered, was but a poor substitute for iron. He found it impossible to construct knives or any cutting instruments out of that metal.

---

* The good reader is reminded again, lest he should forget it, that Friar Justino, the author, as we verily believe him to be, was a Catholic missionary, with strong predilections for his church.

It was altogether too soft. It was even inferior to the hard stones of the country for such purposes, and flints were therefore properly regarded by the natives as of infinitely more value than gold. He did succeed at one time in fashioning some arrow-heads out of this pure yellow metal, which was abundant in places, but it dulled and bent much too readily, and had to be cast aside as of no real value. Gold, said Justino, so bright and cold, and for which so many men their lives have sold, is after all only precious by the common consent of civilized man, its value being entirely fictitious.

So delighted were the young Christian priests of Evora with Manuelo's account of the good Anglos that one of their number, more ambitious than the rest, undertook to give Justino's description of them in verse. His success in the Portuguese tongue was a thousand times greater than has attended its rendition in English, which, owing to the exertion required to give in rhyme a literal and truthful translation of the text, has been nearly an entire failure. The translator, nevertheless, has come almost as near to a proper rendering of the original as did Alexander Pope in translating the Iliad. But of this the reader will be able to judge for himself, since he will have Manuelo's story both in prose and in rhyme. If, however, anyone should lack the time to waste on mere repetition, he can skip over the balance of this chapter.

>Most happy people were the Angelese,.
>They nothing lacked that could their fancy please,
>Or wants supply. Their needs were few and such
>As would be satisfied without too much
>Expenditure of labor, for, indeed,
>There was of labor 'mongst them little need,
>In order to obtain, or to prepare
>What they required for food, and what to wear.
>In sport, and with the arrow and the hook,
>They could procure afield and from the brook
>Whatever was desired, or what caprice
>Demanded for their comfort and their ease.

They were, in fact, contented altogether,
And in the worst as in the best of weather;
For comfort were their houses made, and warm,
And well designed to shield them from the storm;
Fashioned as well against the summer's heat
As to protect against the snow and sleet
Of winter. Nor so made were they that falling
When visited by those most appalling
Earthquakes which sometimes, and too often, came,
They would destroy, or mutilate, or lame
Their occupants. But they were made so light
That all were safe in them, by day or night:
But if, by any chance, a house should fall,
The occupants within could easy crawl
Out from beneath the masses of *débris*,
And, notwithstanding loss of house, would be
As independent as they were before,
For it was little trouble to restore
The structure to the shape it had at first,
And such of their mishaps was not the worst.

Of prisons had they none—they needed none.
Of criminals, so called, there was not one,
For all obeyed the laws with greatest care.
If anyone by chance, a thing most rare,
Incurred the censure of his fellow-men,
Or was unable to make good again
Some wrong, and when that fact became disclosed,
His punishment was always self-imposed.
No man among them all was ever known
To take or use that which was not his own,
Nor was one ever found to do a thing
Which had the slightest tendency to bring
Sorrow unto his fellow-man, or cause
Him pain, or in the least to break the laws
Of human kindness, or a word to speak
Which would bring blushes to another's cheek.

The women were all modest and all good,
And never one by word or action could
Be charged with any impropriety,

Or what would not in good society
Be lady-like, and be by all approved;
In consequence of which they were much loved.

The children were, without exaggeration,
As pretty as of any other nation.
The pupils of their eyes were dark and bright,
But the surrounding parts as snow were white.
So plump, and smooth, and soft the cheeks of each,
They might be likened to a perfect peach.
The lips of many of the little miss_s
Were quite too sweet for anything but kisses.
But then their sweetness was by no means all
In their sweet lips: their graceful mien, and tall,
Lithe forms, could not but be admired,
And these he said always true love inspired.
These blessed little folks Justino thought
Most perfect would have been had they been taught
To say their prayers and read the catechism,
And been, likewise, purgated with baptism.
These things those tender creatures wanted most,
And lacking these, of course their souls were lost.
A sad reflection this for the good friar,
Whose thoughts were not in this, but in the higher
And better world above, where all who know
Just how to worship God are sure to go.

Their knowledge of philosophy was slight,
Nor kenned they much beyond what was in sight;
But then, about all things within their view,
None others better than these people knew.
The world entire of course they could not see,
And therefore were in doubt what it might be.
The wiser of them were somewhat inclined
To think it was a creature of some kind,
A monstrous, living, animated being.
Upon whose back the Anglos were then living;
But on whose other parts and near the side
Some other nations were allowed to ride.
They thought the bloody Dagos and Movos
Were on the parts behind the good Anglos,
And that the Barbos were more near the head,

And therefore might more justly be in dread
Of being shaken off, when this huge beast,
Uneasy from some cause, or when, at last,
He might, after a lengthened sleep, awake,
And rouse himself by giving one good shake.
From such belief concerning this great sphere,
They would not dig it up for very fear
Of wounding the great monster, and thus make
Him angry, and so cause the earth to shake.
In consequence they neither plowed nor sowed,
Nor planted grain, nor seeds, nor reapt, nor mowed,
But were content to gather what they could
For eating find among the hills and in the wood.

The sun they knew it was that gave the heat
That caused to grow whate'er was good to eat.
They could observe that when he moved away,
And by receding shortened each new day,
That vegetation died, or ceased to grow,
And that the hills about were white with snow:
But when the sun returned, the snow would melt,
And plants and living creatures likewise felt
The kind influence of his warming beams,
And how delightful in the spring the streams,
So cool and bright, would course down from the hills,
And thus create the music of the rills.
Observing these the people, every one,
With pagan darkness worshiped the sun
Bow down they would to him, morning and night,
Deplore his absence, or adore his light.

The pale, cold moon, with placid, shining face,
Was all the clock they had on which to trace
The march of time. Her change from new to old
And old to new, thirteen times round, all told,
Marked one whole year for them, in which the sun
From north to south and south to north had run,
And this same guide would fix the occupation,
In different seasons, of this happy nation.
The stars they thought to be not far away,
But why they shone by night and not by day

They could not understand, nor could they tell
What shooting stars were for, nor why they fell.

Their worshiping the sun was the extent
To which their knowledge of religion went:
Whence they came, or whither they were going,
These wretched pagans had no means of knowing.
Their priests were not those pious men of learning,
Who could with ease enlighten them concerning
The life that was to follow this on earth;
And all as well about the second birth,
Which men must have before they can be sure
That they will find above an open door;
About that lake of fire, far down below,
Where unrepentant sinners all must go;
About that city which is paved with gold,
And precious stones, and filled with wealth untold;
About the three in one, the blessed Trinity,
Which may be three, or may be one divinity;
About the future, and the present, and the past,
And what is coming of this world at last;
How it was made six thousand years ago,
The work of six days only, as we know:
Those poor blind heathen, having no such teachers,
Could never comprehend what kind of creatures
Themselves and other human beings were,
And how infinitely superior
Mankind must be to all the brute creation;
How very different in form and fashion,
How much unlike in mind and aspirations
To other living, animate creations.
Justino was about them much concerned,
And, as we know, his good heart daily yearned
To be the bearer to them of the truth,
And which he would have been, had he, forsooth,
Not been by death, alas! too soon cut off,
To render by his actions certain proof
Of his most pious and humane intent,
Regarding that strange land where Manuel went,
And where, together with his native wife,

He spent a part of his eventful life;
Becoming king of all the people there,
And ruling over them with pious care.

LXXVI.

THE SANTOS INVASION.

THREE years, and upwards, had the good Manuelo been thus employed in improving the condition of his people mentally and physically, when he was greatly alarmed at the close of a charmingly quiet day in early summer, by the hurried arrival at the capital of a herald, informing him that his territory was about to be invaded from the north by a large hostile force, but how large the excited messenger could not state, further than that he represented it to be as numerous as the locusts which had the year previously devastated a large part of the Anglos dominions. They were pouring down, he said, on several different lines, and apparently sweeping everything before them. This was all that Manuelo's anxious inquiries could draw from the affrighted courier, but it was far more than he wanted to hear.

To him who had now been, for years, thoroughly engrossed in civil pursuits, and who had lost much of his taste for war and military display, this was most unwelcome news. Whatever the disturbance might be he knew it was not of his seeking, and he resolved within himself to confront the danger without a murmur, as a person in his position should. Accordingly he lost no time in sending out runners in the direction of the encroachment, to gather information concerning the invaders. These were dispatched singly and in pairs, with instructions to ascend to the mountain-tops and observe carefully everything relating to the enemy, and, if practicable, to approach near enough to their camps to ascertain who they might be and what was their purpose. This last delicate duty was imposed more particularly upon two of his astute and trusty young warriors by name, respectively, Loto and Soto. These were to spy out, at any hazard, the strength, armament, and habits of the enemy, and to report as soon as possible. They were furnished with disguises, and with fabricated pretexts by Manuelo, so that in the event of capture they would stand some chance of being spared.

This precaution to obtain desirable information touching the enemy having been taken, Manuelo at once set himself, personally, about the task of reorganizing his army, a task he prosecuted with great diligence. For three whole years had his men been engaged, almost exclusively, in industrial pursuits, greatly to the neglect of military discipline, and even their arms had, so to speak, become rusty. To be exact and to tell the truth, their bows had been long unstrung, their arrows were headless, their spears sprung, and their shields warped. There was no public armory in the country, and in failing to establish one, Manuelo had shown a neglect that seemed now unpardonable for a man in his position. But then all his known enemies had been subdued, and he was in no apprehension of attack from any quarter. The fact is he had seen too much of standing armies in his own native country, in his younger days, to believe in their virtue, and he was the last man to encourage them. But it is clear that he ought, at least, to have kept in constant preparation a sufficient supply of the accouterments of war for an emergency like the one which had now arisen. In this alone he exhibited a weakness unlooked for in one possessing so much wisdom in other respects. He argued that a standing army was always a means of oppression, and the ready instrument by which wicked despots perpetrated wrong and outrage upon their own subjects. Though ostensibly for the defense of the state against foreign enemies, standing armies are more frequently organized for the suppression of liberal sentiments at home. Manuelo maintained that a just king needed no military establishment in time of peace, and he set a worthy example to others by dismissing his own. The safety of a country, in his estimation, reposed in the patriotic hearts of its citizens, rather than in military power, and he was satisfied, as he said, that an army composed of the loving subjects of an upright ruler, improvised for the occasion, was infinitely more reliable than a horde of heartless hirelings, however carefully equipped and disciplined. Such an army he had himself created on two former occasions and in each instance they had proved invincible.

In further extenuation of his neglect to provide an armory and to keep up an active military force, he asseverated, with great earnestness, to Justino, that regular army life was nothing less than a species of slavery, and that, too, of the most abject kind, inasmuch as the common soldier must be entirely subordinate in all things to the will of his superior. Military life, said he, requires the surrender of all independence of action, and even of thought. The very existence of the soldier in the regular army establishment, he continued, is subject to the arbitrary discretion of his commanding officer, and no harmony can possibly be preserved between real manhood and such a life. But what struck him as still worse, and the greatest objection to a standing military organization, was the enormous drain upon the industrial resources of a people, incurred in its maintenance, even in time of peace. Many a nation, he said, had been kept in abject poverty by this means, and millions of subjects, in the most productive of countries, have been reduced to penury and starvation, to gratify the ambition of some prince, in keeping on foot a painted, feathered, and tinseled soldiery. Not such alone as are killed in battle, said he, are destroyed by the standing army, but a much larger number perish in the useless work of keeping the army alive.

Manuelo was unwilling to be the guilty instrument of a tyranny of that sort, hence he had disbanded his forces after his conflict with Mosoto, remitting them, one and all, to the peaceful pursuits of private life. By this course he had secured at the time a larger share of the esteem of his subjects, and had lost none of their veneration for him as a military chieftain.

At his call, now, his loving people came forward with wonderful alacrity, and he soon found himself surrounded with a force of over two thousand as brave soldiers as ever gladdened the heart of a military leader in any country. Even sooner than he thought it possible, they had become thoroughly equipped and were under excellent discipline.

There were enough of the veterans of the campaign against the Movos left to instruct in the usual tactics the younger members of the tribe, and all the men who had participated in the battle of the Warm Springs, as well as those who had fought the Barbos, now turned to most earnestly, to incite by their graphic accounts of these two engagements, enthusiasm in the breasts of their less experienced companions in arms.

The forces were drilled this time in two battalions of a thousand men each, or thereabouts, and besides, there was a small reserve corps, who were to act as scouts and skirmishers. These last were put under the command of the trusty Warno. A better organized army for its numbers, take it all together, it would be difficult to find, and so the enemy, after a few days, and without searching for it, found it to be.

The heralds that had been sent forth to observe the movements of the invaders were now returning one by one, and their reports comfirmed, yes, more than confirmed, all that had been told by the excited messenger who first brought the news. The enemy was approaching by slow marches, but in numbers truly appalling. The first returning scouts had observed them from the mountain-tops only, and were unable to give any definite description of them, so that the Anglos were in great doubt as to who the approaching people might be, but Manuelo's suspicions had been aroused from the start, that they were the Santos, and his suspicions proved to be, in the main, correct, though not quite comprehensive enough to include all the facts. He likewise knew full well what their motive might be, but this was understood by himself and Alola alone; for not to this day had either of them ever disclosed to the people with whom they were living, the escape they had made, nor why they had fled from the land of the swift-footed Santos.

Manuelo knew of no other incentive than revenge on the part of his former friends that could have mustered such vast numbers against him, and his fears were very naturally aroused for the worst. Still, somewhat in doubt, he awaited with as much the appearance of calmness as could be assumed by a person in so responsible a position, the return of one or the other of his two more reliable messengers, before undertaking any decisive movement. Soto was first to make his appearance.

Just at the close of the seventh day from his departure, while the gloomy twilight was fast receding from the western sky, the faithful Soto, with breathless haste, came running into the camp of his friends, and, in words much broken with trepidation, related how he had, two nights in succession, hovered around the quarters of the enemy, and beheld with his own eyes the ominous bird's wing, worn as an emblem by the main body of the invaders. He learned, moreover, that the bird's-wing people had for their allies large bodies of Barbos, and likewise of the Movos, as he supposed them to be, and that the entire army then threatening the Anglos capital comprised many thousand men, all well armed and provided for desperate war. From the best estimate that could be made by the faithful herald, the enemy outnumbered the Anglos at least ten to one, and they were already within the borders of Manuelo's kingdom. Neither this dreadful intelligence, nor the unfeigned commotion in the mind of the trusty Soto, disturbed the apparent equanimity of the king, who was at some pains to soothe the perturbation of his friend, and then, turning about, calmly reminded his warriors, who in full force were there assembled, that not only considerable valleys, but three ranges of mountains intervened between the approaching host and his capital. He assured them—proclaiming the fact in words so loud that all could hear—that however numerous the enemy might be, and even though they outnumbered the locusts, they could be checked and driven back by his little army of heroes, who had never yet been, and never could be conquered. Halting here for breath, in the middle of his speech, a great shout was sent up on that calm summer night, from his two thousand men —such a shout as was never before heard in that place and probably never will be again.

LXXVII.
A BATTLE IN THE CLOUDS.

EARLY on the following day the brave Anglos army, inspired by the applause of all the women of the city, who had come forth to witness and encourage the movement, conspicuous among whom was the tearful Alola, were on their march to intercept the enemy at the first of the ranges of mountains to be crossed on his way, from the place where last seen, in coming towards the city of the Anglos.

Manuelo, though the bravest of men, could not summon up courage to take a formal leave of his affectionate wife. Somehow, in spite of himself, fearful forebodings would come over his mind that he might not see her again, and he dreaded most lest the weakness which he would be sure to exhibit in parting from her in the usual way, might produce an unfavorable impression upon the minds of his men. With illy concealed emotions, therefore, he hurried off to the head of his forces, and from there anxiously looked back upon the comely form of Alola, again and again, until quite out of sight and far away on the plain.

After three days of lively marching, and early on the morning of the fourth day, the forces of Manuelo took possession of the only two known passes leading over the third range of mountains to the north of the capital, not knowing with certainty which of them would be assailed by the combined forces then advancing. Manuelo's army, though small at best, in comparison with the one opposed to him, was thus, at the start, necessarily divided. But his men were judiciously apportioned in reference to the strength of the two positions, some fifteen hundred of the regulars, with the reserves, being posted in the easier of the passes, and only five hundred in the other and more difficult one.

As was expected, the enemy approached the lower and broader of the gaps, the one where Manuelo himself remained in command, the stalwart Warno being put in charge of the five hundred brave men who were sent to occupy the more elevated of the passes. Arranging the forces under his immediate charge in the best possible manner, and in the most advantageous position in the pass, Manuelo quietly awaited the onslaught, which, from the proximity of the enemy, it was apparent could not be long delayed. Before the warm summer sun of that day had mounted quite to the zenith, the main body of the Santos, confiding in their numbers, advanced with steady steps, coming up the gentle mountain slope in solid phalanx, ready and anxious to give battle on any terms, with an adversary whom they regarded as despicably small. But Manuelo, undismayed, watched their every movement from an elevated position, in the middle of the pass, and when the enemy, in large force, were in easy range, he ordered his men in the front rank to discharge their light weapons. The invaders, thus greeted with a perfect shower of darts and arrows from the strong bows of the gallant Anglos, were a little nonplussed at first, and failed to respond at once to the fire. Manuelo seeing their hesitancy, quickly ordered a second discharge, whereupon the foremost men in the advancing columns, staggered by the reception given them, wavered and fell back in some confusion. But they were supported by a large body of Barbos, and the charge was speedily renewed by the combined battalions of the Santos and Barbos, followed up by other allies. Urged on by their ablest commanders, the enemy now came up with redoubled determination, and a terrible conflict ensued in that high mountain gorge. Fortunately for him, there was only room between the precipitous hills on either hand for the employment of just so many men on Manuelo's side as he had in his command, and more, had he possessed them, would have been useless, unless as reserves. So the advantage of the position was altogether with the Anglos, and the combined forces of the enemy were stubbornly held at bay. The battle was maintained long and desperately on both sides, but the assailants, finally, after suffering fearful slaughter, were compelled to withdraw from the carnage. Crest-fallen and dissappointed, they retired to the plains below, whence they had but lately come. Taking with them their wounded and some of their dead, they went into camp, for it was now night.

Manuelo's army, though elated with their success, were not so thoughtless as to be drawn from their position by pursuit of the retiring foe, but remained within their strong entrenchments, hoping that the allies would renew their rash attempt on the following day. But the enemy had been too severely chastised not to consider well of the matter before resuming active hostilities. They were advised of the existence of the other pass—the one occupied by Warno—but had ascertained from their scouts that it also was well guarded.

All the next day was spent by the enemy without any general movement, apparently in consultation among themselves, for the ascertainment of some more practical way than the one they had undertaken, of continuing on the course towards their destination. But the day by them was not wasted. During the forenoon a detachment of the pilfering Movos, some five hundred strong, were observed to move silently off from their camp in an easterly direction, as if towards their homes, and were soon lost to sight.

On the next day the second one after the first battle in the clouds, another attempt was made with equal vigor, to all appearances, to effect a passage of the mountain on the same line with the first. The fight was renewed with the same determination on both sides, and the result must have been a repetition of what occurred on the former occasion, but for a piece of strategy on the part of the enemy, which would have done credit to Scipio himself. While the combat was at its height, Manuelo discovered a cloud of dust rising off in the valley on the hither side of the range, and he was not long in determining that it was caused by a body of the enemy who were approaching to attack him in the rear. The fact was that the five hundred Movos who left the camps of the allies the day before, had gone many leagues to the eastward, and during the night, by forced marches, had passed through the mountains by another and far-distant opening, known to themselves alone, and were now hastening to the aid of their friends. Observing this movement, Manuelo sent word concerning it by a courier to Warno, who was stationed in the neighboring pass, and they (Warno's men) at once rushed down to intercept and punish this band of Movos, for Manuelo could illy spare any of his own fifteen hundred, every man of whom, together with his reserves, was required in the great struggle with the main body of the enemy. Warno's command, which had not yet tasted battle, and who were anxious for the fray, speedily fell upon the equal force of the Movos, and fairly annihilated them, scattering to the four winds so many of them as escaped death. But the cunning Barbos, familiar with wild mountain life, were watching with eagle eyes the occurrences from their side of the range, and seeing the higher pass vacated by Warno, themselves hastily took possession of it with a large force of light-armed bowmen, and nearly all the unemployed reserves of the allied armies followed at once in that direction.

The detachment of the Anglos, under the brave Warno, who had been chastising the Movos, now undertook to regain their former position in the pass, but the effort was in vain. They were this time put in the position of the attacking party, and were now no longer on the defensive, with the choice of the situations, as they had but lately been. Besides, their numbers were limited, while their opponents were as numerous as the locusts and like locusts were constantly increasing. Warno and his followers fought with the desperation of lions, and were ready to sacrifice themselves, every one, but it was of no use. They were contending against impossibilities.

Seeing the desperate situation into which matters were thrown by adverse fate, Manuelo ordered a bold final dash upon the enemy in his front, and put them to flight, whereupon he immediately withdrew his men from the pass, and joining the other division of the army under Warno, on the plain below, they marched together, in good order, across the intervening valley towards the next range of mountains.

As many another general before him, so now Manuelo had been compelled to yield to the force of numbers. It was no worse for him than it had been in the case of Pericles, of ancient fame, nevertheless it was exceedingly galling to his pride. For the first time now had he been worsted, unless, indeed, we except the occasion, long past, when he was in lead of an army of base slaves against the king of the Modens; but that, it is thought, ought not to be considered as a military defeat at all, for was not he the only brave man among them? To have continued the fight at that time would have been to sacrifice himself to no purpose, and its consequences would have been most disastrous, since it would have deprived the world of this valuable portion of its history.

Referring to Manuelo's present distressing discomfiture, Father Justino could not but remark upon what a slender thread hangs the destiny of some men. How precarious, said he, are the ways of Providence, as they relate to persons and to whole armies, and even to nations and to the races of mankind. Out of the slightest circumstance sometimes emanate momentous events, and the most gigantic preparations of men are often brought unexpectedly to naught by the merest trifle. Man proposes, continued the good friar, but God disposes.

LXXVIII.

ANOTHER STAND.

ON the next range of mountains, through which there seemed to be only a single pass, Manuelo the brave took his stand, determined there to defend his kingdom against the ruthless invaders, or perish gloriously in the effort. Every precaution was taken by him, as soon as possible, in the way of posting his men and in fortifying his position. A succession of barricades of brush and wood and stones were speedily thrown up across the road by which the enemy must approach. Behind the strongest of these, and near the summit, his little army, now somewhat but not greatly reduced, was stationed to await the oncoming of the allies, who, elated with their late triumph, must have been impatient of delays. Though considerably crippled by the stubborn resistance they had met with, and now, in consequence, moving, as it were, upon crutches, the enemy were not expected to tarry long in the valley below, although that valley was one of the most beautiful and attractive ever beheld, covered as it was with a thick carpet of greensward, interspersed with flowers, and coursed by a stream of bright, crystal water, bordered with a thick growth of umbrageous sycamores. It was a place that would have beguiled a more sentimental people, but the barbarous allies took little heed of its fascinations, and pushed hopefully on, looking only to the coarser enjoyment of booty and beauty in the capital of their enemy.

News of the discomfiture of the Anglos had gone back with telegraphic speed to the city, causing the greatest possible consternation in the minds of the people, and fairly wringing with distress the poor heart of Alola. With more than womanly discretion, she had taken it upon herself to organize and push forward all the new recruits she could possibly muster, almost, as it seemed, robbing the cradle and the grave to supply them. Old and young alike were drafted into her battalions, and such was her anxiety on her husband's account, that she could hardly be dissuaded from taking command of them in person, and leading them against her former friends, for she knew now of a certainty that the enemy were none other than the powerful Santos.

Alola was the more resolute in demanding the services of the old and infirm of her subjects, from the fact of her having long entertained the opinion that such were precisely the persons that ought always to be sent off to the wars, and not the hale and hearty. She reasoned, that if any persons in a community ought to run the risk of being killed, it should be, not the most useful, but those, rather, whose usefulness on earth had nearly ceased. And these, she maintained, if any, ought to be willing to sacrifice themselves upon the altar of patriotism, since they can be of service to their country in no other way. The sensible little woman could never see the propriety of exacting military duty of such valuable citizens as Manuelo, to the exclusion of persons of no account whatever in the world; nor could she be persuaded of the consistency of the uniform practice of nations, of killing off in wars their very best and most vigorous young men, while the infirm and the useless are permitted to go free.

LXXIX.

LOTO'S STORY.

SCARCELY were his preparations for defense in this mountain pass completed, when Manuelo was surprised and momentarily delighted by the sudden appearance within his fortifications of the other one of his faithful heralds, the sharp-eyed Loto, who in pursuance of instructions had actually penetrated into the camp of the enemy, and had been with them many days, only now making his escape to report to his master what he had seen and heard.

At first Loto was treated by the Santos as a spy, and narrowly escaped execution as such, but by the practice of that native astuteness for which he was distinguished, he won upon the confidence of the leaders in the enemy's lines, and learned all about them and their purposes. His story, as related with trembling lips and blanched, to the impatient Manuelo, was that Mosoto on his first flight had gone directly into the land of the Barbos, and had given that people a complete account of Manuelo and his young wife, both of whom, as we have already seen, were grossly misrepresented by him. Even before the expedition of the Barbos, in which Mosoto lost his life, it is thought that information may have been conveyed in some way to the nearest villages of the Santos, touching the whereabouts of Manuelo and his bride. But whether this be so or not, certain it is that the Barbos, on their return from that war, were not long in dispatching a delegation of their shrewdest and most influential men, including their head prophet, to visit the capital of the Santos, and lay before the authorities of that people a full account of this strange personage, for such Manuelo was to them, and to take counsel of that great nation as to what should be done, or undertaken, to quell his extraordinary and growing power.

From their own sad experience with him in arms, no less

than from the description given of him by the wicked Mosoto, the Barbos looked upon Manuelo as an exceedingly dangerous character, and that opinion had been intensified by the remarkably suspicious circumstances attending his first appearance as an entire stranger among them in company with a young and beautiful woman. They had long since detected the falsehood of his account of himself on that occasion, and they would have placed no confidence thereafter in anything he might have said or done.

The delegation of suspicious Barbos on arriving at the Santos' capital, found to their no little astonishment that both Manuelo and his interesting companion were but too well known to that people. The swift Santos were of course greatly surprised to learn all then told them about the fugitives, whom they supposed to be dead, but their astonishment knew no bounds when assured that Manuelo had actually become the king of a considerable nation known as the Anglos, and that his interesting little wife, their former princess, was queen of the same. They had been constrained to believe originally that both Manuelo and Alola had been drowned in the Bay. This fact they inferred from finding shortly afterwards the canoe in which the pair had departed, floating empty upon the watery waste. It had been driven back across the Bay by adverse winds, and all signs pointed ominously towards the conclusion that its late occupants had perished.

Alola, in particular, was long and sorrowfully bewailed as one dead and never to be heard of again. The then impending Feast of Flowers, which was to have been made especially joyful by her marriage with the gallant son of the old high priest Pokee, instead of being an occasion of gladness, was turned by her untoward absence into one of the deepest sorrow, and so severe was the bereavement to her father, the great chief, that he pined away, and the very next year died of grief. The young and stalwart Gosee, the intended bridegroom, was duly elected king in the place of the deceased father of his betrothed. This event was not at all inconsistent with the character and standing of the man, but it is believed that sympathy for the young brave on account of the loss of his intended (as was supposed, for no one knew that he had been jilted) may have had something to do with his choice as king. But on this point the evidence, from the very nature of things, is uncertain, and the suggestion must be regarded as resting largely upon the naked surmise of Justino, for it cannot be shown at this late day, that any of Gosee's supporters were influenced by such inadequate motives. But surmises, with no better basis, even in matters of history, are often as reliable as positive statements, which are falsely claimed to be founded in facts. Be all this as it may, it is sufficient for our purpose to say that Gosee had been elected the successor of Bear-Slayer, and was king of the great Santos nation when their capital was visited by the aforesaid Barbos delegation. And when the young king became fully convinced by the representations of that delegation, of the treachery of Manuelo, and of the infidelity to himself of Alola, his rage arose to a towering height, and he resolved on vengeance, cost what it might. The cunning Barbos embassadors having accomplished their purpose, returned to their own country satisfied.

A system of secret inquiry was promptly set on foot by the vindictive Gosee, extending throughout all the nations and tribes to the southward of his dominions, and these were carried on for a year or two with the greatest diligence, in order that he might learn all about Manuelo and his people. Spies had even been sent into the Anglos country, but their object had never been so much as suspected by that generous and confiding people. All this investigation was conducted with so much caution by the king of the Santos and his faithful subjects, that it never came to the ears of Manuelo at all, who, in the meantime was enjoying, in conscious security, his ease and dignity in his own kingdom. Not a soul among the Anglos had the least apprehension of the terrible conspiracy that was being, in that cruel manner, hatched up against them.

The emissaries of Gosee found willing listeners among the Movos as well as among the more intelligent Barbos, and both these nations, moved by a spirit of revenge for past discomfitures, were but too willing to unite their strength with that of their more formidable neighbor at the north, to crush out, if possible, the power of the mysterious white king of the Anglos. The fullest preparations having been made by these three nations, and all being in readiness for an aggressive movement, the great army of the Santos, under the skillful leadership of the ambitious Gosee, set out on its march. On his southern border Gosee was joined, in pursuance of previous arrangements, by large forces of the Movos and kindred tribes, and by the Barbos, and the march of the allied powers was continued towards the capital of the unsuspecting Anglos, as the good reader has been already informed.

This intelligent report of the hawk-eyed Loto caused Manuelo inwardly to tremble, but he was not the person to exhibit evidences of fear to his confiding soldiery, and he kept up, as best he might, all the outward appearances of unfaltering courage. He now knew for a certainty the full nature of the enemy he had to contend against, and he felt a little relieved from suspense, though not at all encouraged for the future. He was fully aware that the leader of the opposing forces, the disappointed and jilted Gosee, would be unmerciful towards him and Alola, and he prepared his mind for the worst that could possibly happen, resolving within himself to sell his life for the very highest price he could obtain for it, and it appeared to him, just then, that the market was, so to speak, exceedingly favorable to a satisfactory disposition of the same.

A smaller army than his own, he remembered, had stayed a

much larger force of armed men than that which was being led against him, at the Pass of Thermopylæ, and the pass he was now holding was believed to be as favorable, at least for defense, as the one mentioned in Greek history. Nor did he forget that Leonidas and all his little Spartan band had perished in the noble struggle in which they were engaged. But it was for his beloved Alola that he feared the most, and he could but shudder whenever the thought came over him, as it would at times, of that tender creature's falling into the hands of the revengeful Gosee. The more he pondered upon this matter the more he thirsted for the blood of her tormentor, and he longed for an opportunity to meet him in single combat. He would gladly have settled the whole dispute in that way, but such, alas! was not the custom of those times, nor in that country.

Manuelo likened his enemy to the mighty Attila, who, at the head of an innumerable throng of barbarous Hungarians, Scythians, and Germans, swept down upon the plains of Italy, carrying devastation wherever they went; and as Attila was compelled at the great battle of Chalons to retreat, so Manuelo hoped to drive back this latter-day Hun, the bloody Gosee, with all his wicked allies. But when again he remembered the fate of the Emperor Theodosius, who finally fell, cruelly murdered by the sword of the conqueror, he could scarcely suppress a feeling of horror at his own possible fate, and that of his ever-affectionate wife.

In spite of himself, Manuelo was haunted by these apprehensions, from the time he learned from his faithful Loto that it was certainly his old rival who was so stubbornly opposing him, and his mortification at being once beaten was much the more poignant on account of its having been suffered at the hands of such a person. It is proper enough, right here, to soothe the anxious mind of the reader by stating that things did not turn out quite so badly as Manuelo apprehended, else how could he have given Justino an account of the battle? But then they did turn out badly enough, in all conscience, as will be seen, if the reader will but carefully peruse the next chapter.

LXXX.

ANOTHER FIGHT AND DEFEAT.

THERE was now no time for vain laments. The enemy that had given Manuelo so much trouble was still before him, and flushed with victory. It stood the Anglos general in hand to re-inspire his men with confidence, or all would certainly be lost. Fortunately they, as well as he, could see the strategy by which they had been driven back from their last stronghold, and they could see, as plainly as he, that the disaster they had suffered on the other mountain was owing to no fault of their commander-in-chief, but was the result of the overweening anxiety of the men in the smaller subdivision of the army, under Warno, to take part in the fight, and to chastise the circumventing band of treacherous Movos. It was this unfortunate zeal that led to leaving exposed the second pass in the first range, thus compelling the retreat of the whole Anglos army. Similar tactics on the part of the allies did not seem likely to be practiced successfully a second time, for the circumstances were now somewhat different, and the courage of the men, and their confidence in their leader, were not very greatly impaired.

By the direction of Manuelo, the forces under him were arranged in the best possible manner, the spearmen occupying the front ranks, and in their rear, but on more elevated ground, were stationed the bowmen, in lines three deep. The curious body of recruits, pushed forward by Alola, arrived just in time to receive orders before the battle began, and were stationed in a secure place in the pass, out of reach of the enemy's weapons, but where they would be convenient as reserves, to render what assistance they might in case of an emergency.

The main body of the little army being posted behind breastworks, were positively ordered to withhold their fire until the invaders approached within close range, and by no means to deliver battle until the enemy had discharged his first volley of missiles, many of which it was known would find lodgment within the defensive works of the Anglos. These orders of Manuelo were obeyed by his men to the letter, and the proud advancing foe, not this time with the swift-footed Santos in the van, but led on by their relentless allies, the Movos and Barbos, pressed forward up the steep mountain-side, overcoming the first obstacles with ease. The exulting enemy came on this time in more solid columns than before, and apparently with more determination, though it was plainly to be seen that one detachment of the Movos, a sort of vanguard, anticipating their fate, halted several times, and had to be rallied most vigorously by their officers. The enemy finally approaching, with some enthusiasm, almost to the ramparts of the Anglos, discharged their first volley of arrows and javelins, but with no great effect, when Manuelo's men, in turn, opened upon them with a perfect cloud of spears and arrows, all at the same moment. The enemy went down before this discharge like a row of bricks, which, set upon end, and leaning one against another, the first being displaced, the whole string of them tumble in quick succession. The head of their column was staggered, and as many of them as remained on their feet would inevitably have fallen back precipitately down the pass, but the cunning Gosee, having anticipated the possible cowardice of his allies, had kept in their rear with his whole Santos army, prepared to force his alien cohorts up to their work. Thus prevented from retreating, the enemy's assaults upon the Anglos' strong position were renewed again and again, and every time with the same result. In the meanwhile, the great body of Gosee's army, inspired by the loud exhortations of their commander, were crowding close up to the lines of the Anglos, and were fast becoming a dense and impenetrable mass. Several ineffectual attempts had been made to effect a breach in Manuelo's fortifications, but they were promptly repelled, with loss to the assailants. But now the spears and javelins of the brave Anglos having become exhausted, and their arrows nearly so, they were compelled, as a last resort, and at greater risk to themselves, to seize and return the weapons of their adversaries. The fight, under these circumstances, was wholly unequal, with the advantage on the side of the allied enemy.

In this emergency the raw Anglos recruits, furnished by Alola, were ordered to the front, and they came forward with a fearful yell of discordant voices, old men and boys mingling their cries in the general shout. If these were not as stalwart as soldiers usually are, they were, to say the least, sufficiently armed, and they promptly lent a portion of their weapons to their veteran *confrères*, who were quite as anxious to use, as to get them. This timely assistance to Manuelo's little army, furnished by the remarkable foresight of a woman, was indispensable at the time, and came not a moment too soon.

The battle was now more desperate than ever. It was waged with unheard-of determination, all along the line, which stretched quite across the pass, from side to side, and the victory seemed to hang in the balance, so to speak, for a long time. But just now, and in the hottest of the fight, the athletic and swift-footed Gosee appeared, with his tall plume, upon the scene, rallying his well-disciplined and trusty Santos for a final charge. With stentorian voice he called upon his friends to follow, himself leading the assault. In an instant the breastworks were broken down on the left and right, and Gosee, in person, with one grand bound, made a breach in the center.

An immense number of his men quickly followed, and in an instant hosts of them were inside of the Anglos' works. There they were promptly met by its brave defenders, and in less than a quarter of the time that it takes to relate the facts, the contest assumed the form of a hand-to-hand struggle. Manuelo, with a voice that was heard above the din, exhorted his band of heroes to still greater exertions, and they fought with the desperation of tigers at bay. But numbers will always tell in the long run, and the Anglos were finally overpowered. Manuelo himself was hastening to confront with his own weapons the powerful Gosee, when unfortunately, stepping upon a smooth rock, that lay there wet with blood, he slipped and fell. No sooner did his men see their leader prostrate than, supposing his fall to have resulted from an enemy's spear, they beat a retreat. As when some huge bull, invincible to ordinary foes, is attacked by a whole swarm of bees whose hive is unluckily overturned by the proud monster, is powerless to resist, and from necessity is compelled to retreat, and who with head in air and loudly bellowing, hastens away, pursued by the buzzing throng, so the noble band of Anglos, forced by the multitude of the enemy to flight, made off from the field. The day was lost. The allies were victorious, and Manuelo was a prisoner. He regretted, at the time, though not subsequently, that he had not been slain then and there.

The allies quickly made their way through the now unobstructed pass, and poured down, still in countless numbers, upon the valley below. The shattered forces of the Anglos, in confused and unequal detachments, made the best of their way, in hot haste, towards the near and only remaining range of mountains intervening between their homes and the hosts of the enemy, intending as they went to make one more and a final stand before surrendering all.

Early the next day most of the Anglos, assembled upon this last mountain height, were prepared in mind for any exertion that might be required of them, but, alas! they were now without a leader. Even Warno had been killed or captured, they knew not which, nor did it make any difference to them just then, since he was not there to advise and assist in their present dire emergency. Like Manuelo, he had been left behind, and the fate of both remained a mystery for some time.

The passage of this last range, the lowest of the three, was much more difficult of defense than either of the others had been, and consequently the brave Anglos were vastly more in need of a directing spirit than they had been on the former occasions. Nevertheless, they hastily completed such preparations as they were able to make in the brief time allotted them in order to dispute the passage of this mountain with an enemy, elated with successive triumphs, hurrying forward, confident now of his ability to achieve another and any number of victories.

Gosee, however, was too good a general to incur the danger of an unnecessary sacrifice of his men, and accordingly he deployed a portion of his forces to the right, and another portion to the left, sending them up and down the valley to find other passes in the range, with directions to them to push over, however precipitous the ascent, and to attack the Anglos occupying the pass in the rear, while he, with the main army in hand, was to advance in a direct line and force his adversary to extremes. His plans were readily understood by the intelligent Anglos, who were especially familiar with this range of mountains, and they acted accordingly. Leaving a small force of their best men in ambush, as it were, merely to check the onward march of the enemy, the main body retired reluctantly to the city. The news of the second great disaster to the Anglos had preceded them, by several hours, and the proud capital on their arrival was found in the greatest possible commotion.

About the only persons who had been left at home were the

women and children, and they were all alarmed beyond expression. There was weeping, and wailing, and wringing of hands, as each fond wife, mother, sister, or daughter, inquired of the returning soldiers touching the fate of her husband, son, brother, or father. Yes, and there were anxious inquiries about the old grandfathers and the little boys whom Alola had sent to the front in the desperate emergency. But the bereaved would have been more numerous had the Anglos army been less ably commanded than it was. And besides, being better acquainted with the country, many more of them escaped, and presently made their appearance in the city, than could reasonably have been expected. The return of each one, whose absence at first led to the belief that he had been slain, was the signal for rejoicing among his friends, and there was some little merriment amidst the general gloom. But as night approached, thick clouds of impenetrable darkness seemed to hover over that doomed city like birds of evil omen. Its army was broken into fragments, and no longer of much use. Its king and guiding spirit was absent—either slain or captured. A numerous, angry and ruthless enemy was at its very gates, and Justino was entirely correct when he said there was very little left upon which to hang a hope, if indeed hope was not already suspended.

LXXXI.

THE CITY ABANDONED.

A SORROWFUL time indeed had now fallen to the lot of the Anglos, who but yesterday, so to speak, were so very happy. From an exalted state of prosperity they were precipitated into the darkest abyss of despair. As on some bright summer afternoon a black cloud suddenly appearing in the western horizon, quickly overspreads the whole heavens, amidst lightning flashes and peals of thunder, deluging the earth with rain, compelling husbandmen, in great haste, to save their property from the destructive floods, so the sudden advent in their territory of the allied enemy caused the Anglos to bestir themselves and now to flee for their lives. A severe earthquake shock, overwhelming their city in general ruin, could hardly have been more surprising. Their country was overrun by hostile feet; their beloved chief was, they knew not where, nor whether dead or alive; their capital was about to fall into the hands of a powerful and unrelenting enemy, and there was apparently no relief from the impending catastrophe, and no power to stem, even for a brief time, the fast inrolling tide of misery.

If there was one single circumstance wanting to make their distress complete, it was that the Dagos were not engaged with their other adversaries in the general work of devastation. This small shadow of comfort was left to this distressed people in the midst of all their sorrow. But it was no merit of the Dagos that they were not so employed. That revengeful tribe would have been but too glad to participate in the indiscriminate plunder of the rich Anglos homes, had they, like the Movos, been invited to do so. But fortunately, they were not. On account of their remoteness from the land of the Santos, and not by reason of any want of inclination on their part, they were left out of the calculation when the war was begun. In truth, up to this time, and for some period afterwards, the Dagos rested in profound ignorance of these hostilities, and of the great disaster that had befallen their neighbors at the north, so completely had communication between the two peoples been broken off.

The flood of consternation in the doomed city was augmented by the return of individuals and straggling parties from the front. Members of the brave little army, some alone, and others in squads, some wounded and others not, but all tired and foot-sore, kept coming in as the night waned, until at last the excitement arose to such a pitch that it can better be imagined than described. In fact, an adequate account of it would be impossible, and Father Justino has wisely omitted the attempt, concluding, doubtless, that any effort he might make in that direction would result in disastrous failure.

But amidst all that was transpiring on that momentous occasion, there was one cool-headed person; one who appeared to be equal to the emergency, and whose judgment was no less clear in storms than in sunshine, and that person was the gentle Alola. In the absence of her husband, all responsibility was resting upon her delicate shoulders, and she felt the full weight of that responsibility. She was, in this terrible emergency, wrought up by a keen sense of the obligation of herself and Manuelo to that good people, to the exercise of more than masculine fortitude, and her remarkable strength of purpose and goodness of heart never shone forth with such brilliancy as on that most trying occasion. She, at least, wasted no time in vain lamentations. Though having infinitely more reason to be sorrowful than any other person in the city, she, among them all, displayed the least weakness.

Without waiting for the return of all the men who had gone to the war—and, indeed, to have waited for all would have been to wait to all eternity—but what Justino intended to say was that Alola, without waiting for the return of all the soldiers of the Anglos that had been spared by the weapons of the cruel enemy, ordered every preparation to be made, as speedily as possible, for abandoning the place. She caused to be packed, in convenient form for transportation, everything that would be most useful in the flight, and all that could be borne away by her people; and that which might be at all serviceable to the enemy, she ordered to be destroyed. When, early the next morning, all was in readiness, and every man, woman, and child supplied with as many of the necessaries of life as he, she, or it could carry, the whole population, bearing with them, so to say, their *lares* and *penates*, with many loud lamentations and floods of tears, bade farewell to their pleasant homes, and filing out of the western exit of the city in groups of families, and detachments, the strong helping the weak and infirm, but none far sundered from others, they entered upon their distressful line of march towards the sea-shore. Longer delay was impracticable, for the combined army of the enemy, though not yet in sight, could not be far away, and the van-guard might, in a few hours, burst upon the plain, and soon thereafter arrive in the suburbs.

Similarly sad experiences, peradventure, had been the lot of cities before that time; but never, in all history, had a people greater occasion to bewail a sorrowful fate. In the rear of the long procession, surrounded by a little band of faithful soldiers, was the queen herself, she being the last to leave the doomed capital. This had been the scene of her greatest triumphs. There had she enjoyed a measure of happiness that had fallen to the lot of but few of her sex, and she thought it befitting that she should be the one to bid final adieu to those scenes. In doing so the poor woman could not conceal her emotion. Overwhelmed with sadness, she lingered long in the beautiful apartments of herself and her lord, and there, alone, for some moments gave vent to her grief in copious tears and loud lamentations. Thus within her own doors occurred the most heart-rending event of that terrible day. Summoning courage at last, and banishing her tears, she followed the silent procession of her people, and in a few hours they were all beside the great ocean, which, in its boundlessness and depth, it is thought, might furnish some slight illustration of the sorrow and sadness of the Anglos. Continuing along its shores, they made but a few leagues the first day, for the march was encumbered at the same time with small children and large supplies, and their progress was necessarily slow. The whole retinue camped by the sea the first night, and the grief of the people was soothed, in some measure, by the gentle music of the breakers. The second day the march was continued by the ocean-side, and likewise the third.

LXXXII.

THE PENINSULA.

EARLY in the fourth day of the hegira, the fleeing Anglos, already weary with the march, and some of the more infirm ready to give up in despair, came in sight of a curious geographical formation. It was a peninsula extending far out into the sea and connecting with the main-land by a narrow isthmus. At a considerable distance from the principal shore, the peninsula widened out into a broad area, which could be approached only by persons passing in single file over the rocky neck. Alola in an instant saw the advantage of this position, and without much delay marched her people onto the peninsula, the women and children proceeding with great caution lest they should tumble into the deep on either side. This peninsula being a broad and beautiful table-land, or *mesa*, as written in the original, was supplied with wells of water, from which the sharp-eyed Alola observed it had been occupied before, and she concluded that it had, in past times been the resort of some people similarly circumstanced, but concerning such use of it even the oldest men among her subjects knew nothing.*

In pursuance of orders the camps were pitched on this stronghold, and the sacred fires were lighted upon an altar hastily erected of rough stones. With but little delay, thanks were

---

*It has been ascertained on diligent inquiry that no such geographical formation exists at the present day, or, at least, none can be found anywhere along the southern coast of California; but that matters not, nor does it discredit the story in the least; since without doubt the waves and earthquakes of these last three hundred and fifty years, have broken down and removed the isthmus, or narrow neck, entirely, and what was once a *paene insula*, is now *tota insula*, or a complete island, which is there still; and what is conclusive of the question, it is in the same location exactly as when visited by the queen of the Anglos, in the early part of the sixteenth century.

offered up by the high priest to the sun and moon, and whatever lesser deities and saints belonged to the calendar of the pious Anglos, for this their apparently providential deliverance from wicked enemies.

A sufficient guard was then stationed at the isthmus to prevent any encroachments, and the good queen and all her weary followers, feeling now perfectly secure against danger of every sort, slept the night through. Her mind was now relieved of a great burden. The innocent people under her charge were at last in a place of safety, and she felt like defying Gosee and all his wicked hosts. She deemed she had now fairly eluded her relentless pursuers, and she would have joined heartily in the general rejoicing, continued from the day before, had it not been for the absence of her unhappy husband, who, though far away in person, was seldom absent from her thoughts. Alola knew not how near the enemy might be on her track, but she was sure they would follow without much delay. She reasoned wisely that the disappointed Gosee would never falter or turn back until he had her in his possession; at all events, so long as there was the least hope left of accomplishing that purpose. Her gratification was most in the thought that from her present secure place her brave soldiers could sally forth and harass the enemy and be as safe, on their return, as if ensconced in the fortress of Gibraltar.

Though considerably demoralized at first, and broken in spirit by their successive defeats, her warriors, nevertheless, were the same men who had fought so gallantly on former occasions, and she was confident they would still be able to do great execution against the common enemy—common, did we say? surely it was a most uncommon enemy for the good Anglos. There was one consideration, however, in this connection that pleased her not at all. She remembered that her former friends, the Santos, were reputed to be the swiftest runners in the world, and it would hardly do, therefore, for a force that relied upon retreat for safety, to come in collision with them at any great distance from home, and she feared her men might be able to inflict upon the allied powers less annoyance for that reason.

The good queen was unremitting in her exertions to provide, and lay in supplies of every kind that might be needed within her fortified place, so that it should not be reduced by starvation, in case of siege. Men, women, and also the larger children, of both sexes, under her charge, were sent out into the nearest hills and valleys to gather provisions, and all the necessaries of life, and in a short time there was laid up in this camp an abundant store. On the borders of the peninsula, all around, close down by the sea, shell-fish abounded, and in the deep waters, near the shore, other fishes of all sorts could be taken in numbers, and the beleaguered would have that resort for sustenance in case of great need. Thus fixed and provided, Alola, the fair, was secure in these her new quarters.

Scarcely had the requisite preparations for long confinement in this islandic home been completed, when the Santos scouts began to make their appearance on the main-land, and in a day or two longer a large body of the combined forces of the enemy hove in sight. These were under the lead of the jealous Gosee himself, who, exulting in his late victories, was in hot pursuit of the fugitive queen, whom he confidently expected to capture, and whom he fully intended to lead back to her native country in triumph. As she had treated his suit with disdain by running off with his rival, so he was resolved now to visit upon her the fullest measure of punishment, in the form of contumely and reproach. His ambition was to possess himself of her person, as now he had that of Manuelo, and by humbling her before all the people, he thought to heal in some measure the gaping wounds in his honor. Learning, while yet in the

Anglos city, from his scouts, the direction she had taken, he, impatient, tarried only a day and part of another, at that place, and then pushed on to overtake her, which he felt certain in his own mind of doing, knowing full well that her flight would be impeded by the children and old people she had felt compelled to take with her. A man, he thought, might have abandoned these to their fate in so great an emergency, but a woman, and least of all Alola, he was certain would not, and he followed her up with renewed confidence of success.

Already, in his imagination, was she bending before him in the deepest humiliation, her dark eyes streaming with tears, begging for mercy at his hands, when he arrived in front of the peninsula with his army—but here his pleasant delusion was suddenly dispelled. Gosee took in the situation at a glance, for was he not an experienced commander? and he was greatly perplexed to know just what next he should do. At first, he essayed rashly to cross some of his troops over the narrow neck of land that led out to where Alola was entrenched, but her trusty men were on guard and promptly repelled his advance, casting several of the invaders headlong into the briny waves. Being dumfounded with disappointment, and in great doubt, Gosee stamped about for a while, and then ordered the allied forces to go into camp for the night where they were, and called a council of war. Neither he, nor the wisest of his subalterns, were able to devise any means by which possession could be obtained of Alola's new quarters. Some of his warriors advised that the place be blockaded at once, in order that, all supplies being cut off, the queen would be compelled, after a little, as they thought, to surrender at discretion. But this calculation, like many others in war, was made without sufficient information. Alola had prudently provided against just such a contingency. Nevertheless, a siege was concluded upon; for the victorious Gosee had come too near his game to forego the chase, while there was yet the shadow of a hope left of a capture. He was not the man, after advancing thus far, to be balked in his purpose at last, and that too by a woman, if he could help it.

In the midst of this perplexity, on the following day but one, and while Gosee, like a prudent general, was taking observations upon the situation of his antagonist, he was greatly surprised by the sudden appearance, on the neighboring portion of the peninsula, of Alola herself, who, arrayed in her gayest attire, attended by a troop of brilliantly-dressed young women, and all surrounded by a guard of brave warriors, approached, as nearly as safety would allow, to the main-land, and there, standing upon a high bluff, with clear and distinct tones addressed her former lover, the new king of her native country, and successor of her noble father, who (that is to say) Gosee, was attentively watching her movements from the main shore, and eagerly listening to catch her every utterance; for he knew at once, from her majestic bearing and beautiful appearance, that it was none other than the long-absent Alola. Directing her burning words to her cruel persecutor, she severely reproached him for waging an unjust war against a people who had never, in the slightest degree, molested him or his kingdom. She plainly told him that the blood of many of his own subjects, who had been slain in this cruel war, as well as that of not a few of her own, was upon his guilty head, and she warned him that the vengeance of the offended gods would surely overtake him in his wicked career—and herein she seemed to speak with the voice of prophesy.

She said, with much emotion, for she could not entirely suppress her feelings, and her voice was broken as she proceeded, with sobbing, that if it was on account of her elopement with the good Manuelo that he waged the war, still it was unjustifiable, since the laws of his country were grossly unreasonable, in so far as they enforced matrimony upon unwilling parties;

and that such laws, no matter where found, ought not to be respected; that they were in direct conflict with a great law of nature, and that, not their infraction, but obedience to them, would be criminal. She told him, emphatically, that she had never loved him, and never could, but that her love for Manuelo, as Gosee himself might have seen if he had had his eyes open, was from the first, pure, holy, and irresistible, and that she had now no regrets for anything she had done, and had never felt any compunctions of conscience on account of absconding with him.

She then demanded to know where her husband then was, and with thrilling tones warned the proud king that if Manuelo was yet living, as she verily believed he was, it would be unsafe for either Gosee, or any of his men, to harm, or permit to be harmed, so much as a hair of his head; that if Manuelo should be killed, or maltreated, she, who was now quite beyond the reach of all danger, had genius enough left to avenge such a wrong, and she would live for that purpose alone, during all the balance of her natural life, and when dead, haunt him for the crime.

She then coolly informed him of what he had already suspected, that he might as well break up his camp at once, and go hence about his business, for he could never enter the peninsula, or make a captive of her; that she had anticipated his tactics and had laid in an ample supply of provisions for her people, and could hold out in her impregnable station much longer than he could afford to maintain the siege. Finishing her speech, she was on the point of retiring, when Gosee, who had been listening with open mouth and ears to every word she had uttered, now with lying and deceitful tongue replied that her dear Manuelo, upon whom she had so graciously condescended to bestow her charms, instead of upon himself, though a prince imperial, was then dead, having been killed at the pass in the mountains, and that she could make up her mind never to see him more, unless in the land of the spirits. Alola shuddered when he assured her that the body of her beloved husband was at that very moment being torn by hungry vultures, on the field of that desperate strife. The heartless Gosee then reproached her for being the cause of the premature death of her venerable father, by her willful violation of the laws of her native country, and ended his deceitful harangue by complimenting her on her splendid personal appearance, telling her that he had never seen her look so fine before in his life, and that, though he had no disposition to flatter her, far from it, yet he could not help saying that the Anglos nation had done themselves great credit in selecting for their queen a person of so much beauty and attractiveness, and finally, that, as a native Santo, like herself, he was proud and delighted that the choice had fallen upon one so worthy of the place.

Alola, for the moment, was in doubt as to the motives of Gosee in the utterance of such very kind and agreeable words; but she deigned not a reply, but as she left her high stand, she waved her hand towards him, as much as to say, "Go away," or, as Justino interpreted it, " Get thee behind me, Satan."

This remarkable interview ended where it began, for neither party was, as to the other, further or nearer than before. The siege was maintained for several days longer, without any event worthy of mention in this hasty narrative, when one bright morning the camp of the allies was observed to be broken up, and their forces marching off over the neighboring hills, as if the siege were entirely abandoned. The enemy were all soon out of sight from the peninsula; but before they quite disappeared, the Anglos soldiers, who were always on guard, observing the movement, sallied forth in considerable numbers, well armed, and pursuing, fell upon the rear guard of the receding foe, to the end of annoying him and nothing more, for it was not their purpose to become involved in a general battle.

LXXXIII.

A DESERTER.

THESE brave Anglos warriors contented themselves with harassing the retreating enemy, in the manner described, during the greater part of that day, and after inflicting no little punishment upon him, they leisurely made for their stronghold on the peninsula. But on their way back they picked up by the road-side a straggler from the enemy's ranks. He had feigned to his friends to be lame, but was really a deserter from the Santos corps. This man had fortunately listened to the speech of Alola and was captivated by her arguments. Being a native of the same place as herself, he had known Alola in former years, in fact during all the period of her childhood, and was strongly in sympathy with her. His admiration of the lady had always been excessive, and it was not at all diminished when he learned the facts about her subsequent history. He was an admirer of heroism, whether in man or woman, but in all his life he had never heard of so fabulous an exhibition of it as was witnessed in her individual case.

This man being remembered by Alola, was freely admitted over the narrow isthmus into the peninsula, and in response to Alola's anxious inquiries, gave to her then and there a full account of Manuelo's treatment after his capture, for he was not killed, as Gosee had falsely stated. She was, as you may well guess, most eager to hear about him, and listened to the story of the deserter with tears in her eyes. Seated on a tawny lion's skin, in the largest wigwam, in the presence of his captors, but addressing his words to Alola, he said that when gallant Manuelo unfortunately tripped and fell, at the battle in the steep pass over the second range of mountains, he was instantly seized hold of by a detachment of the Santos soldiers, many of whom remembered him well, and some of them, in spite of all attempts to inflame their minds against him, still entertained for him a very high regard. In past times he had graciously instructed them in the useful arts, and among those arts were the wonderful improvements in the fashion and construction of their wearing apparel. Remembering these things gratefully, the last thing they would do would be to inflict upon so useful a person unnecessary harm. But the feelings of Gosee towards him, and for abundant reason, were entirely different. Manuelo in fact had been his successful rival in the affections of the fairest, wisest, and best of all the damsels of his kingdom, and Gosee was ready and anxious to visit upon him the vengeance that was rankling in his heart. Incited by such hatred, he would have rushed headlong upon Manuelo as soon as he was observed to fall, had he not been restrained by a quickly gathering crowd of his Santos soldiers, who closely hovered about the prostrate white man, and perceiving that their king had blood in his eye, resisted his advance by force, protecting Manuelo. The *melée* that ensued was terribly exciting, till Manuelo regained his feet and was prepared to defend himself. So hotly revengeful was Gosee that he raved like a madman, and his purpose could with difficulty be thwarted. He was determined at every hazard to compass the death of his more fortunate competitor for the fair hand of the princess, but the numbers against him were too great, and he was compelled to desist. Manuelo's life for the time was spared, but his mighty enemy was by no means disposed to give it up so. It was the principal burden upon Gosee's mind, until in camp that night, on the hither side of the mountain, the question was again raised, now with more deliberation, as to what disposition should be made of the distinguished prisoner, when, fortunately for Manuelo, and the literary world, the Barbos and the Movos both put in their several claims for the distinction of putting him to death by torture, for both these peoples, like the bloody Gosee himself, were boiling over with revenge. They recollected, as they had good reason to, the chastisements that had been inflicted upon them in the past by his hands, and a violent dispute arose between them as to which should enjoy the satisfaction of taking his life. Each of the allies based his claim upon the fact of having been in the van of the attack, and having in consequence suffered most from the resistance of the Anglos, and perhaps from the weapons of Manuelo himself, and both were extremely persistent.

But for this unexpected quarrel, which ran very high at the time, the deserter assured the trembling Alola that Manuelo, a prisoner, unarmed as he was, must have given up his life that night, inevitably, and with tortures probably unheard of. A period, however, was finally put to this dispute, said the deserter, by a force of the Santos, who came forward and claimed the prisoner for themselves, by virtue of their greater numbers and their superiority in some other respects. This demand of the swift-footed Santos was not to be resisted, and the designs of both the allies were thus frustrated. When the lucky Manuelo was once more in the hands of his former friends, the bloody designs of Gosee were likewise opposed, and the prisoner's life was spared. In fact, the commander-in-chief of the allies was too much engrossed at this hour in the disposition of his various forces, to give further attention to his distinguished captive, for discontent, from different causes, and dissatisfaction on account of their losses, were fast creeping into the camps of the cohorts. Serious complaints were heard among them, growing out of being compelled to take the brunt of the fight, while most of the glory, they spitefully alleged, was being appropriated by the selfish Santos. Quiet was at last restored among the clamorous allies, who slept that night upon the hope of an abundance of plunder and pillage within the next day or two, which they expected surely to find in the rich capital of the Anglos.

On the following day the movement in advance was resumed, and on the evening of the very day it had been deserted by its inhabitants, the doomed city was entered by the triumphant hordes of the enemy. Hurrying forward for the purpose of sacking the town, the invaders found much less to gratify their desires than they had been led to expect, and out of revenge for their disappointment they turned to and wickedly destroyed or desecrated whatever there was left.

Gosee in particular was terribly annoyed to find that he had been eluded by his game, and in his rage he stormed so loudly about, as was said, that the whole city was shaken from its foundation. With the utmost confidence had he counted upon the capture of Alola, and when the kindly deserter, who was relating these facts, came to describe to that person the conduct of her wicked pursuer, she could but join in the general rejoicing of those present. The vindictive Santos high chief was most overcome with anger when he visited the magnificent apartments of his former betrothed; as he did without delay, and found that the beautiful bird had flown. It was a poor and a petty revenge to tear to pieces with his own hands whatever was recognized as having belonged to her, and his conduct only excited the contempt of the queen herself, when listening to this account of it. Remaining in the city only that night, but without finding much sleep for his eyelids, the fiery Gosee pushed forward on the following day, as we already know, in pursuit of the fugitive queen, leaving Manuelo, in the meantime, under a strong guard of the Barbos, in his own mutilated and deserted capital.

As may well be supposed, the loving Alola was overjoyed to learn from this kind Santos deserter that her noble husband had been spared, and was yet alive, and apparently safe. So happy was she made by this intelligence that, in recognition of the great obligation, she permitted the deserter to reverently kiss her soft hand, and he was more than satisfied for all the risk he had run in bringing the welcome information. It was a compensation he had not been looking for, and was therefore all the more gratifying.

What was thought at first might be a feint on the part of Gosee in withdrawing from the siege of the peninsula, proved to be a veritable retreat. The situation, as he had found it, was discouraging enough to him and his impatient allies, and he despaired of ever being able to reduce the place, or to capture the wily Alola. Ashamed to be seen withdrawing by the same route he had come, he took a more circuitous one by night, and made his way back to the capital of the Anglos, disappointed and crest-fallen, and the more so from being worsted by a woman. Finding not the wherewithal in the towns of the Anglos to recruit his men, as he had hoped, Gosee tarried but a short time in the country before turning his face northward, for the season was now fast advancing. Hovering about in the enemy's country, therefore, but a few days, to gather up such supplies as he could find, he mustered his wearied and hungry warriors in front of the city, and without a word either of congratulation or encouragement, he gruffly ordered the march to begin, for their homes, over the same path by which they had come some weeks before.

Disappointed in the main object of the expedition, Gosee sullenly lingered behind in the silent city; for though he had Manuelo in his charge, he wanted Alola the more, and reluctantly departed without her. To his great mortification, he afterwards learned that this noble little woman, leaving a colony on the curious peninsula, to the end that she might always hold the same as a secure retreat for her people, in case of another disaster like the last, had returned to her cherished capital, and by the exercise of extraordinary energy and foresight, had restored it to its former condition of prosperity, and even more. There she continued to reign in the absence of Manuelo, but always with a hope of his return, for the good woman knew full well that if it was ever in his power he would hasten back to her arms.

LXXXIV.

MANUELO A PRISONER.

BUT poor Manuelo was now a prisoner of war in the hands of his most cruel and vindictive adversary, and was being carried back to the land whose laws he had broken, and from which, years agone, he had fled. A captive he had been before, but not under such intensely disagreeable circumstances as the present. When with the Modens he had been merely restrained of his personal liberty, but now in addition to the loss of his individual freedom, he was compelled to undergo the humiliation of being held by his quondam friends, and for what they considered a gross breach of good faith on his part, and what he himself was constrained to regard as somewhat in the nature of a violation of the laws of hospitality. The mortification which he suffered, on this latter account, was a thousand times more cutting to his sensitive nature than would have been ordinary captivity, or than had been his painful servitude with the cruel Modens. But there was no help for him now. Ignominiously bound, to prevent his escape, and under an ample guard of the myrmidons of the cautious Gosee, he was forced to keep along with the returning army of the Santos and their mercenary allies. He was, in fact, about the only trophy of the disastrous campaign worth naming, but it was regarded by Gosee as no mean achievement to take back to his capital the reigning king of the country against which he had led the war. Though not particularly proud of the expedition, on account of his failure to capture Alola, Gosee was at least glad to be in possession of the person who had treated him so disdainfully, and had cheated him of the love of that agreeable young princess.

It was some consolation to poor Manuelo to have the company, in his distress, of his faithful Warno, and a few other Anglos veterans, who, like himself, were being led into captivity, but who, unlike himself, knew not whither they were going.

On the borders of his kingdom, the haughty Gosee dismissed his allies, the Movos and the Barbos, and then prosecuted his march towards the great city on the Bay, located, as we remember, over against its entrance from the ocean; and the progress of the returning army of Santos was thereafter without incident.

Arriving at the capital just in time for the autumn feast of ripe fruits, the disconsolate Manuelo saw, on that occasion, many of his old friends, by some of whom, prisoner though he was, he was greeted with kindly words and tender expressions of regard, but by none with more real sympathy than was shown him by his former betrothed, but slighted, Noña, who happened to be among the visitors and recognized him this time instantly. From her he learned many things about his early friends, the Yonos, from whom he had been so long absent, and for whose welfare he had never ceased to feel the deepest solicitude, as he truthfully assured her. Noña had been happily married, for three years and upwards, to a younger son of the high priest, and was already the mother of two interesting children, a boy and a girl, who were always with her, and who shared with their mother the hearty congratulations of her former betrothed. Manuelo made her and her excellent husband the bearers of numerous greetings, from a full heart, to their people, and particularly to his reliable friend, the elder son of the high priest, and to his indiscreet wife, who had been the cause of so much annoyance in times past; but concerning whom he was now especially gratified to hear only the most favorable reports. Manuelo was informed that the priest's son had returned alone from the fishing excursion, entered upon by the two some half dozen years before, and in his account of the same, stated to his anxious tribe that he and Manuelo had been driven, by adverse winds, quite across the Bay, and that

Manuelo had positively refused to return, and it was with some reluctance, he was told, that the Yonos had given up their claim upon him, but they had almost forgotten after a while that such a person as Manuelo had ever existed.

But for all Manuelo could do, and notwithstanding the undisguised friendship of a portion of the people of the city for him, the king, the hard-hearted Gosee, remained bitterly hostile, and not only he, but some of his guilty retainers, were ever disposed to heap indignities, of one sort or another, upon him.

Manuelo could illy brook their many taunts and insults, but there was no relief, since Gosee had become a popular king, and powerful withal, and his subjects were afraid to offend him. Having been a king himself, Manuelo possessed too much good sense to find fault with his treatment, or to suppose that the present king of the Santos was wanting in a provocation. But this was poor consolation to one who was kept constantly under the closest watch, and, oftener than was needful to prevent his escape, was bound hand and foot. His sufferings under these inflictions put upon him by the royal prerogative of the tyrannical Gosee, were so very great that life itself was fast becoming intolerable, when one day, that autumn, a strange spectacle made its appearance. Two large foreign ships were observed coming into the harbor with all their sails set and colors flying. The whole population were much alarmed at this most unusual sight, and great commotion followed, especially in the capital. These two monstrous vessels, side by side, like two great swooping birds, sailed around the broad Bay, and at last dropped their anchors directly in front of the city. In due time six boats, three from each ship, filled with armed sailors, were sent to the shore. These men, arrayed in shining accouterments, with proud step, and with cutlasses drawn, marched directly up to the town, where Gosee, the king, tremblingly awaited their approach. It was presently discovered that the strangers were of the same race of people as Manuelo himself, who in consequence, was at once released from his confinement, and gladly brought out to converse with them, and to demand of them what they might want.

The ships were two proud Spanish men-of-war on a cruise up the coast, and had entered the harbor, in the name of their king, to take possession of the country, which to them bore the appearance of being a land of pagan barbarity. They were greatly surprised to find in such a place, and with such a population, a person who was able, after a little exertion, to recall and converse with them in the Spanish tongue. In appearance, his dress being the same as the natives, Manuelo was hardly distinguishable from the rest of the people of the country, so long had he lived among them, and so completely had he adopted their habits and customs, and it was with some difficulty that the strangers could be made to believe that he had ever been a Spaniard like themselves. But his account of himself soon convinced them of the fact, and they then greeted him with many demonstrations of kindness.

It rejoiced Manuelo's heart beyond measure to be able to speak kindly words to his countrymen on behalf of the swift Santos, with whom he had been so long acquainted, and thus to protect them from the harsh treatment that Christians, in those days, were in the habit of inflicting on all unbelieving nations.

But towards the haughty Gosee he was less kindly disposed, and boldly informed the Spaniards, in the very presence of the king, though in the Spanish language, that he was a cruel prince and a barbarian withal, and that he ought to be deposed. In pursuance of this information, the guilty Gosee was directed to leave the country, on pain of being treated as an enemy of the great king of the Spaniards, and on his sullen departure, a younger brother of Alola, a veritable prince, who, in the last few years had grown to the estate of manhood, was duly installed, in the place of Gosee, as king of the swift-footed Santos nation.

This young king, whose name was Tonee, acknowledged the supremacy of the Spanish crown, which the arbitrary Gosee had refused to do, and he was promised the support, in his reign, of as many great ships, like those now in sight, as might be needed to make his authority secure. Tonee entered upon his administration with great eclat, and the event was celebrated by salvos of artillery from the two ships, which, thunder and lightning, as it was thought to be, was never forgotten by those simple-minded people. When the ceremony was over, it was believed that no one would ever thereafter dare to dispute the right of Tonee to the throne, and as far as known no one ever did.

On the elevated ground near the palace of the new king, a large wooden cross was erected, large enough for actual use, had such been required, and in all respects resembling the original; and there, in the presence of the young king, *Te Deums* were sung, in which that considerable personage and all his household took part, as best they knew how, and they were duly taken under the protection of the Spanish crown.

LXXXV.

CARRIED OFF.

THE two great ships remained in the Bay as long as was deemed necessary to firmly establish the rights of their royal master, the king of Spain, to this newly discovered territory, as they called it, and then, with colors flying, and with booming artillery, they sailed away, taking Manuelo with them. Manuelo, be it said to his credit, left this country at that time with a great deal of reluctance, but he was overpersuaded by the captains of the two vessels, who were exceedingly anxious to carry him along, as a true witness at home of the vastness and importance of their conquests. Father Justino was sure that he never would have left the land that contained his lovely Alola, but for a promise, which he exacted in the most solemn manner from the captains of both ships, that they would surely return at an early day and bring him back—a promise, however, which Justino believed they never intended to keep, and which, at all events, they never kept so far as known at the present time.

Having accomplished the object of their cruise, which was to find and take possession of, in the name of the king, the best harbor on the northwestern coast of America, these two great vessels of war, with all sails unfurled, and with cheerfulness on board, bent their course towards some home port, too anxious to give to the Spanish authorities an account of their eventful voyage. There was cheerfulness, we said, but the cheerfulness was not universal on board; there was one person there full of despondency, and with a heavy heart.

On the fourth day out, when the ships, sailing together, came opposite the country of the Anglos, Manuelo sorely repented him of his rash act, and wished heartily he had remained on land. From the quarter-deck of the great vessel the poor man looked off with longing eyes towards his kingdom, now the kingdom of Alola, which lay spread out like a map before him, until, overcome with anxiety, he appealed to the captain of the vessel, in the most pitiful terms, to be put ashore. As the beautiful image of his loving wife came up before his distempered imagination, he was excited to the brink of madness, and with bended form he moaned aloud, bewailing his sad predicament. So earnest became his importunities, at last, that the prudent captain directed the ship to be headed out further to sea, and away from the coast, lest Manuelo, in his uncontrollable frenzy, should leap from the deck down into the waves with a view to swimming ashore. The hard-hearted captain, never having himself felt the pangs of disappointed love, disregarded the appeals of the distressed Manuelo, and, impelled by a favorable breeze, hastened on his voyage, thus dissevering the very heart-strings, as it were, of 'his unwilling passenger.

It is fortunate for Alola that she did not know her poor husband was there, else her end would surely have been hastened by drowning in the ocean that bore him away.

In a very few weeks the good ships arrived safely at a port, supposed to be that of Acapulco, where the fame of Manuelo was soon spread abroad, and a report of his wonderful adventures reached the ears of the Dominican friar, Justino, who in due time sought out the disconsolate sailor, and in return for Christian blessings liberally bestowed, easily persuaded Manuelo to relate his experience in full.

Many days were consumed in the work, but Justino wrote down, word for word, the whole of that strange, eventful history, just as it appears in the manuscript, and no occasion exists therefore now for repeating the same.

When the story was completed, the good Dominican, exhausted by the labor and broken in health, took passage for home in the very same ship that had brought Manuelo from the coast of California. In due time, with the precious scroll in his charge, he arrived at his native city of Evora, where, as we know, he died and was buried.

Manuelo was left by the good friar Justino in far-off Acapulco, but what became of him afterwards is not certainly known, though Justino remembered that the last seen of him he was fitting out, on his own account, a small schooner, of which he himself was to take command as captain, and proceed with all haste to Upper California. If successful, as the voyage probably was, since it was favored with the earnest prayers of pious Justino, as well as by propitious winds at that season of the year, the schooner reached its destination in safety, and Manuelo the brave was again happy in the embrace of the fair princess Alola.

Table of Contents.

		PAGE.
I.	The Beginning	5
II.	The Next Chapter	12
III.	Manuelo	17
IV.	Something Else	18
V.	Native Habits and Religion	19
VI.	Their Sports	23
VII.	Chapter Seven	25
VIII.	The Subject Resumed	28
IX.	The Abandonment	29
X.	Providential	31
XI.	The People Described	32
XII.	Matrimonial Affairs	33
XIII.	Their Habitations	34
XIV.	Their Names	35
XV.	A Doubtful Trick	37
XVI.	His Departure	41
XVII.	His Majesty	43
XVIII.	The High Priest	45
XIX.	Embarrassments	46
XX.	Pretensions	47
XXI.	Native Weapons	49
XXII.	The Kingdom	50
XXIII.	The Capital	52
XXIV.	Their Occupations	55
XXV.	Setting the Fashions	57
XXVI.	Their Sundays	59
XXVII.	Sun Worship	61
XXVIII.	Festivities	63
XXIX.	About War	68
XXX.	The Modens	70

CONTENTS.

		PAGE.
XXXI.	Some Reflections	72
XXXII.	Fishing	76
XXXIII.	A Shipwreck	77
XXXIV.	A Sea Fight	79
XXXV.	Santos Industries	80
XXXVI.	Some Legends	82
XXXVII.	Winning a Sweetheart	84
XXXVIII.	A Bear Fight	86
XXXIX.	Trials	91
XL.	A Change	96
XLI.	Avoiding Danger	98
XLII.	Another Tack	101
XLIII.	War Brewing	102
XLIV.	A Prediction	103
XLV.	The Cause of the War	105
XLVI.	A Dilemma	107
XLVII.	Preparations	108
XLVIII.	The March and Battle	109
XLIX.	Captivity	114
L.	The Retreat	120
LI.	Some Rehearsals	125
LII.	An Apology	128
LIII.	With Old Friends Again	129
LIV.	Jealousy	131
LV.	Strategy	136
LVI.	Neglect	140
LVII.	Prologue	141
LVIII.	A Dream	143
LIX.	The Plains	147
LX.	San Francisco	154
LXI.	The People	161
LXII.	The City	164
LXIII.	Dress	173
LXIV.	The Return	186
LXV.	A Flight Considered	195
LXVI.	The Elopement	203
LXVII.	The Barbos	221
LXVIII.	The Anglos	229
LXIX.	War with the Dagos	238

CONTENTS.

		PAGE.
LXX.	Trouble with Mosoto	245
LXXI.	Manuelo as King	255
LXXII.	Against the Movos	257
LXXIII.	Returning Home	263
LXXIV.	Mosoto's War	267
LXXV.	The Anglos Described	277
LXXVI.	The Santos' Invasion	285
LXXVII.	A Battle in the Clouds	290
LXXVIII.	Another Stand	295
LXXIX.	Loto's Story	297
LXXX.	Another Fight and Defeat	302
LXXXI.	The City Abandoned	307
LXXXII.	The Peninsula	311
LXXXIII.	A Deserter	318
LXXXIV.	Manuelo a Prisoner	323
LXXXV.	Carried Off	327

www.ingramcontent.com/pod-product-compliance
Lightning Source LLC
Chambersburg PA
CBHW021205230426
43667CB00006B/566